From
Crisis
to
Creativity

6/06

Other Works by Dr. Feldman:

Lessons in Evil, Lessons From the Light

Speaking of Health Audio Cassettes for Coping:
    Adult Medical Series
    Children's Coping Cassettes: "Education for Self-Care"

From
Crisis
to
Creativity

Taking Advantage of Adversity

Gail C. Feldman Ph.D.

 BookPartners
Wilsonville, Oregon

Permission to reprint is gratefully acknowledged from the following:

Judy Chicago for her poem "The Merger," originally printed in *The Dinner Party*, New York: Anchor Books, 1979.

Elisabeth Kübler-Ross for the Richard Allen poem in her book *Death is of Vital Importance*, Barrytown, NY: Station Hill Press, 1995.

Agnes Martin for her personal interview, sayings, writings.

Mr. Dieter Schwarz for use of materials from "Agnes Martin, Writings" accompanying the exhibition "Agnes Martin: Paintings and Works on Paper, 1960–1989," Winterthur, Switzerland: Kunstmuseum, January–March, 1992.

Cover design by Richard Ferguson
Text design by Sheryl Mehary

BookPartners, Inc.
P.O. Box 922
Wilsonville, Oregon 97070

Lovingly Dedicated To:

Dr. Elisabeth Kübler-Ross, Psychiatrist

> *The dying experience is almost identical
> to the one at birth.*
> *It is a birth into a different existence.*

Agnes Martin, Artist

> *As the river runs to the sea, and the plant
> grows to the sun,*
> *So do we flow and grow and exist.*

Contents

Creativity is defined as "the art of growing self-expression."

The author's discovery that the stages of grieving mirror
those of creativity is described. Psychological defenses may
prevent us from resolving grief and manifesting our full artistic
and emotional potential. This chapter highlights inventor **Elias
Howe**.

Modern and ancient stories illustrate how it is possible to
experience devastating loss, metabolize the feelings about that
loss, and move through the stages of grieving to accept a new
and expanded sense of reality. Highlighted are **Job, Demeter**,
and **Persephone**.

The first stage in the grief and growth process is often
denial. Denial is resistance to change and disavowed grief. With
awareness, we can dismantle our defenses—our early program-
ming to live "lies of limitation,"—and we can overcome
obstacles to successful living. Highlighted are the lives of
Siddhartha, Einstein, and the artist **Celia Rumsey.**

The second stage in the grief and growth cycle is anger.
Anger as a protective defense can be used to buttress denial, or
it can be used as assertive energy, helping us to express and
transcend our grief. Highlighted are **Muhammad, Gandhi,** and
van Gogh.

The obsession that stalls us on the path to grief resolution
and creative self-renewal is referred to as "paradigm paralysis."
When our energy is unblocked, the incubation of new ideas and
plans is under way. The transformation of this energy allows for
the passionate pursuit of one's chosen work. **Krishna** and
Michelangelo are highlighted.

Depression is seen as unresolved grief and as a block to
higher creativity. This chapter focuses on coping with death,
suicide, trauma, and relationships. The life of Mexican artist
Frida Kahlo illustrates the persistent determination to
transform pain and depression into expressions of self and love.

Acceptance is the last stage in the grief and growth cycle. It
signals the ability to accept a changed reality and accept love
into one's life again. The resilience of **Jacques Lusseyran,** the
blind resistance leader and concentration camp survivor, is
described, along with that of the blind sculptor **Michael
Naranjo. Confucius,** the teacher of the "arts of peace," and
Jesus, teacher of love, are highlighted.

At the end of every journey through despair or disappointment, one's life energy can be transformed to its unlimited
potential. This potential for inner peace, a sense of purpose, and
love we may call wisdom. Job's wisdom, "I have spoken of
things I did not understand, things too wonderful for me to
know..." was accompanied by a restoration of abundant life and
love. New Mexico artists **Agnes Martin** and **Judy Chicago** are
highlighted, along with the life story and poetry of a New
Mexican student, **Sarah Dixon,** whose life exemplifies "determined overcoming" and transcendent living.

Preface

There was bad news and good news on the day of my birth. On September 21, 1941, the Nazis encircled Leningrad, preparing to starve the city to death. But in New York, the Museum of Modern Art added Vincent van Gogh's painting "The Starry Night" to its collection.

I grew up on the only dead-end, dirt road in San Diego. It was, however, San Diego and beautiful city parks and magnificent beaches served as my playground. Money was scarce, but when my mother sent me to the store for a loaf of bread, she only had to give me eight cents to pay for it. When I was eight years old and my parents divorced, Mother, who'd only completed the tenth grade, went to work in an aircraft factory. I was lonely much of the time, but I learned a great deal about independence and resourcefulness. My sister, Judy, older by four years, focused her anger on me, but that was offset over the years by a tremendous bond of affection. We are now like twins. I thank her for coming along with me on many of the research trips for this book.

Every aspect of my early life served as a stimulus, for growth and resilience. Each frightening experience was like an inoculation, strengthening my immunity against subsequent harsh events. Here's an example: The first time my mother went on a date after her divorce, she took me to stay with Uncle Ellis, my great-uncle. My sister was living with our grandparents for a time because she couldn't be "controlled." I know now that in the 1940s divorce was seen as a human disaster. My perfectly respectable mother suddenly became suspect, a threat to other wives. We had to be out of the neighborhood so that no one could see her engaged in the nefarious business of dating. Uncle Ellis went to bed shortly after she left, but I couldn't close my eyes. I crept into the room where Uncle Ellis slept, sat by his bed and watched him breathe until my mother returned.

It makes me laugh now, but I know I was terrified. I'd already lost one parent, and now my mother was gone. This ancient uncle would most likely choose this night to die, and who knows what would happen to me then? I survived this abandonment, and then it only took one more incident to cure me of my fear: Mother was called in the middle of the night, from my neighbor Gloria Metrovitch's house, and she came to walk me back home in the moonlight. After that, I became the sleepover queen of San Diego. Bringing my own pajamas and pillow, I would settle in the bedrooms of one or another of my numerous girlfriends. I settled in so frequently in Karen Wickstrom's room I should have been paying rent.

And that brings me to the topic of lifelines, buoys, and boats. In every person's life there are those who serve as lifelines, hauling that person through rough seas. Many people in San Diego became extended family by buoying my confidence, pulling me through emotional storms, and quietly insisting that I could do things I didn't think possible. Karen Wickstrom Karros and her mother, Mayrel, have been there for me since I was in kindergarten, their house a safe harbor right across the street from McKinley Elementary School. My other friends along the way, Maggie and Bob White, Janice, Jolene, Betty, Marilyn, Mary Jo, and all the high-school sleepover gang I write about in chapter 5, have floated along beside me offering constant encouragement.

My teachers at Hoover High School gently nudged me to apply for scholarships to college, insisting that I continue my education when I secretly thought that only the rich kids in Kensington Park were smart enough to compete beyond high school. No one in my family had ever attended college. My professors and supervisors at San Diego State University reinforced my sense of competence during my mental health internships and helped me believe that I could complete a master's degree at the University of Southern California. There are far too many people to list here who were instrumental in bringing me to the point where I could return to college to earn a Ph.D. and eventually write books. I hope you know that you live in my heart.

My dearest friend in Albuquerque, Marcia Landau, is a standout in the lifeline department. She has supported me, day and night, through every crisis in my life. She shares my joys as well. I thank her for patiently reading my early manuscripts.

My husband, Bruce, has helped me to grow in endless ways. Our long-term love is a challenge that continues to engage us. The births of our two daughters, Nicole and Megan, brought new lifelines. I felt I could have died satisfied knowing I'd made the world a better place by bringing them into it. What a delightful surprise it has been to find that even happier moments came with every year of their growth, until now I count them as my closest friends. Niki teaches me about patience in love. Megan inspires me with her incisive intellect.

I wish to thank Jim Levine, my initial agent, for his help in publishing my first book, *Lessons in Evil, Lessons From the Light*, and Thorn Bacon, my current editor, for his confidence in the success of this second book. Lastly, I wish to thank all of the people I write about in this book who shared their grief, growth, and personal creativity with me. Special thanks to artists Agnes Martin, Celia Rumsey, and Michael Naranjo, and to student Sarah Dixon. I stand in awe of every one of you and I thank my guardian angels for bringing you into my life. I am mindful of the fact that we teach what we need to learn and in moving from crises to creativity I remain an attentive student.

Gail Feldman
July 1998

Introduction

I'm ready for the new millennium. I'm eager. A bright beginning beckons to me like a first birthday party. Not that the world will change. Disasters and devastation may well occur at the same rate in the next thousand years as during the past thousand years. Death will continue to be an unwelcome visitor. Accidents will shake our confidence in the safety of familiar places. Disappointment will sometimes stalk us. Life includes regular doses of painful experiences.

I've discovered that the antidote to despair and depression is personal creativity. I believe we develop our capacity for creativity by recognizing grief as the natural response to life's crises and by embracing our own individual manner of expressing the emotions of recovery. Self-expression propels us on this path. The benefit of transcending grief through greater creativity is an expanded capacity to give and receive love.

For me, nearly each of the last ten years has been marked by a personal loss. I entered the 1990s anticipating certain milestones: my two daughters leaving home to go to college and then out into the world; entering my fifties; reaching my thirtieth wedding anniversary; celebrating twenty-five years as a practicing psychologist. I couldn't have foreseen the events that would stop me in my tracks—incidents that would cause me to evaluate my life, my relationships, my work, my values, and my coping skills.

I couldn't know that one of my closest female friends would die suddenly of an asthma attack, one of my patients would sue me, my best male friend would hang himself, my father would die of cancer, my marriage would falter, and my oldest daughter's sweet boyfriend would sequester himself in a tiny garage and die of carbon monoxide poisoning while grasping his last love letter to her.

The quiet convulsions of grief I experienced were no different from those of my friends and patients who have suffered similar losses and, I'm sure, not even close to the agony of parents mourning the death of a child. As I made my way through the stages of grief and recovery, I became alert to the depths and plateaus of my emotions. I noticed my need for distractions—outdoor adventures, classes, novels, films—activities that would transport me temporarily out of a world of loss and show me ways to overcome my sorrow.

I began taking piano lessons. For me, learning music was like learning a foreign language. It was fun to be really bad at something for the first time in my life. I felt deliciously silly being the only adult performing at my teacher's recitals. The children would play their piano pieces from memory and I would play haltingly, barely able to read the music.

I began to take myself less seriously.

I started to see how every form of creative expression helped me to overcome my grief. I noticed that as my bereaved patients healed, they too grew bolder in the ways in which they expressed themselves. Some of them seemed to become physically bigger, as though they had taken off outgrown winter coats. As more comfortable room was made for inner peace, their joy seemed to take up more outer space.

The "necessary losses" we experience in life include changes that we don't often associate with grief. Moving from one normal developmental level to another can cause sadness and disappointment, as well as anticipation and joy. A young child may feel twinges of regret over leaving the dolls in her room and going out to ride bikes or play soccer. Although my daughters were excited about becoming teens, they each hit a depressive pothole when they began menstruating and realized there was no going back to childhood.

When I was five years old it took me several years to recover from the loss of my best friend, Mona. She moved away and disappeared from my life forever. Losing friends, parents, toys, teachers, pets, health, good marks, a sense of security, or a cherished dream—all setbacks, major and minor—necessitate growing through grieving to prevent, as author Sam Keen put it, "the grief becoming a grievance."

I have discovered that as we learn to accept change as a fact of life, and accept grief and growth cycles as a definition of the process that makes us "change-resilient," creativity increases. Every time we manifest our personality—some aspect of how we think, what we think, who we like, what we do, how we see and solve a problem, how we express our feelings—every single way we "Insist on ourselves!" as Emerson would say, we paint a picture for the world to see. The stronger and bolder these pictures become, the more they mirror our courage to face crises and overcome them, using life energy in the service of growth.

It's time to relax our judgment about "negative" experiences and recognize that while we can't choose what happens to us, we can choose how to respond. As legendary actress Mary Pickford once said, "This thing we call failure is not in the falling down, but in the staying down." Resilient children and adults to not stay down. They learn how to grieve over life's bumps and bruises, stand up, and display a new self, a new creation. With resilience, we present our calling card to the world, and it says, "I'm up and I'm getting better!"

What do I mean by crisis? I mean a life change that produces stress. The physiological effects of stress involve a release of hormones that create the "flight or fight" response, which prepares the body to sense danger, outrun a predator, or defend against attack. Immediately following a crisis, the body should be able to return to its previous, comfortable state. However, driven by the hectic pace of modern living, too many of us live as if we are in constant crisis, with stress levels that take a toll on our health and stifle our creativity.

The physical reaction to crisis is the stress response, the emotional reaction to crisis is grief. Much of this book is about the need to engage in the "grieving feelings" in order to process or metabolize crises and adapt to change. The act of living means facing constant change. Whether we perceive it as positive, or negative, change provides us with an opportunity to shed outmoded defensive styles, experience our deepest emotions, ponder mortality, and express our individuality as we emerge into the light of awareness and choice. One measure of maturity is the willingness to recognize the effects of change, cycle through resistance to acceptance, and in the process discover new opportunities for learning and creativity.

What do I mean by creativity? I mean any form of self expression that helps us overcome stress and transcend turmoil. I mean developing a conscious awareness of one's emotional reactions. I mean choosing to transform the energy of grief into energy for personal growth. The word "create" means to "cause to come into being," to "originate," and being creative means "having the power to create" originality in thought and behavior. For simplicity's sake, I define creativity as "the art of growing self-expression."

Recognizing that grief cycles mirror the creative process can give us a hopeful vision of the future. Using anecdotes from personal experience, case studies drawn from my professional work as a psychologist, biographical accounts of artists and historical figures, and literary analysis, I hope to show you how great good can come from grief. This book is intended to empower you to bring a unique expression of yourself into stronger focus.

As part of the natural world, we cycle through seasons. There is no avoiding fall and winter. They exist for us as a time of darkness, rest, germination, incubation, and renewal. We tend to think of the metaphor of human growth and seasonal change as applying to the course of an entire life span. I prefer to emphasize that every time we cycle through challenge and change, we are presented with an opportunity, psychologically and emotionally, to release past fearful beliefs in failure and greet the present with a greater sense of awareness, competence, and wisdom.

We are all "works in progress." Wherever we are in life is where we need to be at this particular moment for maximum learning. There is no better time than the present to develop your signature self-expression, your personal form of responsiveness to the world. Come along now and learn to take advantage of adversity.

Chapter One

Grief Cycles and the Creative Process

*"We die and we die and we die in this life, not only phys-
ically—within seven years every cell in our body is
renewed—but emotionally and spiritually as change seizes
us by the scruff of the neck and drags us forward into
another life. We are not here simply to exist. We are here in
order to become. It is the essence of the creative process; it
is in the deepest nature of things.*

— Susan Howatch

Everyone suffers. In addition to death and taxes, the other
constant in life is suffering. And most suffering is due to
change. Everything in the world is changing constantly. Some
changes we simply cannot understand. We may ask: Why this?
Why me? Why now? What on earth is the meaning of this
suffering? These questions have moved and motivated great
thinkers and formed the foundations of the world's religions.

While preparing a lecture on creativity one day, I had an
epiphany: a simple, yet profound realization that the stages of the
creative process parallel the stages of grieving—that even as we
experience grief, we are incubating an expanded self. The ancient
alchemists used the term "blackness" to characterize the first stage

of creativity. How ironic that during the first stages of creating or inventing something new, we usually haven't the vaguest notion of how to go about accomplishing our goal! As we take the first steps, there appears to be no movement at all.

In a similar manner, during the first stage of coming to terms with life change or loss, numbness holds the mind in check, and supports a temporary illusion that there are no ripples on the lake of our consciousness. The protective defense of denial provides a holding pattern as we gather enough strength to orient ourselves to change. The first step of facing change appears to be avoiding it. But the struggles we encounter during the process of change are inevitable. I believe they are no less than the manner of life itself.

How we ultimately perceive and handle a change—as a negative crisis or a positive opportunity to grow—can mean the difference between falling victim to stress, despair, and depression, or becoming empowered by transforming the energy of our grief into creative expression. I'd like to illustrate this with the story of a little boy I saw at the Albuquerque Child Guidance Center in the mid-1970s.

It was odd to see a child this young be so quiet. There was no fidgeting, not even the occasional foot swing or a tentative peek around the room with curious eyes. Seven-year-old Joey stared at his lap as his mother explained why she'd brought him to the center. As she spoke, I noticed her clothing—a long skirt with a large silver concho belt, a long-sleeved velvet blouse and silver and turquoise jewelry. Joey's bowed head was much smaller than his mother's, his brown skin darker, his thick black hair cropped short, unlike his mother's, which was captured in a band at the back of her neck. Their appearance boldly announced their Native American-Hispanic background.

When his father was killed in a tractor accident the previous year, Joey stopped talking and participating in school activities. Joey's mother informed me that their large extended family lived on a ranch and that Joey was taken to the funeral, where he hadn't shown any emotion. Several days later he became completely withdrawn.

I suggested that Joey and I spend some time together in the playroom. He followed me dutifully, sat down with his shoulders hunched, and kept his hands in his lap. I put plain paper and crayons on the table and asked if he would draw me a picture of one of the animals he liked. He drew a dog. With further encouragement, he drew cows and horses. I then told him that I understood that his father had died and he must miss him terribly. Could he draw a picture of his father? He made an elaborate stick figure wearing a cowboy hat. I then asked if he knew how his father had died. He nodded. When asked if he might draw a picture about what happened, he set to work making a huge tractor and a tiny man on the ground. He worked slowly and meticulously on his drawing. Tears began falling down his cheeks as he worked on the picture. By the end of our time together the tears were flowing freely and little sobs were jerking his entire body. I offered Joey tissues and asked if he wanted to take his pictures home. He wiped his face, shook his head no, and left the room. I never saw Joey again.

Joey hadn't spoken one word to me, but when I called his mother several weeks later she said that he had become himself again. "I don't know what you did to him, but he got better," she said, greatly relieved. Joey was talking and participating at school. She mentioned he'd also started playing with clay again.

"What do you mean, 'playing with clay'?" I asked.

"Joey's dad used to bring him adobe mud from down by the river, starting when Joey was real little. He always liked to make animals and little things with his dad. We used to call him 'the Adobe Kid.' It makes me feel better to see him playing that way again.

A small wave of happiness washed over me.

Following that conversation I began to wonder what happened so that Joey "got better." Could it be that the simple act of putting crayon to paper cured his mournful heart? Is it possible that his sparse drawings, like one stick pulled from a small pile blocking a rivulet, allowed the flow of feelings to resurface and reenter the stream of life? Art as communication is a theme in the thinking of esteemed psychoanalyst Anna Ornstein. She sees art as providing its creator with the "feeling of being understood, mirrored, and validated." In this sense, Joey entered a sacred space where he could reconnect with his painful feelings and use art as his voice to communicate grief in the understanding presence of another.

◡ ◡

My mother's generation seemed to accept drastic change as a fact of life. The absence of any formal schooling beyond the tenth grade never stopped my mother from imparting common wisdom about life change and loss. After my grandmother died and we were going through her cherished possessions, my mother showed me a collection of pictures of the babies and toddlers in our family who had died. Infant and child mortality was very high around the turn of the century, before the advent of penicillin, immunizations, and surgical procedures. In each picture, the deceased child was laid out in baptismal gown and bonnet. They looked like dolls to me, beautifully arranged as though they had been photographed for an antique doll catalog, instead of to document their brief lives. Each garment of white cotton with crocheted, lacy borders had been hand sewn by one of the older women in the family.

"This one died of scarlet fever," my mother mused. "And I think this one died of whooping cough. Sometimes the country doctor just wouldn't know why they died." She came to a picture of a young woman and stroked the picture, as though the touch would bring back more memory. "Jenny was one of my favorite aunts. She died in childbirth when she was just twenty. My grandmother was a fine midwife and delivered many babies, but Jenny hemorrhaged and Grandma just couldn't stop the bleeding. I remember hearing the men work late into the night hammering the boards together for the coffin."

"How did people like Grandma and her mother cope with so much loss?" I asked her.

"Death was a fact of life in those days. Grandma used to quote the Bible, Ecclesiasticus, about 'a time to be born and a time to die; a time to weep and a time to laugh.' Our modern society has forgotten that grief is just a part of the life cycle."

Dr. Elisabeth Kübler-Ross, in her groundbreaking book *On Death and Dying*,[1] taught us about this cycle. She described five stages of thinking and feeling that we must move through in order to come to a sense of peace about loss. The stages of grief are:

Denial—Anger—Bargaining—Depression—Acceptance

At first, I could only understand this process in the context of death and dying. Over a period of years, I began to apply the Kübler-Ross model to coping with loss generally: a lost childhood, loss of work, loss of self-esteem, loss of parental love, lost wishes, and even a lost soul. Psychoanalyst Leonard Shengold calls the effects of childhood abuse "soul murder," in his book by the same name.[2] While most of us, fortunately, haven't been brutalized to the point that we wonder about the integrity of our souls, all of us have had to face disappointments that call into question our ability to cope.

When I received a call one morning informing me that my friend Shelly had died the night before, I couldn't comprehend the truth of it. How could she die? She was strong and healthy. She was a brilliant pediatric cardiologist. She was the mother of the two children who grew up like siblings to my own children. She had asthma, yes, but asthma is not supposed to kill people.

Denial, the first stage of grief identified by Dr. Kübler-Ross, protects us from being overwhelmed by loss. We simply can't acknowledge change that brings with it implications that we are not prepared to handle.

The second reaction to grief is anger. When the full realization of our loss takes hold, we feel outraged. We feel so at a loss that we may let our thinking run wild. We'll blame anyone, including God. Someone must be held responsible. Someone must right this terrible wrong and restore what is ours. We feel frantic and want anything but peace. We may even want revenge.

The release of stress hormones, at this time, drives some people to physical violence. Suicide is certainly an expression of unresolved grief, and it is impossible to estimate how many highway deaths are actually unconscious suicides. In some cultures, people used to tear their clothes or cut their bodies to release the terrible tension. Animals go through a stage called "protest," when a loved one dies. They may howl or screech to discharge the pain of loss. Human babies protest the early separations from mother by crying, howling, or having a tantrum.

In the third stage of grief, which Dr. Kübler-Ross called "bargaining," we turn to rationalization. Strong emotion hasn't worked to restore our loss, so we'll try cunning. Maybe we can make a deal with God. "If I promise to leave my money to the church, please, God, let me live long enough to see my first grandchild," or, "I'll devote the rest of my life to helping others, if you take the cancer away." When the loss seems final, as in the death of a loved one, obsession may take over. The mind ruminates, going over and over the details of certain aspects of the trauma.

I have changed Dr. Kübler-Ross's term "bargaining" to "obsession," in the grief and growth and creativity model, because I think that ruminating over loss is a universal reaction to any disappointment, regardless of how large or small. Who hasn't been caught up in mulling over what should have been said during an argument or what should have been done to prevent an accident?

There may be a long list of "if only"s: If only I hadn't let her go out that night...If only I hadn't let him take the car...If only I had insisted on another opinion the diagnosis might have been picked up earlier...If only I had paid attention to this one detail the lawsuit might not have occurred...If only I had pushed Shelly to take better care of herself... This obsessive phase is another way that we process our grief.

Baby monkeys who lose their mothers go through a time, after the protest phase, called "searching." They look and look, trying to find the lost love, just as human toddlers, when their favorite blanket or stuffed animal disappears, will tear their room apart searching for the beloved object.

The fourth stage, depression, is the one people relate to most easily. In our society it is quite typical for someone to say "I'm depressed." It would be unusual to hear "I'm grieving," except in the case of a death, and it would probably be considered arrogant to say. "I'm busy being creative." And yet, often, when we feel depressed, we are actually grieving a loss or a disappointment, and we are working to create a new acceptable reality. At these times, however, we may be conscious only of our hopelessness. We may feel lost. Or, we may feel nothing, completely numb. Or the pain of profound sadness may result in tears that seem to never stop. Infants who have lost their mothers and do not have adequate nurturing literally fail to thrive. In these extreme cases, they go into developmental arrest, stop eating, and die. Their grief actually kills them.

A part of us dies during a grief cycle. But, like the salamander that has lost one of its small weak limbs, we discover that the lost part regenerates. We have grown a more resilient self.

During the fifth stage of grief, acceptance, we discover a new reality, a reality filled with possibility. And with this new dawning, joy re-enters our life.

My cardiologist friend Shelly was also a docent at the Albuquerque Zoo. To celebrate Shelly's memory, her mother, Sarah, and her numerous friends instituted "Zoo Boo," an annual Halloween event. Face-painting, apple-bobbing, costumes and haunted houses offer children a safe and exciting time, accompanied by the sounds of lions, leopards, and elephants. And each year Sarah looks to the sky and says, beaming, "I know Shelly's enjoying this day with us."

When we come through a period of mourning, there is no question that we're able to function on a higher plane of understanding, of synthesis. As we move through major, or minor, grief and growth cycles, we become more clearheaded, stronger, and more positive about who we are and what we believe. We are constantly recreating ourselves in this way. Those who process disappointments readily seem to be more flexible, optimistic, and happy. What appears an insoluble or threatening problem to one person, to a good griever is a fact of life that can be an exciting opportunity for creative problem solving.

To illustrate how this process works with even a simple life change, let me tell you a personal story. After having lunch with friends in Santa Fe one afternoon, I stood up and realized my earring was missing. "It can't be gone," I thought. "It's my favorite! It'll be here on the floor somewhere" (denial). My friends and I got down on the floor and searched all over, but no earring. I sent them off with plans to meet later and I began to backtrack along the streets where we'd been walking. I was getting more and more annoyed about spending time searching for my earring instead of enjoying the day with my friends (anger). As I walked along, I begin obsessing about how the backing on the earring had been loose. I knew that, and yet I didn't fix it. If only I'd paid attention (obsession). As I realized that I probably would not find my earring, I felt very sad. A true feeling of loss came over me, but immediately I thought, "How silly it is to let such an insignificant loss upset me" (depression). After a few minutes, I had an *Aha!* I would simply wear the remaining earring with a different one! That's a new style, I thought. I immediately felt better, relieved, and a sense of regained equilibrium and lightness spread over me (acceptance).

There are many dramatic stories of people who have overcome tremendous problems to achieve high levels of creative functioning: people like Helen Keller, and other physically challenged people who learn to paint with their toes, or by holding a brush in their mouths. The life stories of some of these people are vivid illustrations of resilience. But for the most part, I'm addressing "normal" people with the "normal" problems of everyday life. Problems that they encounter range from catastrophic losses that interrupt routine functioning, to brief blips on the computer screen of life, the kind my mother referred to with her version of swearing.

"Good Grief!" she'd yell, as she grabbed a pan to put under a leak in the kitchen plumbing. As a child, I couldn't understand what was good about grief. It's taken all this time for me to figure out why she would call grief "good." Now I know why people who grieve well live well. They have learned to express their thoughts and feelings about change without fear of drowning in the deeper inner realms of being. Grief, properly understood, then, is a link to our creativity. Good grievers are choosing to live in the light of what I call "creative competence."

We have no way of knowing how long it will take us to move through a cycle of denial, anger, obsession and depression. It can take minutes or years to accept change and embrace new realities. What I am suggesting with this model is that these cycles are ongoing throughout our lives. I believe that the human growth and development process involves learning to move through the cycles more and more quickly, and furthermore it means experiencing deep emotions that become transformed into compassion and understanding for one's own life journey, as well as the journeys of others. The desire to come to terms with life change is a profound one: it originates in the depths of one's being; it is pervasive and extensive.

When people do not grieve, the stress response sets in and eventually they become physically ill or so chronically resentful they make others ill. Researchers have found that tears contain stress hormones. When we "have a good cry" we are releasing these hormones and facilitating adaptation to new realities. We're proving that we are full of life energy and not afraid to show it.

Again, we face this grief and growth development not only during coming to terms with death and dying—we face it every day when we are confronted by disappointments or setbacks and we respond by learning. The path of grieving contains ruts that we fall into, and we get hurt and doubt our ability to get out. We must learn to recognize when we are choosing to not get out. This is what I mean by awareness.

According to St. Francis, "the long dark night of the soul" leads from "blackness" to the light of re-creation. Many people get lost in that dark night and some people get so comfortable in it they choose to stay there. The greatest lesson of my life is the awareness that how we choose to cope with every change, from small disappointments to enormous losses, reflects a psychological, moral, and spiritual creative journey. I hope this book can provide a road map for that journey.

While the discovery of the parallel process of mourning and re-creating the self is an intellectual one, learning the truth of it is deeply emotional. For many years I had been helping my clients reframe what they called depression into unresolved grief. For example, Bonnie, a teacher, came for psychotherapy for "chronic depression." During childhood she had met with a number of common difficulties, such as several moves, which had made her school and social adjustment problematic. Her mother was fairly remote emotionally, but her father, in spite of frequent travels, was caring and emotionally available for Bonnie and her brother. Her adult life was marked by a divorce to which she felt she had adjusted quite well. When I asked about children, Bonnie replied while blinking back tears. She had a daughter and a son. Her nineteen-year-old son was killed in a car accident five years ago, she said.

"Bonnie, do you suppose your depression might be unresolved grief?"

"I don't know how it could be," she answered, sighing. "That happened five years ago!"

"So, you think grief goes away just because time passes?" I asked.

"I just never thought about it before," Bonnie said, wiping her eyes. "Everyone says that cycling through one year should be enough grieving. But, I never went through all those stages I read about. I never did get angry."

"How we move through grief is very personal," I told her. "While one person may seem to cope quite easily with a significant loss, another is completely thrown by a life change that doesn't appear as important. Losing your son is obviously deeply significant. Do you think you should be angry, and if so, why?"

"I couldn't be angry with Billy, even though the accident was his fault. It was late and it'd been raining. He was probably going too fast and drove off the road. I couldn't be angry with his girl-friend for surviving. Pauline had over one hundred stitches in her head and was terribly traumatized. I've never been able to even feel anger toward God. All this just happened."

"The stages of grief are meant as a guide," I said. "We may get stuck in one area or another depending on our personality style. Your tendency is toward depression, so that's the area of grieving you'll have to be aware of. I know a man whose daughter was murdered many years ago. He's still as angry today as he was at the time it happened, because his personal style of coping tended toward anger. His anger represents his unresolved grief.

"Hospice workers have taught us a lot about the meaning of healing. We think it means getting over an illness or an injury. But hospice worker and poet Stephen Levine teaches that getting over our *fear* of death, or our woundedness as expressed by depression or anger, is the true meaning of healing.[3] Allow yourself to 'do' your grief in your own way."

Bonnie came to realize that she was not trapped in depression. She needed to open her heart and fully grieve fro her beloved son. With that accomplished, she was able to transform her life and give her teaching career her full focus. She reclaimed her energy, and creativity infused her classroom. She enjoyed preparing assignments. Student participation increased. She reestablished friendships with other teachers. Bonnie left her sadness in the past.

Another woman, Maurine, was referred for supportive psychotherapy after her car was hit by a truck and she sustained serious back and leg injuries. We discovered that, in spite of other physical traumas in her life and the pain of living with an alcoholic husband, she had never healed from the loss of her most cherished child who had died in a motorcycle crash nearly sixteen years earlier! As she allowed herself to grieve by becoming aware of her feelings, her body as well as her soul slowly healed.

We all have "crisis credentials." Along with achievements, honors, and graduations, our enrollment in the course of life brings setbacks, crises, and seeming failures. I encourage you to examine your crisis credentials to discover how your inner strength has brought you through grief and growth cycles to a new level of creative self-expression.

I have two friends whom I think of as capable of being stand-up comics. Each of them has cycled through a difficult grieving process, one related to the suicide of her father, the other due to the mental illness of her mother.

Grace was the anchor in a family constantly blowing off course. Her mother suffered from schizophrenia, so Grace had to care for her younger siblings when her father was away on temporary duty with the navy, and she tried to protect them from the results of his bouts with alcohol when he was home on leave. She left the family when she was sixteen and put herself through college, studying computer engineering.

Grace had finally created a comfortable life when her husband announced that he wanted a divorce. She spent several years in psychotherapy acknowledging her feelings and processing her grief. She began to meditate regularly and finally found inner peace, knowing that she would truly be all right on her own.

What surprised me about her growth is that she became funnier than ever, doing imitations of comics and corporate executives.

"I don't remember you being this funny in the past," I told her. "And I didn't know you as a kid. Were you like this in school?"

"Hah!" she replied. "I never opened my mouth in school. I was a total nerd. I loved numbers. There were no feelings attached to them."

"Well, I think you ought to become a stand-up comic," I said.

"I'm too tired to stand up," she said, hands on hips, with a Richard Simmons lisp. "What I'd really like to do is open a small tea house. Of course I wouldn't serve people, I'd just sit and drink tea with them," she replied.

Although it's fun to be entertained by Grace and to call her Gracie, after comic Gracie Allen, the real gratification we feel is that she's happy. Her life energy is flowing in the proper direction, toward creative self-expression.

Life energy can flow in the opposite direction as well. As creativity guru Mihaly Csikszentmihalyi says, "The chief obstacle to a good life is oneself." I believe we can be trapped in misery by unresolved grief. Some people even choose to embrace the dark side of life, albeit unconsciously, by holding on to their anger and hate, projecting blame for their problems onto others. They come to believe that evil is more powerful than love, and that domination will dissolve their fear.

Most of us wish with all our hearts to escape from grief and disappointment as quickly as possible, to emerge with renewed vitality and a strengthened capacity for love. However, sometimes we get lost in a dark area of forest, not realizing that there is a path to a friendly castle on the other side of the woods. The forest in which we lose our way represents the first four responses of the grief process: denial, anger, obsession, and depression. These four areas of behavior actually serve as protective defenses. We use them according to need, like body-armor, while we're jousting with loss, life change, and new realities.

Inventor Elias Howe

Growing through grief sometimes feels impossible and unpredictable. We may feel stuck in depression and suddenly find ourselves back in anger, or quite comfortable in denial, ignoring the implications of our loss, when suddenly obsession takes over. During a focused creative project, we might achieve a long-awaited *Aha!* only to find ourselves thrown back into blackness because of our inability to manifest the discovery. Elias Howe's experience with inventing the sewing machine is a good example of how these creative stages may work.

Howe was familiar with the cotton industry and the machinery of the mid-1800s. He wanted to develop a machine that could sew clothing. Putting together parts that would drive the machine was not a problem. He got completely stymied, however, by the problem of how to get the thread through the material. He experimented and deliberated over how he might achieve his goal. Howe moved from germination of the seed of an idea, through periods of frustration and anger, and through times of nagging obsession and depression. Even though it seemed as though he would never fulfill his dream, all of his struggles can be seen as part of a process of incubating a resolution. During incubation, the creative process is taking place below the level of awareness.

One night, Elias Howe had a nightmare. He was being chased by primitives who were throwing spears at him. As he ran away, he turned to see a spear coming right toward his chest. He looked closely and noticed there was a hole near the end of the point. *Aha!* His block to understanding how to complete the machine was overcome. Whereas in hand sewing the thread goes through a hole in the large end of the needle, for the machine, the opening for the thread needed to be near the tip of the needle. It took Howe five years to achieve this creative solution, plus another grief and growth cycle to establish the patent rights to his work. But his creative effort led to a revolution in garment manufacturing.

Dreams can bring breakthrough information to us, as well. My friend Diane Campbell, told me the following dream that she had during her divorce and gave me permission to share it: "I'm climbing a very steep mountain and I've come a long way up. I notice that my backpack feels heavier and heavier. I keep going, but more slowly, one handhold at a time. My shoulders and arms begin to ache from the heaviness on my back and I wonder if I'll be able to make it to the top. Finally, I can't imagine why my pack is so heavy and I turn my head to look. I'm astounded to see that I had been growing huge, beautiful, white wings, and I simply let go and fly."

What an important reminder that with each grief and growth learning cycle, we become better at transcending habitual tendencies to indulge in what some call "the lower emotions." Frustration, anger, obsession, depression, and self-doubt can be carried like a heavy backpack, weighing us down. It's a relief to know that we can escape that load and fly.

There are three dimensions of movement from crisis to creativity. The first level is the crisis itself that necessitates grief. The second is the transformation of energy into creative self-expression, and the third dimension consists of powerful possibilities for transcending troubles and manifesting love.

The creative process calls us to open to the inner world. Coping with change does not mean adapting to whatever happens in the outside world. The intention to change internally illuminates possibilities in every area of life This creativity, which I call "the art of growing self-expression," is what leads to full-capacity living. It requires the willingness and the courage to analyze your personality style to see where you get stuck on your way to creative competence.

Most people have a tendency to fall into a pattern when reacting to stressful events. More men than women fall into anger. More women than men fall into depression. When we are grieving we are all blind to the higher good that a challenging life event might bring.

Looking at the following Grief and Growth Chart to find where you characteristically get stuck in life will help you to discover your "neurotic style," or to put it more kindly, your "paradigm paralysis."

Grief and Growth Chart
From Crisis to Creativity and Transcendence

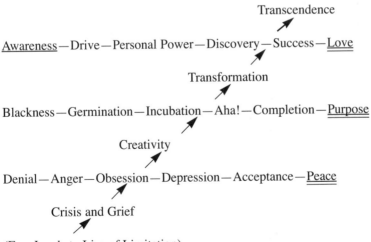

(Love Leads to Powerful Possibilities)

Transcendence

Awareness—Drive—Personal Power—Discovery—Success—Love

Transformation

Blackness—Germination—Incubation—Aha!—Completion—Purpose

Creativity

Denial—Anger—Obsession—Depression—Acceptance—Peace

Crisis and Grief

(Fear Leads to Lies of Limitation)

The word "awareness" is underlined to highlight the fact that awareness is always the beginning of transforming life energy from negative thoughts and emotions to positive ones. Awareness brings with it possibilities for transcending problems. Solving any kind of dilemma begins with awareness. Seen in this way, every act of learning, creating, and personal growth is accomplished with awareness as the starting place. Awareness should not be confused with understanding. Understanding may come further along, during the *Aha!* stage of creativity, or during the acceptance stage of grief, or possibly many years after a particular life experience.

While we all bounce around handling a host of different feelings during crises, most of us have a tendency to flounder in one particular area. Make a mental note about which reaction you habitually fall into: denial, anger, obsession, depression, and pay particular attention to the following chapter that pertains. Knowing that there are options will help you on your way to taking charge of personal change.

With each cycle through grief and growth, one's creative competence increases. Higher energy, clarity of purpose, and inner peace result. I believe that as we become "good grievers" we move through the cycles more quickly. We don't fall as deeply into grief, we transcend fear more easily, and we emerge with a greater sense of renewed purpose. Kathleen, a professional performer, stated it well as she was summing up her gains in therapy: "I no longer get so upset when I'm upset," she said.

If there are only two states of being, love and fear, as is taught in *A Course in Miracles*,[4] I see the grieving process as one of fear and the creative process as one of love. This perception provides a "touchstone" for cutting through confusion about feelings. In response to any life change, I can ask, "Am I dwelling in fear, or am I feeling love?" in order to catch myself in depression or obsessive thinking. If the answer is "fear," I know I need to push up my periscope to see the creative work I am doing. I need to provide a context for myself in which to know that *because* I am allowing life to touch me, and *because* I allow my feelings to flow like a cool fountain on a hot day, I will soon be functioning in a stronger way.

When I catch myself obsessing, for example, I remind myself that I am busy incubating solutions and that my unconscious mind can take care of that. I then look to the top of the Grief and Growth Chart to remember that I must also be working on a greater sense of personal power. I can trust that the love connection will return.

As we learn how to grieve effectively, we are unblocking energy, allowing it to flow from our own deep pool of creativity within and become a rainbow of creativity without. Our alchemists gold is a true transformation: a stronger, happier, wiser self.

The quest for transformation requires intention. It rarely happens quickly or easily. My funny friend Grace, early in her quest for grief-relief, did a five-hour long sitting meditation. When I next saw her, she said, "I was doing fine for the first two hours, then I started getting back pain. I'm talking serious back pain! I decided if this is what it means to get in touch with my Higher Self, I am in big trouble!"

Grace eventually figured out that besides some arthritis in her lower back, she had pain that was an expression of feeling trapped in a depressive position of being hurt by those closest to her. As she resolved her life-long pattern of internalizing hurts, she discovered her true nature; the light and loving spirit that comes through to others.

Most of us wish that an *Aha!* insight would come to us in the same dramatic way that it came to Elias Howe, and immediately resolve our problems. However, the *Aha!*s that move us along through grief to acceptance and creative change are more likely to be happening consistently, but subtly. As we develop our awareness and pay close attention to life events we will be able to see them, nonetheless.

Angie, a market researcher for a large company in southern California, was devastated when the corporation downsized and she was left running the department alone. She had no idea how she would be able to handle the work. Over a three-year period she discovered that the budget allowed her to contract for the help she needed and even expand her vision and objectives. She was able to provide work for the best in her field and found herself promoted in salary and position.

"Three years ago, I was thinking I'd have to change careers. Now I have more work than I can handle, more networking with others in my field, and I love it!" Angie had found her creative niche.

Maggie, a childhood friend I hadn't seen in many years, made a slightly more dramatic discovery involving death. She was telling me about the death of her mother, with whom she had been very close. "I'd never thought very much about death and when my mother was so ill with her cancer I just thought death would bring relief from her suffering. I was really angry, though, that this was happening to her. The night she died, she seemed to be in a coma and she kept calling out to my father. He died many years ago. At first I thought she was just hallucinating or something, but I began to get the strangest feeling that she was actually seeing him. She died quietly about an hour later.

"I realized as I was making the arrangements for the funeral that, in spite of all the work facing me, I felt peaceful. I've begun to consider the possibility that my father was there waiting for her and that some of the stories I've read about the afterlife may be true."

Maggie's periscope had been pushed up from grief to acceptance and awareness of the creative possibilities in death. Her *Aha!* began the process of healing moving her beyond her fear of being without her mother and her fear that her mother would suffer while she was dying. She accepted instead the possibility that her mother was being reborn into a spiritual life.

Coming to trust that these grief and growth cycles are guiding you in just the right direction requires not only awareness but also trust and patience. Healing our fear of life change may take an entire lifetime. The heart's purpose, however, is to reach the light of self-acceptance and inner peace. While I can't provide the exact how-to's, the grief and growth concept can be an assuring frame of reference as you develop your creative competence. I encourage you to reframe your depression or other grieving feelings into a natural creative process. You will see that there is meaning in your reaction to every life change. You can discover your spiritual nature, and that discovery will bring a sense of purpose and a calm feeling of inner peace.

Daily Creative Discipline
(Grief Cycles and the Creative Process)

1. As soon as you wake in the morning, make two **positive statements,** one about yourself and one about the world or the community in which you live.

2. Spend at least ten minutes each morning in meditation, contemplation, yoga, prayer, relaxation, self-hypnosis, stretching, exercise, or some method of **inward-focused attention.**

3. During that time, think of a personal trait you have disliked in someone else and look for one way of understanding that person's behavior. This type of creative thinking leads to transforming negative feelings into **awareness.**

4. During your morning break, think of a personal trait you have disliked in yourself and find one way that behavior has protected you or helped you to cope with a difficult life experience. This type of flexible thinking will help you to achieve **self-acceptance.**

5. Whenever you find yourself in anger, obsession, or depression, allow yourself to become curious. Ask yourself if you might be in a grief and growth cycle, mourning some disappointment, old or new, large or small. Open your mind to any awareness of inner wishes for greater drive, personal power, discovery, or **success.** Ask yourself each day, "What is the best thing, the most amazing thing, that can happen to me?"

6. Keep a stack of white paper and a box of crayons easily accessible. Each evening, without thinking of form or style, **make a drawing of the prevalent feeling state** of that day. Date and file.

Chapter Two

Murphy, Job, and Other Tales of Creative Competence

For the human spirit is virtually indestructible, and its ability to rise from the ashes remains as long as the body draws breath.

— Alice Miller

Some of our most enduring stories, from antiquity to the present, illustrate the personal transformations that can take place when one completes a grief and growth cycle and moves on to creativity. This process is so deeply rooted in our history, we need to draw on the knowledge to sustain us through our own cycles of suffering. Before I tell the ancient stories, I'll allude to the modern equivalent: Murphy's Law. There are two models of movement through grief and growth that I'll be describing: Murphy's Law of Misery and Job's Law of Life. With Murphy's Law, everything that can go wrong does go wrong, but there is always a sense that one's head is above water and the water will eventually recede. When Job's Law of Life hits, it hits like a cyclone, leaving recurrent feelings of drowning and total devastation. The loss is simply overwhelming. The "good" in grief is easier to accept with a Murphy's Law experience, as things seem to right themselves more quickly and the learning is more immediate.

Murphy's Law of Misery

A friend of mine once had to endure a decidedly Murphy's Law day. Jonathon is a psychiatrist and internist in Los Angeles. On this day, he was caring for a small boy who had accidentally drunk lye. He was very worried about this child's survival. The child went to surgery and Jonathon needed to be available for the post-operative care. His wife Molly was also in the hospital that day for a breast biopsy. There's a history of breast cancer in her family. Jonathon had to take a break and drive to pick up one of their children from school out in the Hollywood Hills.

As he was winding through the hills, wishing he could stay at the hospital, his pager went off. There were no businesses anywhere in the area, so he finally found a fire station. He used the phone and learned from his answering service that one of his psychiatric patients was standing on top of a building in Los Angeles preparing to jump. He needed to be in four places at once! He wanted to be with his wife, with the sick child, with his own child, and with his desperate patient all at the same time. He proceeded to his child's school and spent the next hour on the telephone before completing his parenting duties and getting back to the hospital. He had one very long day. He felt pressure in his head and tension throughout his body.

That night and over the next few days Jonathon talked to Molly about the details of each of the mini-traumas of that day. He spent time listening to her tell of her experience with the biopsy. He expressed his feelings of frustration and anger that he wasn't able to spend more time with her. He went out and bought a mobile phone, new technology at that time, in order to diminish some of his stress about being out of contact with his patients and his family. As Jonathon and Molly shared their thoughts and feelings, the grief connected with these events was processed, digested, metabolized. Instead of burying reactions and building resentment, each expression of coping and tending the feelings from this "down day" was a demonstration of creative competence.

Jonathon had had a "Good Grief!" kind of day, the kind that becomes a good story after one has survived and been strengthened by the creative use of emotions.

Job's Law of Life

Job, on the other hand, barely survived, and definitely could not relieve his stress by buying a mobile phone. You remember Job. According to the Bible, he was the greatest man in all the East. He had thousands of camels, oxen, sheep, donkeys, and slaves. He had seven sons and three daughters, and his personal hell lasted many, many days. And it was deeply personal. Before one messenger bearing bad news could depart, the next arrived. His donkeys and oxen were stolen and the herdsmen killed. His sheep and the shepherds were destroyed by a lightning storm. A group of bandits stole his camels. And finally, the worst news imaginable: during a feast, the roof literally fell in, killing his sons, their wives, and his daughters. All his earthly belongings and his children, gone.

And what was Job's response? He fell prostrate and said, "The Lord giveth and the Lord taketh away; blessed be the name of the Lord." And with that, Job enters the first stage of grief—denial. How do we know that reaction is denial? Why couldn't Job, who was a very devout man, immediately be at the last stage of grief, acceptance? Because we read in the rest of the story that Job becomes angry and rages at God. He becomes obsessive until he sounds paranoid. He becomes deeply depressed and falls ill…all the stages of grief with which we are familiar.

While Job is trapped in his shock and pain, three of his friends, the first psychotherapists, come to try to help out. First, they are so overwhelmed by his misery and by seeing the complete downfall of such a great man that they tear their clothes and throw dirt around (they go into the heavy-duty grieving rituals that were practiced at that time). Then they, along with Job, become mute for seven days. I think that symbolizes the numbness that often sets in during the initial stage of profound grief. Notice the number seven.

In the biblical story, seven days is the length of time required to create the world.

When Job begins talking again, he curses the day of his birth. Then he begins ranting against God, adding, "Every terror that haunted me has caught up with me; what I dreaded has overtaken me. There is no peace of mind..." (Job 3:25-26). Job tells us that he has been living in fear, dreading the loss of his possessions. Even before the catastrophe, fear had destroyed his peace. He's no longer silent, but in the defensive mode of anger. Job's wife moved ahead of him into her grief when she said to Job from the depths of her rage, "Why don't you just curse God and die!" This expressiveness must have been frowned upon, because that's the last we hear of her! (Job's wife is linked to the feminine God energy, Sophia, in chapters 4 and 7.)

Job brings his anger into the next stage of bargaining when he wishes for someone to mediate with God, "impose his authority...so that God might take his rod from my back" (Job 9:33-34). This reminds me of the story of a man who is running from a tiger. He comes to a cliff, slips over the side and grabs onto a branch. He's hanging there looking up at the tiger and turns his head to look down. There's nothing but a vast chasm. He shouts to the heavens, "God! Please help me! Tell me what to do." A deep voice answers slowly, "Let go!" The man is stunned. He asks feebly, "Is there anyone else up there?" Fear not only destroys inner peace, it destroys faith.

So we hear Job's anger, his ruminations and obsessive thinking. We even hear paranoia when he says to his friends, "...what gifts indeed have you that others have not? Yet I am a laughing-stock to my friends—a laughing-stock, though I am innocent and blameless..." (Job 12:3-4). And then the proof that he is no longer taking responsibility for his thoughts: "they are all in league against me" (Job 16:10).

His friends, the first therapists, take turns trying to talk sense to Job, reasoning with him, telling him things aren't so bad, and by the way, who does he think he is being so self-righteous that he blames everyone including God for his troubles? Needless to say, it doesn't work. Only Job can decide, when he is ready, to move forward through his grief.

My Revised English Bible refers to this grieving process as "Job's Complaint to God." Basically, it's Job working his way, with a good deal of anger and whining, through the grief process. And isn't that what most of us do? If we become more aware of this dynamic, we may be able to move more quickly and with less suffering to the completion of a cycle, acceptance of a new reality, and subsequent peace of mind.

I believe the story of Job is a metaphor for the states of mind we experience during the processing of difficult life events. Eliphaz, Bildad, and Zophar, Job's friends, represent the obsessive thoughts we can't get free of in the middle of a period of grief. Job's paranoid projections represent his self-hate, and we're given reason to believe that Job, like most of us, made mistakes that he deeply regretted. He finally becomes ill and hopeless in his depression.

The young man, Elihu, who chastises Job for being more righteous than God, represents Job's intuitive self. He speaks of the importance of learning lessons in life and acknowledging the power of universal law. Finally, Divine Intelligence, which may also be Job's Transcendent or Higher Self, speaks: "Gird your loins, brace yourself, and stand up like a man!" (Job 38:3). I think that means to hike up your pants, or get a grip, and take responsibility for your life. And in a moment, Job sees the light of truth, asks forgiveness, releases the past, and accepts the present.

We're told that in that same moment, all his possessions are returned two-fold, and that he lives another hundred years. In other words, when Job gives up defensive reactions to his losses, he accepts responsibility for the present and is transformed. As he matures, his family matures. He is at peace and his life is filled with abundance once more.

The entire story of Job is about his painful emotional reactions. Forty-one chapters are spent describing his grief. The very last passages refer to the acceptance of a new reality, a profound illumination, a discovery that "I have spoken of things which I have not understood, things too wonderful for me to know" (Job 42:3).

A dear friend and colleague, David, is a psychiatrist with whom I shared office space for the fourteen years before his retirement. He used to listen to me explain my life problems. My "whining post" would listen carefully and with great patience while I looked at the impossibility of my situation from every angle. Finally, he'd nod his head and say, "Gail, this is gonna make a man out of you." We'd laugh together over some unspoken insight about my inevitable survival.

What David was saying is that with every grief and growth cycle of life, I would become a stronger individual. Like Job, I would suffer but then move through my grief and eventually become transformed by an awareness of things that had been "too wonderful for me to know."

Surviving traumas or coming to terms with personal conflicts gives us a stronger, clearer sense of who we are, what we stand for, and how we express ourselves. There is greater awareness that our spirits are safe in the world. Energy accessed through grieving is freed for creative self-expression. We are free to choose the powerful possibilities of creative competence and love rather than remain in "lies of limitation," believing we are trapped in some emotion not of our own making. When Job alludes to "things which I have not understood," I'm certain he is referring to the realization that all change and loss are part of creative cycles that bring us ever closer to loving connectedness with other souls, with ourselves, and with Divine Energy.

The Grief of Demeter, The Power of Persephone

Later in history, during pre-Hellenic times, we find the story of Demeter and Persephone that gives us further insight into this cycle of grieving, creativity, and rebirth. Demeter is the Earth Mother, the mother of what evolves in the present as well as in the future. As such, she is rich in creative potential and nurturing abilities. She has a daughter, Persephone, who is an adolescent, joyous and playful. Persephone spends her time in the meadows, reveling in her curiosity, her youthful energy, and her spontaneous discoveries.

In the first version of the story, Persephone is playing one day and hears outcries of anguished people. That evening she tells her mother, Demeter, that during her play she has heard people weeping. Demeter tells her to not pay attention to such things. But, the next day, she continues to hear the weeping. She looks until she finds a crack in the earth, and she discovers lost souls in the underworld. Her compassion leads her to make the descent into Hades's domain to help these souls find their way to the light.

In a later version of the story, Persephone is playing in her field when Hades rises from the underworld in his dark chariot drawn by black horses and steals her away without leaving a trace. Whether it is Persephone's conscious intent to go "under" or whether she is stolen away, naturally Demeter feels distraught and destroyed. She begins searching for her daughter everywhere on earth. She searches the mountains and the oceans. She crawls into caves bearing a torch. She finally sits down exhausted and bleeding, the light in her life extinguished.

Hecate, an old woman, comes to Demeter and tells her that she has heard her daughter being abducted. She didn't see what happened, but she heard something. Maybe it would be wise to go speak to Helios, the Sun. Together they go and Helios says that Persephone was given to Hades as his bride by none other than great Zeus, the king of the gods, who thinks it would be a good marriage for Persephone.

Demeter is inconsolable in her grief. She withdraws from life, wanders far from her home in Crete, and takes a job as nurse to the son of the King of Eleusis. While she has regained enough energy to nurture a child again, her deep mourning has caused the earth to become barren. There is no food and the earth's people are in a very bad way. They are losing faith in the gods and threatening to stop honoring them. Zeus begins sending every god in the pantheon of gods to Demeter, begging her to restore fertility to

Earth. One by one they come, pleading with Demeter, but she ignores them.

Finally, out of desperation, Zeus sends Hermes to talk to his brother Hades. Hermes tells him he must return Persephone to her mother in order to restore seed and growth to the earth. Zeus is willing to compromise with Hades. If Persephone has not eaten any food while in the underworld, she may return to her mother permanently. But if she has eaten food there, she will belong to both worlds.

In one story, Hades forces her to eat a pomegranate and she swallows six seeds. In the other version, she eagerly eats of the pomegranate, ending her self-starvation, when she learns she is being returned to Demeter. Either way, the story ends with her having to cycle between spending time with her mother and spending three to six months each year in the underworld with Hades.

This story gave the people of ancient Greece an understanding of winter, the seasons, and the natural balance of life and death. Modern Jungian psychologists Clarissa Pinkola Estes and Helen Luke expand on the significance of the story by relating it to personal development.[1] Like Job, Demeter has to confront her fear and loss. She tries to avoid the dark side of life by suggesting that her daughter ignore the suffering she heard while playing. But the desire for knowledge of the entire spectrum of the human experience can not be denied. Persephone, who symbolizes the bright, young, creative, energetic part of ourselves, gets separated from her nurturing source.

Whether intentional behavior leads us into the depths, or whether we are victims of someone else's violence, we sometimes cycle through times of blackness. Our creative juices are dried up. We suffer pain and lost hope. We feel barren. But like Demeter, we must search, and we must learn to trust that our creativity, our spirit, can never be taken from us for all time. Hecate, the old crone, represents the intuitive side of our nature. Hecate heard something happen to Persephone. She didn't know exactly what had happened, but knew how to discover the truth, from Helios, the

Sun, the Light.

Demeter processes her grief in a manner similar to Job's. She is angry, depressed, and obsessive. Each of the gods tries to reason with her, just like Job's friends did with him. Cajoling and reasoning have no effect on the deep emotions, however. As the French mathematician Henri Poincare once said, "It is with logic that we prove, but by intuition that we discover!" Demeter uses her intuition to help her search and then again as she constructs a new life for herself. We are told that her search took nine days, symbolic of the nine months of pregnancy.

Demeter's beloved daughter Persephone, her life spark, is restored to her when she accepts the reality of the life and death cycle, the awareness that every creative urge begins with darkness, germination, and incubation. The conscious mind must give way to the mysteries of the unconscious. There is an integration of all parts of our psyches when we accept responsibility for this process. Knowing that we are not only Demeter, but also Persephone, Hades destroying our creative urges for a time, Helios the Light, and the intuitive old Hecate, gives reassurance that spring will come again and our creative urges will bloom and bear fruit in summer.

Trusting change, believing in intuition, having faith that life will unfold in just the right ways...these attitudes require cultivation. Especially during the first stages of change and creativity, it is imperative to place your pain in a larger context, the context of this creative and transformative cycle. Pinkola Estes reminds us that "there can be no renewal without death, without entropy, without reduction and regression."

The alchemists knew that the first stage of the creative process is actually blackness, the Latin *Nigredo* or *massa confusa,* total mental confusion. Even during the subsequent stages of germination and incubation, ideas come together and then break apart, leaving us again in blackness. Feelings of shame, guilt, obsession, and depression can lead to withdrawal and physical breakdown. But then the discovery or *Aha!* stage, the stage the alchemists called *Citrinitas,* the flash of gold, leads to a breakthrough. The *Aha!* breakthrough can appear as simply as waking one morning and feeling well, intact, and comfortable. Or, it can appear dramatically in a dream, like that of Elias Howe and his sewing machine needle, or scientist Niels Bohr dreaming the structure of the atom, or chemist Friedrich Kekule, daydreaming on a London bus and discovering the structure of the benzene molecule. At the point of an *Aha!* breakthrough, everything is right with the world again. Fertility is restored. Our juices are flowing.

Five phenomena seem to be occurring during the discovery phase of creativity: (1) a state of relaxation, (2) suspension of critical thinking, (3) heightened imagery, (4) time distortion, and (5) associational flow. These aspects of creativity are described further in chapters 7 (p. 165) and 8 (p. 203). These states are most likely given favorable ground when we cease resisting a life change. At this point the mind is freed for creative thought.

At the end of psychotherapy when people review their progression from unhappiness to contentment, these experiences are often mentioned: greater relaxation, lessened tendency to be judgmental, no time pressure and greater enjoyment of associations and imagination. "I'm not frantic to be on time," one man said, "I just live *in* time." One woman said, "I don't know when the obsessions and compulsions stopped. They just seemed to get more infrequent, and one day it dawned on me that I wasn't in that state of tension, of worrying and having to clean things constantly." Her energy was flowing into a self-expression she never dreamed of— art and the ability to speak her mind to her family.

An architect who was recovering from childhood molestation by a priest said, "My nightmares have stopped. My depression has lifted. I feel free for the first time." This man could immediately see the result of his increased creative energy. "My work is moving in a direction I never expected," he shared. "I had this insight that after the abuse, I never felt 'at home' again, either in the Church or with my family. Now, I'm designing my first real home. It feels wonderful."

I believe the *intention* to heal our fear fuels our focus on difficult emotions and eventually enables us to reach acceptance and inner peace. If one is determined enough to change, it will happen.

In the mid-1960s, when my husband and I first moved to New Mexico, I conducted adoption studies for the State Human Services Department. In most cases, it took at least two years to find an infant for a couple, in addition to the years they spent trying to have children of their own. But many times, after the couple adopted a child and relaxed into parenthood, the mother became pregnant. Why?

I believe it has something to do with grieving and growing, ceasing to struggle, and continuing to focus on one's vision of happiness. Inner peace and an unconscious opening to new possibilities result. And, in some cases, a literal miracle of creation occurs.

Whether you are moving through a Murphy cycle or a Job cycle, recognize that your emotions are part of the dynamic energy of life. Learning to understand, respect, and accept this energy, both the "negative" and "positive," will add balance and peace to your life. Trust in the process of change. Believe in yourself. Know that you have a place in the world. Practice faith in the way your life is unfolding. Love life and you will be astonished by your increasing ability to create your own true Self!

Daily Creative Discipline
(Creative Competence)

1. Think of one disappointment or loss you are currently dealing with. List three possible outcomes. Make sure one is outrageously **positive.**

2. Push the periscope up on the Grief and Growth Chart to see the corresponding aspects of **creativity** with which you are working. Tell yourself you are incubating a more vibrant, expressive, irrepressible you.

3. Think about what needs to happen in order for you to move closer to accepting what now seems like a negative experience in your life. Flip it upside down in your mind and see the **possibilities** for expanding your world.

4. Envision yourself in the future, when this cycle is complete and you have come to accept a new reality. Feel the full responsibility of living in **joy,** working, playing, having a clear sense of your life **purpose.**

5. Remind yourself each day that you are on an **exciting personal journey.** Trust that you have an internal and external guidance system in place, facilitating your learning and your growth.

6. Write a **brief story** in which you are the main character living a "Murphy's day," a "Job's year," or a Greek tragedy. Remember that even gods and goddesses had very bad times, but their stories always end, like Job's, with restoration. How does your story end with a new beginning?

Chapter Three

Denial: To the Light of Awareness

*It is one of the triumphs of the human that he can know
a thing and still not believe it.*

— John Steinbeck

Denial is disavowed grief. When Job prostrated himself on the ground and said, "The Lord gives and the Lord takes away; blessed be the name of the Lord," he was behaving automatically, according to his beliefs and his cultural upbringing. The connection to all he had known that spelled safety, security, love, and the Divine, had been annihilated. Although he must have felt utterly destroyed, in order to go on functioning at all he tried to affirm his connection to God and to adhere to the grieving rituals of his day.

Denial is like treading water in the middle of an unknown sea. There may be no fear and a belief that we'll have no problem reaching land. Sometimes the resistance to awareness is so great we can delude ourselves that we're not even in the water but on firm ground, even though those around us are quite aware that we are wet and being moved by deep and transforming tides. We dispute a new reality to reassure ourselves that nothing is really changing, while in actuality we are in the midst of powerful change.

Denial is protective. It is the first psychological defense that every one of us develops. When toddlers cover their eyes and say, "You can't see me!" they are exercising the power of the mind to block out reality. Using this defense mechanism, children can normalize the most hurtful of worlds. A parent's neglect or abuse becomes simply the way all parents are. Poverty and loss are merely the ways of the world. Without the protection of denial, we would all commit suicide in childhood. Denying a harsh reality holds us while we grow our resilience.

Once we are grown, denial becomes the belligerent know-it-all, bellowing, "I know what I know! Don't bother me with the facts!" This is the part of the personality that proclaims, "I don't get ulcers; I give them." There is also an opposite, bland form of denial: "I am not angry. Everything's fine." A crisis is more likely to be acknowledged in order to protect people we love than to nurture ourselves toward creative competence. A person in denial, however, creates a toxic atmosphere by refusing to discuss or acknowledge problems.

We all sense the tension between denial and awareness, and are tempted to stay in fear and experience the world as "giving us grief." This tension characterizes our ambivalence about change. At the same time that we want to explore the world, we want to settle into comfort and security. We thrive on challenge, but we are also creatures of habit. The wish to master new areas of learning is usually conscious; the stumbling blocks are unconscious. Because difficult problems and adjustments may come with change, denial is our automatic, first-line resistance against that change.

Our ambivalence about awareness is expressed in the saying "Ignorance is bliss." At the same time we are eager to increase our awareness of the world, we dread the difficult process and long for simpler times, when learning meant riding a new bicycle or baking brownies in an Easy-Bake Oven. We often yearn to live in the innocence of childhood, where we can rediscover the bliss of watching floating clouds on a peaceful summer day. Adults never entirely get over the tendency to hope that problems will go away if they are simply ignored.

Denial as a psychological defense protects us from feeling overwhelmed by perceived threats to our psychological and physical integrity. The cognitive and emotional ways we block awareness range from silence, numbness, forgetting and avoidance, to intellectualization, rationalization, and loud protestation.

In one family therapy session, the father, a politician perceived by his family as being intimidating, became increasingly agitated as he listened to his grown children describe their difficulty communicating with him because of his anger. Finally, he shouted, "I am not angry!" to which we could only giggle and call his attention to the obvious (which he still could not see). Denying our own behavior, someone else's behavior, or other difficulties simply blocks the movement of life energy toward creative purpose.

All children have to believe that what they experience in their families is normal. A child's mother, father, or parent-surrogate represents the entire world to that child. A mother is our lifeline to feelings of sanity and safety. Adult survivors of child abuse tell me that they thought all families were like theirs. They automatically denied they were being mistreated. Thirty-eight-year-old Tom said, "I just thought all the boys in the third grade got beaten when their fathers came home from work." On another level of awareness, the child knows that what is happening to him is cruel and capricious. The psychological defense of denial helps us feel safe as children. Once grown, however, we must slowly replace denial with awareness.

Opening our eyes to confront difficult issues is the first step in mastering our fear of change and accepting new realities. Barbara, a therapy client who survived childhood "lessons in evil," consciously denied her family's satanism for a long time.[1] It was only after she was an adult with many years of therapy that she was prepared to acknowledge the meaning of her nightmares and flashbacks. Barbara could acknowledge her mother's abuse because it was her grandmother with whom she had a maternal bond. But when she finally accepted that her grandmother had also betrayed her to the cult, she was inconsolable in her grief. "Her satanic beliefs are about her," she cried, "but not loving me has to be about me!"

Obedience to the family rules had been Barbara's survival mechanism. Barbara still believed what her family had indoctrinated, that everything they did to her was her own fault; therefore, she must be unloveable. As an adult, she was struggling to release the lifeline she no longer needed, the self-doubt her family had carefully nurtured. In order to completely heal her fear, she ultimately had to give up denial in favor of the awareness that her grandmother was unable to love her appropriately and was unable to place Barbara's needs before the requirements of the cult.

Living in denial means living a lie. I call these beliefs "lies of limitation." As long as we believe the lies, we are stuck and completely stalled on our paths of creative competence. As long as Barbara believed the lies that she was responsible for the cruelty, she believed herself incompetent and undeserving of inner peace and worldly success.

Everyone understands the immediate reactions of shock and denial when a loved one dies suddenly. Upon hearing that my closest male friend, Robert, had committed suicide, I began saying repeatedly, "No! No! No! I don't believe that!"

I couldn't believe it. We cannot accept profound change quickly. The mind needs time to take in the new information, to reprogram. We need time to begin to process the grief response. The most enormous change, the loss of a beloved partner or child, seems impossible to accept, even over a long period of time. Ellen's first response to the suicide of her husband, Robert, was numbness.

"Sometimes I feel anger boiling down deep, but mostly I feel nothing. I'm numb. My body's shut down and doesn't seem to be working. I can't sleep or eat. I'm like a zombie."

Ellen and Robert had a secure, long-term marriage and two nearly grown daughters. No one knew that Robert's business investments were failing and that he could not face financial ruin. The oldest son of an alcoholic, Robert had become the financial kingpin for his parents and siblings and expected to continue his hard-won tradition of wealth and generosity. But he had never grieved the loss of his own childhood, and so he hadn't learned emotionally how to process disappointment and discover his own level of creative self-expression.

Ellen's body initially felt like it had died along with Robert's. Gradually, the pain of rage let her know that she was very much alive. She was furious with herself for not being able to help Robert, and angry with him for having given up on life. Ellen told me that her therapy gradually helped her understand why Robert couldn't handle his terror of financial change. She opened up to an awareness of his silent suffering and to her own denial of the problems and inability to acknowledge the financial turnaround. In this case, moving from denial to awareness and acceptance meant forgiving herself and forgiving Robert for not knowing how to cope with change.

Ellen's striving to get through the emotional mud puddles of her grief gradually unblocked her creative energy. Five years later, she has a new degree in Fine Arts and an ability to draw and paint that came as a total surprise. "Art history was really my interest, but I had to take studio classes for my degree. I was amazed that I could actually create decent drawings."

Ellen now feels, for the most part, that she has come to accept losing Robert. She sometimes misses him desperately, feels twinges of anger and guilt, or finds herself obsessing about some details of their relationship, but she has clearly come through grief and growth to a higher level of creative competence. She has acknowledged the past and now faces the future. In so doing, she has found a new career. She even toys with the thought of moving to the Far East, an area of the world that has always intrigued her.

One year after Robert's death another dear friend, Shelly (whom I introduced earlier), died one night of an asthma attack. Although she was an outstanding physician, I knew her more as a mother. Our first babies were born nine days apart in 1969 and grew up like brother and sister, sharing the same caretakers, schools, and summer camps.

Just as my husband and I and our mutual friends had denied that Robert might be facing a crisis and in a state of grief, we denied the severity of Shelly's physical problem. We teased her about her devotion to her animals in spite of the wheezing and congestion they caused her. Never did we acknowledge that her situation could be life threatening. While assuming responsibility for Robert's or Shelly's deaths would be grandiose and unreasonable, I will always regret that I didn't recognize their problematic situations and express my concern.

We may be barely aware of our tendency toward defense and denial, or have no awareness at all. It took me more than a year to begin writing this book in its current form. During that time I knew that the transformation of grief into creativity and transcendence was the topic I wished to write about. I wrote energetically, only occasionally noticing that those who read my drafts were not as enthusiastic as I'd hoped. One day I realized I was not writing about creativity and transformation at all; I was still processing my grief over the experiences of the previous two years. I was denying the impact of the deaths of my friends as well as the unfairness I felt as a psychologist about the suffering of abuse victims versus the seeming success of some of the perpetrators. I was pulling the reader into my own grief cycle. I had to set aside the more than one hundred pages I'd written and begin again, striving to get through my "blackness" to an acceptance of pain and death as a fact of life.

It is important to remember that we do not necessarily move linearly through the stages of grief and growth and creativity. We may go back and forth between phases within a cycle for years. Candace, whose father forced sex upon her from the time she was two until she was twelve, when he suicided in front of her with a bullet to the head, cycles between denial and depression. "Dissociation is my form of denial. When I'm dissociated, I don't know anything about the incest. When I'm aware, I'm catastrophically depressed. I also have a lot of painful physical symptoms that express my terror."[2]

Notice that Candace is aware enough to know where she is in processing her grief. She has faced enough of the traumatic realities to be successful in many areas of her life. However, at this time, she still needs the protection of denial, the ability to dissociate from the memories, as she grows stronger.

When we are in denial, we are silently saying, "I am not able to cope with or accept the reality of this problem right now." Not only individuals, but groups of people and entire societies can unconsciously choose denial. During my book tour for *Lessons in Evil, Lessons From the Light,* nearly every media appearance I made was marked by a debate wherein my opponent's goal was to discredit Barbara's story of having been abused in an organized satanic cult. I reminded audiences that it has only been since 1962, when the "battered child syndrome" was described, that Americans have acknowledged child abuse. Prior to that, we stayed comfortably in our collective denial by calling these children "accident prone." It took another twenty years for Americans to begin to acknowledge that children could be sexually abused in their own homes.[3]

Resistance to facing individual evil is understandable. And as psychohistorian Lloyd de Mause has shown, the social drive to deny organized evil certainly makes sense.[4] The threat to our personal safety and that of our children feels too great. During the 1940s and 1950s, for example, some Americans adamantly denied valid reports of an organized group of extortionists and murderers called the Mafia.

While it is helpful to remember that people in denial are in the first stage of grief and will possibly move beyond it, it is clear to me that denial is the breeding ground for disordered behavior. For it is in "the underworld of creativity,"[5] staying in unresolved grief, that stagnation of energy can lead to immoral behavior. In order to apprehend our own evil, we must be willing to become aware of the areas of life in which we lose our footing and become fascinated by the descent.

My friend Lynn returned from a personal growth workshop where she had walked on hot coals.

"What was it like?" I asked her. "Did you really do it?"

"Yes. It was interesting because I was going along just fine until I looked down and became fascinated by the red burning embers. That's when I felt my feet starting to burn. I quickly looked up and went on."

Some people don't go on. They come to believe in the threat and the power of the heat. They embrace the fire of personal impulse instead of looking up and forward to the light of self-control, growth, and group well-being.

Perpetrators of abuse choose to live in this first area of grief: denial. Those who violate others are unable to see the possibilities inherent in change, loss, and most of all, love. They do not reach the maturational level of "generativity," which developmental psychoanalyst Erik Erikson describes as "the desire to care for others and for the next generation."

Denial is where evil lives. Goethe reportedly defined evil as "militant ignorance." I have amended his definition to "militant narcissism and the absence of love." Remember the story of Narcissus? He was the young man who adored his own reflection and then pined away because he could not have a relationship with himself. When the focus of our lives is narrowed to the point of fulfilling only selfish aims, empathy is forfeited. The following story from the therapy of a sexual abuse perpetrator illustrates how denial and narcissism go hand in hand:

Psychologist Daniel McIvor was interviewing a man who had committed multiple sex offenses. The man had agreed to the following written statement: "I have never taken part in any kind of sexual activity I would consider to be immoral or wrong."

When Dr. McIvor reminded him of why he was in treatment, he chuckled and said, "Oh yeah, I forgot for a moment."

In Dr. McIvor's words, "This is a very clear example of how effortless it is for a sex offender to compartmentalize as large a chunk of reality as needed to protect one's self or minimize discomfort."[6]

If the multitude of studies identifying victims of sexual abuse as one-in-three women and one-in-five men are even close to accurate, think of the numbers of perpetrators, most of whom are also abuse victims, there are in our midst. They are our families, our neighbors, ourselves. When I was six years old and my mother braided my brown hair into pigtails, I played with a little girl across the street who was only four and had enviable blond curls. Once I found some excuse to grab her hand and pull her behind the house. I pulled her pants down and spanked her. I didn't forget the feeling of excitement and power. I was, no doubt, prettier, stronger and smarter than she, I thought.

The smug feeling of having taught the younger girl some kind of lesson quickly evaporated when I was confronted by both of our mothers. My protestations of innocence were not accepted and I was sent to my room to think about what I had done.

This episode followed the only time my father had spanked me in a similar manner. I was "living what I had learned," reenacting the experience, playing the perpetrator instead of the victim, toying with sadistic feelings, trying to compensate for feeling weak by gaining power over someone smaller.

Several years ago my father, then in his eighties, took me to Sea World when I was visiting him in San Diego. We were sitting under a tree, people-watching, when a mother chastised her child and the father whacked the child on the behind. I asked my Dad if he remembered spanking me that time when I was six. He thought for a moment. "No, I don't, Honey. But if I did that to you, I'm really sorry," he said.

I was surprised and touched. My father, the gruff retired cop, like my grandfather who was unable to say "I love you" until he lay on his deathbed, had let down his armor and softened. I had expected him to deny that he had spanked me and to change the subject. Instead, he was willing to open up to the awareness that maybe he had done something to hurt me. My father's long road from denial to awareness of his tender feelings resulted in his own greater inner peace and closeness with others, a creative achievement I never thought possible.

The move from denial to awareness and acceptance caused a remarkable release of self-creative energy in another man, a man no one would have thought could be transformed. Andrew, a retired metalworker, was referred to me for individual therapy after his wife threatened to leave him. His grown stepdaughter was remembering times as a child when Andrew had molested her. A dedicated family man, Andrew had married Helene and adopted CC when she was five years old. Her birth father had died when she was a baby. Three sons were added to the family and all were grown and had children of their own.

Andrew's boyish round face made him look younger than his nearly seventy years. When he talked about CC, he got teary-eyed and nervously twisted his hands. "I know I did things to her that I shouldn't have," he said. "I was gentle with her, though, and it was never out of anger. I felt sorry for her."

It was true that Andrew felt sorry for her. He identified with CC's having been abandoned by her father because his father had abandoned him, not through death but by continual absence. His father's absence left him the target of his mother's frustration and his older sisters' disdain.

Intimacy with a young girl enabled him to identify with and become briefly like his image of a girl—soft, loveable, close to mother and protected by father. While Andrew could remember some aspects of the molesting, he had little memory of his own childhood and large blocks of time were absent from his mind. What he knew for certain was that he had worked his entire life to please others. He never learned to be aware of and to express his own feelings and longings.

Over the next several years, Andrew focused tenaciously on learning about his behavior and the psychological reasons for it. He worked in a behavior therapy program designed for sex offenders and group therapy focused on preventing relapse. He participated in couples therapy, and he would even occasionally go the West Coast to meet with CC and her therapist. He spent many hours composing letters, attempting as best he could to explain his behavior to family members and to ask for their forgiveness.

When a niece came forward to say that she, too, was one of his victims, Andrew was relieved as well as saddened. He had told me about her when I'd questioned him regarding other children he may have molested. Although his memory for the specific events was poor, he insisted that CC and his niece Mary were the only ones he violated. Andrew and Helene talked with their sons and daughters-in-law about this new crisis and met with me to plan a course of action. One of their decisions was to send Mary a monthly sum of money, enough to help pay for her therapy and medication.

After years of hard work, Andrew came in one day beaming. For the first time, CC was allowing her own daughter to spend a week with them during the summer. She had checked with me first to ensure that her father's rehabilitation was on track. CC worked in the mental health field and knew the sad statistics on how often pedophiles repeat their offenses. As Freud taught us, the "repetition compulsion" is an attempt to master our fear. Andrew, however, no longer lived in fear of abandonment and disgrace and no longer needed to control his fear through a misguided empathy with little girls. He was not compelled to repeat the old behaviors. He had learned to build bridges to family members, and most of the family, including extended family, appreciated his courage and strength in confronting his past behavior

One year after Andrew completed his therapy, he brought me a gift, a beautiful abstract metal sculpture that he had made. He sheepishly told me he'd never considered himself "creative," but since his retirement his wife had encouraged him to continue to put to use his skill with metal. He said he was always surprised by what he created and pleased by the praise he received from others. Andrew had given each of his family members one of his creations.

Releasing old self-protective patterns of denial and opening up to awareness means giving up the comfort of the known. People who choose creative competence take a risk when they give up denial and move into the blackness of the unknown. Andrew risked the rejection of his family by acknowledging his behavior. But it was only by taking responsibility for his mistakes that he was able to ultimately earn their respect. He had to grieve his childhood and the miserable effects of his childhood. He had to live with fear, anxiety, and depression, recognizing for the first time in his life that he had always been fearful, anxious, and depressed. Now it could end. His self-creations signal the birth of a new beginning.[7]

Siddhartha

Siddhartha, who became Buddha in the sixth century B.C.E., chose a completely different path to transcendence and enlightenment.

Siddhartha left his family to learn about suffering. We're told that he was born a prince and that his father, wishing to protect him from being aware of human suffering, would not allow him outside of the palace. Several times Siddhartha convinced a guard to let him go beyond the palace walls, where he viewed sickness, old age, and death. He became obsessed by his longing for a way to cope with the suffering in the world.

Siddhartha finally left the palace for good and lived for seven years in the forest practicing renunciation. Among the ascetics with whom he lived, tormenting one's body was believed to be the way to become free of one's body. In addition to constant meditation, Siddhartha renounced food and all physical comfort. He tried every form of self-mortification, becoming increasingly shriveled and ill. Suffering in order to rid himself of suffering did not liberate Siddhartha from worldly pain, however, so he abandoned the commune. As in the story of Job, Siddhartha obsessed about the ways to obtain enlightenment and compulsively put himself through all the purification rituals of the time. Like Job, he became emotionally and physically depressed and ill, to the point of death. Later, Siddhartha resolved to sit under the Bodhi tree and not get up until he comprehended truth. Finally, alone, shaded by his tree, Siddhartha attained the *Aha!* of his creative endeavors. He discovered the state of nirvana, or freedom from the illusion of separateness and sorrow.

When Siddhartha awakened to his connectedness with all things, he was given the title "Buddha," which means "Awakened One." He had learned that there is no suffering because suffering stems from a belief in darkness, separation, desire, and need, which is all an illusion. Buddha became aware of his oneness. In spite of being told that no one would understand his teachings, Buddha taught for forty years about the freedom, harmony, and peace of living as one in the present moment.

What we are aware of becomes the truth for us. There are four noble truths associated with Buddhism. The first is that all life consists of discontent or suffering. The second teaches that all suffering comes from a belief in being separated from God, one's Good, one's Source. The third truth holds that there is an escape from suffering. The fourth truth states that liberation comes from "nirvana," which means overcoming the sense of separation and claiming connectedness to all things. Mindfulness, or awareness meditation, is one of the paths to nirvana, or oneness.[8]

Siddhartha came through a cycle of desolation and grief and became transformed through his awareness. In Buddhism, it's noteworthy that ignorance, or a lack of self-awareness, is considered to be a greater failing than sin or making mistakes. Buddha affirmed that through awareness, sudden enlightenment is possible. Keep in mind, however, that Siddhartha spent years on his spiritual path before achieving enlightenment. Can we call that sudden? Most of us, like Siddhartha, or Barbara, or Andrew, also require many years following a crisis to metabolize our grief reactions before we become aware that we're safely on our path to enlightened, loving living.

If love is the answer, how to become aware is the question. Notice again that on the Grief and Growth Chart, awareness is the first step toward overcoming the defense of denial and the blackness of inertia and isolation. Only when our psychological defenses are lowered are we able to comprehend with great insight. When Siddhartha dropped his belief in the need to struggle, which was a denial of God, he sat down under the Bodhi tree, and opened up to a complete faith in the oneness of all things. He transcended the sorrow of separation.

When Siddhartha accepted this spiritual reality, his creative task was complete, and he was transformed in his new belief.

The transformative results of psychological growth are: achievement of inner peace, a sense of purpose, and recognition of love as the overriding principle of life. These results of nurturing the soul will be described further on, in more detail. For now, envision these terms like a wedding cake that you hold out in front of you, as you follow your path to a marriage of successful integration of grieving and creative transformation.

Impatience is natural. Even Job was impatient. It was Elihu, in the Biblical story, who urged Job to be patient, let down his defenses and listen and learn from his experiences. We must handle our emotional defenses with great respect. They develop early in life and stay in place in order to protect us from our fear of change and the terror of trauma. Impatience with ourselves or others, or worse, hatred projected inward or toward others, simply prevent the growth process. Recognize that whatever stage of grieving and transformation you are in is exactly where you need to be at this time.

Susan, an energetic mother of four children, had devoted her entire life to her family. Shortly after the last child left home, Susan was diagnosed with ovarian cancer. Miles, her husband, supported her in every way through chemotherapy and radiation. He attributed Susan's stoicism to first-stage-of-grief denial. As month after month passed, however, he became more aware that Susan was refusing to acknowledge the presence of the cancer in any way.

"I thought at first that it was good, that she was going to really fight this thing. But she wouldn't talk about it, ever, with anyone! It became really sad for me and the kids and the extended family. No one could share their grief with her and she couldn't process her grief with us."

Susan died without ever talking about her two-year process of losing her health, her vitality, her family, her Self. And her family suffered a double tragedy: losing Susan to death and losing a source of emotional connection to her before her death.

This extreme example serves to remind us that, like subplots in novels, there can be grief within grief. Susan's family had to accept her death, but they also had to overcome the emotional disconnection that had to have existed on some level even before her illness. We're also reminded here of the need for compassion. It is not our place to try to dislodge others from the safety of denial. We can only grieve and grow ourselves, being aware as we strive toward a changed reality.

Artist Celia Rumsey

Some realities are more difficult to accept than others; the bright light of awareness is too intense, like trying to look at the sun without eye protection. When I entered Celia Rumsey's 1997 Santa Fe art exhibit, "Chronic," my impulse was to close my eyes rather than look at the assault of hospital-white light. The starkness of this light screamed illness-as-isolation. Sculptured body parts—feet, fingers, and artificial limbs—surrounded the show's compelling centerpiece, a modest baby crib containing a diapered, desiccated piece of flesh. There is no sense of wholeness here, or of holding. There exists only the fragmented remains of abandonment. The artist tells her story:

"I remember when I was three. Right after my birthday I was put in the hospital for three months. I was alone in the room. It had chocolate-brown linoleum on the floor and up the walls to a brown molding. The walls above were painted dirty pink. There was a small white window with a tube radiator underneath. The doors were brown. I don't remember any toys, but I think there was a chair. I was in a white crib with white sheets. The nurse would come in the middle of the night, flip on the light, pull down my underpants, and stick me with a needle. She'd turn out the light and leave. I was always hungry."

Celia Rumsey has had approximately seventeen thousand shots since that time. She had been diagnosed with diabetes in an era when little was known about regulating insulin levels, a time when "chronic" illness was more likely to prove "fatal." She was also at an age when children are unable to understand that their behavior has nothing to do with causing or continuing illness. "I thought I was a bad girl, and because the doctors would seem to be upset whenever I'd go into insulin shock, I thought they were saying it was my fault, I had done something wrong."

On this fiftieth anniversary of her diagnosis, Celia Rumsey's art demonstrates that she is doing something quite right. A vivid awareness of the emotional pain she has harbored for so long is finally being carefully expressed and articulated. The defectiveness and rejection she felt as a sick and isolated child has been transformed into healthy involvement in her community. It has been a long and arduous journey from the hospital crib to contemporary art, but her creativity mirrors and keeps pace with her physical trials and triumphs.

It is interesting that Celia's earlier work as an artist portrayed no hint of the anguish brought on by her physical illness. After graduating magna cum laude in art history from Bryn Mawr, she won a coveted Fulbright scholarship to Paris. During her nine months there, she lost forty pounds, turned yellow, and became deathly ill. "After all my scholarly achievements, I felt totally defeated. After twenty years with diabetes, I learned I had a second illness to manage, Addison's Disease, and eventually there was a third, hypothyroidism, which rounds out to a condition called Schmitt's Syndrome."

Celia Rumsey's plans to attend Columbia or Yale for a doctorate in art history collapsed along with her health. However, over the next several years at home in New York, she was able to take painting courses at the Museum of Modern Art, the New School for Social Research, and the Art Student's League. Her fascination with Eliot Porter's nature photographs—"his lyrical, precious pictures," she calls them—provided the impetus for her to move to New Mexico and paint landscape. "Landscape and space gave me a sense of freedom. I wanted to paint the beauty of larger forces of which I was a part. I love the concept of ecology, the interdependence of systems. I wanted to see the world as perfect and I wanted to be perfect in it. I never painted figures or faces. I think I couldn't face what that face would be feeling."

An entire body of work grew out of Celia's lack of readiness to face her feelings about her illness, to square off with loss and arrange the remnants of her dreams into an acceptable life collage. Wading through and working through her frustration, like cleaning up after a flood, took years. Her art proves that in every stage of emotional passage through grief, even in denial, if the artist is great, great art will emerge. And if we aren't trained artists, we can still find creative outlets for the fearful tension that accompanies trauma.

Inner torment is not a prerequisite for creativity, as some have believed. As journalist Samuel G. Freedman wrote, "There is no question that many creative artists, perhaps the vast majority, are centered and sane. The image of the self-destructive artist not only invites futility or death but denies the value of disciplined craft." We do not have to be ill or disturbed in order to be creative. Whether we have a temporary crisis or a seemingly long-term profound reversal of fortune, every artistic communication becomes an act of mastery over a passively experienced trauma. This act of mastery is the transformation of emotion and defensiveness into creative self-expression.

Celia's first art show, watercolor paintings based on Eliot Porter's landscape photographs, took place in New York City in 1971. She painted watercolor landscapes for about ten years, and then after her move to New Mexico painted landscapes from her own photographs taken from road trips, and then aerial photos from small planes flying above the Land of Enchantment. This phase of her work lasted about twelve years. "I was busy painting the beauty I thought the world should be. Once, when I was in Paris, I painted a self portrait. I don't consider myself beautiful, but in that painting, I was very beautiful, angelic-looking." Although Celia may have been denying the negative impact of her physical illness at that time, it seems clear that her awareness breakthrough allowed her to express her vivid understanding of the beauty of the earth and of her own strong spirit.

"The landscapes were metaphors as well as expressions of beauty," she told me. "The tectonic plates expanding and contracting, the planet pushing and pulling, were like the forces in my life." Celia's brother, Peter, died of diabetes at the age of forty, following ten years of painful struggle with neuropathy, retinopathy, loss of teeth and hair and digestive function, kidney failure, dialysis, and hospitalization. "I had a terrible time coping with his death because I loved him and because I have the same disease he died of.

"When my favorite dog died in 1994, I began taking a sculpture class and found myself meticulously sculpting body parts: many, many fingers, because of the finger-sticks one does daily for testing insulin levels; feet, because of the amputations; bones and internal organs. This focus, facing the ugly reality of this illness, led to the current show, 'Chronic.'"

When I asked Celia for her reflections on the stages of grief other than denial, she explained how they overlapped and yet were distinct. "This work is about defiance. I will not drown in my anger and depression. I will not let this illness get me down. I've had tons of anger and rage about having to cope with diabetes. It's like having a second full-time job, demanding and exhausting. When I was young, the anger could become self-destructive, though. I used to do a lot of obsessing about finding a man who would take care of me, having a perfect home and perfect children. I'd make wishes for that, on the moon, on birthday candles. Now I'm obsessed with creating balance in my life. I've learned that I just had to get off the couch and stop being furious and depressed and obsessed with the injustice of my illness."

"How do you view the last stage of grief and growth, the 'acceptance' that I align with the concept of 'success'?" I asked her.

"For me, the success is in having learned to care for myself. I feel very proud that I am self-sufficient. I'm also proud that I've had the courage to do this current work. It takes courage to confess to the world how this illness feels, the impact that it has. In terms of acceptance, I think I've finally accepted responsibility for my life. I don't blame anyone and I don't look for anyone to make it better."

Faced with the possibility of a shortened life, Celia shares her beliefs about life beyond death. "Well, I believe in God," she told me, "an amorphous God, Zeus, Buddha force or power. And because I visualize everything, I see an energy field of midnight blue, a heaven like a constellation, an elliptical format of light pinpricks or pale gold on a deep midnight blue/black volume, stirred up like the Milky Way. Of course these are just symbols of the energy, the way I might paint it. I also believe that when people pass into that sphere they become omniscient; they can see all the intrigues and confusion and can understand them. And I believe that love bonds continue. My mother was my lifeline in this lifetime, and I believe my brother is my cord of continuity to the spirit plane. I believe he watches over me."

"Do you see yourself painting again someday, or will you continue your current work?" I asked.

"Oh, I will definitely paint again," she replied confidently, an angelic smile spreading across her face.

As we confront challenge, change, and growth, personal accounts like Celia's, enduring stories from antiquity, and the messages of world religions all offer comfort. The belief that the soul continues beyond this lifetime suggests that every experience provides important lessons. Our task is to keep learning the lessons. With this focus we can release any guilt we tend to have for not being able to cure our illness, resolve our depression, forgive our abusers, become enlightened—in short, for not achieving sainthood during this lifetime. We are busy learning.

No learning takes place without a sense of safety. Feeling safe is a prerequisite for the normal development of infants and children. A safe inner and outer environment in which we are loved and accepted is always the key to disarming denial. I believe that the concept of nurturing one's "inner child" has been embraced by so many because most people hunger for a greater sense of safety. We must learn to provide ourselves that safety. As we become more aware of creating a feeling of being safe in the world, we can operate more consistently on the higher planes of creativity and transcendence. At those levels we are aware of choices. We choose to leave behind denial and other defenses. We choose to use our energy to discover our present life purpose.

Using awareness of what psychologists call "ego states" to nurture our inner selves may help us move down the path beyond denial. The primary ego states are the "inner child," the "internalized parent," and the "adult." We grow up learning the most about how it feels to be a child and how it feels to identify with our parents' power. This understanding provides a solid footing. If the long period of childhood includes a dose of dysfunctional parenting, however—and most of us are victims of victims in this regard—we may become firmly entrenched in our inner-child fear and the judgment of our internalized parent. Our defenses live with us on those levels.

While it is difficult for most of us to understand how the brain chemicals contribute and react to depression, we can more easily recognize this form of unhappiness as a fall back into a child ego state, a state where we have little awareness of simply being in a transitional time of grief that will pass as naturally as the seasons.

The "ego state" model of the personality, the concept that we function from inner child, internalized parent, or adult ego states, is one way to assess our behavior and feelings. If we consider that the "inner child" and the "internalized parent" ego states are those with which we have the most experience, we can see that a normal reaction to life stress, or fear, is to fall back into one of these two positions. The inner child feels helpless and hopeless in the face of worldly authority and experience. Threatened emotional or physical loss produces fears of abandonment or annihilation. By reflex, the grandiosity of the internalized all-powerful parent seems like a safer place. In the "Parent" state, we can be judgmental and autocratic. We can be smug and self-righteous. Depression grows from the inner dialogue between child and parent as one affirms the immaturity and incompetence of the other. The disconnection from our adult self, that part of the personality that contains every kind of intelligence and competence, becomes unbearable. We are also isolated from our Transcendent Self, the halo above that nourishes us with intuition and divine inspiration.

Be aware of the tendency to feel trapped in the feelings of the inner child and the judgment of the internalized parent, the parts of our personality where our defenses erect barriers to growth. In deep grief, we are vulnerable to living in ongoing misery. Remember that as a grownup you are capable of moving into your adult self with mere intention. The choice to be optimistic and oriented to solutions places you above defense, fear, and limitation. It moves you toward transforming depressed or lowered energy into the discovery of powerful possibilities, success, and the spirituality of the Higher or Transcendent Self, where love lives.

The Higher Self or the Transcendent Self can be thought of as part of the personality psychologists call the "observing ego." This part of oneself helps to observe and practice appropriate behavior in order to maintain a safe distance from fear. I believe it is also the connection to our spirituality and, as Siddhartha discovered, to oneness and connection with God. It is drawn like an angelic halo.

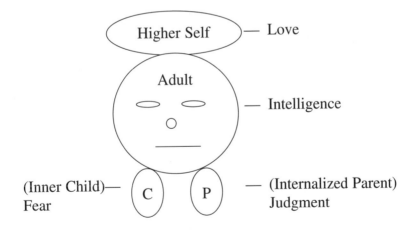

Think of a time when you were able to mentally wide-angle your view of some event or performance in order to observe how you were doing. The experience is like having an inner coach, a mentor providing just the guidance you need to go on. My oldest daughter, for example, had an excellent ski racing coach in high school. During that time, when we were on a ski vacation in Colorado, we were standing on top of a mountain looking down at a steep chute, an area designated for very expert skiers. I noticed that she was talking to herself. She planned a route through the trees and continued to self-coach all the way to the bottom. She was using her observing-ego to function at her highest skiing ability. She was using her Inner Coach, her Higher or Transcendent Self, to maintain trust and confidence.

The following year, on the same mountain, we found a young woman seemingly paralyzed at that exact spot. She could barely speak and could not move. We stood there and talked with her for a long time, encouraging her to breathe deeply and become aware of her inner strength. Finally, she was able to ski one short stretch at a time with us to the bottom.

Awareness keeps us in the present moment and provides us with the opportunity to function from our most mature aspect. Our fearful child and our judging parent typically keep us in the shame and guilt of the past, or the worry and anxiety of the future. The inner child doesn't know how to change. It requires the courage of the adult-self to overcome the fear that has been buttressed by years of self-doubt. To be a child is to be vulnerable to believing "lies of limitation." Until they have the capacity to reason, children believe what adults tell them.

Research suggests that eighty-five percent of what children hear is negative. They are told what they cannot do or scolded for doing something considered "bad."[9] So it is not surprising that children of any age learn to blame themselves when life's path takes a downturn. We believe the negative messages. We learn to live in limitation instead of believing in grand possibilities. At any time, however, no matter where we might be in our grief and growth and maturation process, we can use vision and intention to come into an awareness of truth.

Holly, a successful mortgage banker, recalled a happy childhood but periodically struggled enormously with her physical appearance and her public speaking. "It's seems crazy to obsess the way I do about my hair. But the only negative remarks I remember my mother ever making were about my hair and not knowing what to do with it to make it look nice." We struggle with negative input from our parents to determine whether there is any truth behind the disapproval. With awareness, we can evaluate those appraisals. In order to reach full self-expression, we must distinguish between truth and lies. We must learn to place comments in the proper context.

Holly recognized that her mother's remarks about her difficult-to-manage, frizzy hair were about the hair, not about Holly's character. While the comments were true, they were not intended to damage Holly's self-esteem. Those who are abused as children learn to recognize that their parent's accusations that they were bad and deserved to be hurt were lies manufactured to cover their own guilt.

In our child-ego state, we are especially vulnerable to self-doubt, guilt, and shame—emotions that cement into place our false beliefs about being unloveable. We must handle our inner child gently and with endless understanding. The more loving and accepting we are of our inner selves, the more likely we are to transcend fear and grief and find the truth.

Recall that it was when Siddhartha stopped demanding, struggling, and self-abusing that he achieved nirvana. He simply sat down with the intention of awakening to the truth. He had come through a grief cycle; he was ready for transformation. We're told that he gave in to his desire to eat a meal as well. We must pay attention to the wishes of the inner child. In the midst of our striving, a small voice says, "I'm hungry. I'm tired. Feed me. Put me to bed." We can ignore the voice and deny our true wishes, or we can choose to listen to those needs. It is when we are most respectful and attuned to the needs of our inner child that we feel safe enough to function lovingly, perceiving possibilities for adventure and the sense of purpose that comes with awareness.

When Siddhartha gave up denying his inner needs and Job gave up trying to deny his mistakes, both became their divine natures, one with God, released from fear, awake to the meaning and purpose of life.

Albert Einstein

Albert Einstein, one of the greatest thinkers of our time, embraced a life of continual creativity and self-expression.

Einstein was relaxed and comfortable with his interests. He declared that, as far as he was concerned, imagination was more important than knowledge. He played mind games and pretended he was riding on a stream of light. He could be so absorbed in his thoughts that time would cease.

Albert Einstein is a stunning example of someone who drove his interests to the edge, never limiting the awareness of possibilities. Although some judge Einstein harshly for being insensitive to his family, Max Born, his friend and fellow physicist, evaluated Einstein dispassionately: "For all his kindness and sociability, and love of humanity, he was nevertheless totally detached from his environment and the human beings included in it."[10] Referred to by one biographer as "the perennial child,"[11] Einstein was able to rise above his reactive emotions and live on the levels of creativity and transcendence. From childhood on, he never denied his curiosity or his opinions. Notably, he had an abiding interest in and respect for the child's mind.

It was Einstein who suggested to psychologist Jean Piaget that he study children's intuitive notions of speed and time; this research enriched our knowledge of children's cognitive development. Einstein reportedly said that we know all the physics we will ever need to know by the age of three. He elevated the realms of imagination, fantasy, and intuition to valued scientific functions.

Einstein used his own mind as his playing field. He had no laboratory. His special theory of relativity came from numerous mental thought experiments (*Gedanken* in German). He could become absorbed with his experiments for hours, days, and years. He credited his child-like thought patterns with leading him to the special theory. Einstein made no apologies for his child self. His unabashed endorsement of child-like thinking supports the idea that inner security enables us to leave the blackness of denial behind in favor of awareness and discovery. Lies of limitation are not believed by a fearless child.

What most of us don't know about Einstein is that his awareness was focused on "...how God created this world. I am not interested in this or that phenomenon, in the spectrum of this or that element. I want to know His thoughts, the rest are details."[12] Einstein was deeply spiritual; all his life, he pondered the construction of the universe, the substance of light, dark, space, time, and the meaning of existence. The value he placed on every aspect of creation translated into a deep abiding love of humankind and nature. Einstein was living proof of how far our minds can take us if we heighten our creative competence. While most of us would not aspire, like Einstein, to understand the mind of God, we can all intend to understand our own minds and hearts. We can be open to the possibility that our creativity, the ways we declare ourselves in the world, is our connection to God, our gift of love.

Although it may seem paradoxical, nurturing the inner child is a sure route to the Higher Self, the proving ground of love. The reason for this has to do with being awake and aware of our current needs and desires. Being attuned to the moment and responding to our wishes, instead of denying them, moves us beyond grief to self-care and transcendence.

Remember to *honor* your reactions to life change. *Be gentle.* It is not possible to force awareness. Resistance or threat will only result in strengthening the fears related to change. *Melt the fear* with relaxation methods (discussed in chapter 8) and positive thoughts. Any practice that will allow you to regularly achieve a natural altered state of consciousness will allow you to gradually transform fear and defensiveness into self-acceptance and creative awareness. It is in learning to value every part of ourselves that we resolve the tension between the wish to deny our creative potential and remain small, and the wish to become aware of our desire to grow and become magnificent.

In recognizing that all parts of us are actually one, we awaken to the fact that in our child states we *need* love, in our internalized parent states we *want* love, in our adult states we *choose* love, and in our Transcendent or Higher Selves, we *are* love.

Daily Creative Discipline
(Denial to Awareness)

1. For an entire day, notice any negative reactions to life events. Write down what these events are and how you would like them to **change.**

2. For another entire day, be aware of just your **negative reactions**—even the hint of a negative thought. Then flip it over into a positive. At first you will think you are rationalizing or being a Pollyanna. At some point, however, you will see and feel a difference in your outlook. You are cracking the door open to a **new awareness** of perception.

3. Think of one belief that you hold to strongly, if not stubbornly, one that some might say you're being "defensive" about. Pretend that you are to **debate** this issue, taking the opposite position. List three points you will make.

4. Imagine you are a young Siddhartha and you are lost on your path to inner peace and a sense of life purpose. Each time you detect harsh judgment toward yourself, use your **creative imagination** to sit down under your own great protective tree of life, breathe deeply, and trust that an insight, an **awareness** will come to you.

5. Pretend you are Einstein and practice seeing each experience of the day through the eyes of the child you were at age five. Notice how the child responds to these events. Notice any delighted amusement you feel because of the child's spontaneity. Be sure to record these **enlightened thoughts.**

6. Take a piece of your white paper and color different sections with crayons until the entire page is colored. Take a black crayon and color over the page with black (you can

also paint across the page with black tempera paint). Now, use a pointed object, like a letter opener, and make a design. Notice the feeling of **pleasure** as the colors show through the blackness. When complete, write three or more word associations that describe your image and its meaning for you. Save in your file.

Chapter Four

Anger: The Drive to Wholeness

Anger and hatred are obstacles to the good heart, obstacles to compassion.

— Dalai Lama

Anger is life energy. Our anger can fuel our passions and propel us down the road of our life purpose. The same adrenaline rush that helped our ancient ancestors outrun wild animals can be harnessed to accomplish extraordinary feats. The mother of a teenage boy was able to save her son's life when the car he was working on slipped off the jack and fell. The outrage she felt at the possibility of losing her child was channeled into superhuman strength, and she was able to lift the car off of him.[1] For those crucial moments, the melding of aggression, constructive action, personal power and love created a miracle.

Since the only constant in life is change, focusing life energy into love power becomes a momentous and ongoing choice. Anger can be the fuel for creative action, as with the mother who lifted the car to save her son. Passionate energy can be infused into every activity and every moment of the day. However, when angry energy is surging below the surface and we are stalled in our grief or disappointment, we cease to grow.

Howling pain often announces awareness of our wounded-ness. Philosopher Ken Wilber says that "...pain is, in a sense, the first grace, because most people won't really begin spiritual practice until they're in dire straits. That pain is a wake-up call, and it serves its notice faithfully."

The story of Job graphically describes every stage of his emotional reactions to devastating, painful life change. The emotion that comes through with the most force is his anger. Following the seven days when Job is mute, he begins his "complaint to God" by cursing the day of his birth: "Perish the day when I was born...Why was I not stillborn...For now I should be lying in the quiet grave, asleep in death, at rest..." (Job 3:1, 11, 13). He goes through three cycles of speeches complaining and lamenting the unfairness, the bitterness of life. He says his resent-ment is so great that it outweighs the "sands of the sea" (Job 6:3). Job accuses God of "raining blows on me without cause" (Job 9:17). He calls God a perpetrator, raving that "He leads peoples astray and destroys them" (Job 12:23).

Whoever assigned the moral of "patience" to Job must have read a different version of the story. In truth, one of his friends admonishes him twice about his impatience (Job 4:2,5), suggesting that during the good times Job is strong and supportive of others, but when adversity strikes, "...you are impatient... Fools are destroyed by their own angry passion" (Job 5:2).

Job persists, however, in processing his grief. He voices sixteen oaths denying any moral misdeeds and with intense intro-spection delves into the darker side of his personality, the side that projects blame onto others and resists responsibility for change.

Job's drive to wholeness is demonstrated by his tenaciousness as he drains every vestige of rancor, resentment, and rage from his being. Through full expression of his hurt, anger, and fear, Job becomes a more complete human being.

The Book of Job is best seen as a meditation on growing wise. In order to learn the most from this meditation, let's consider every aspect of the story as an expression of Job himself. In the beginning, a Divine dialogue takes place within Job between Satan, the Adversary or Obstructor, and Job's Higher Self. Job makes the unconscious decision to allow himself to experience the "long dark night" to test his faith and to grow through pain and grief in order to learn to manifest his Transcendent Self.

Following his trials, Job initially denies his pain, then he becomes vehement in his anger and self-justification. I think it no accident that Job's wife expresses her anger first. This represents the need for Job to embrace the feminine side of himself. One influence of Greek culture on Jewish thought during that era was the concept of the feminine embodying wisdom. "Sophia," the Greek word for wisdom, is the co-eternal, co-creating principle of God. She is written about in Proverbs, "When he established the heavens I was there," (8:27) and in Ecclesiasticus, "Hear the praise of wisdom from her own mouth..." (24:1); "She will come out to meet him like a mother; she will receive him like a young bride. For food she will give him the bread of understanding and for drink the water of wisdom" (15:1-3). Wisdom is described as "a loving spirit" (Wisd. of Sol. 1:6), as "Holy Spirit" (Wisd. of Sol. 9:17), and in the following most beautiful prose: "For wisdom moves more easily than motion itself; she is so pure she pervades and permeates all things. Like a fine mist she rises from the power of God, a clear effluence from the glory of the Almighty..." (Wisd. of Sol. 7:24-25).

Job, then, in order to become whole, must embrace his feminine nature. In William Blake's "Illustrations of the Book of Job," God speaks from the whirlwind, to Job and his wife together, at the end of the story. The message is that Job can only find wisdom when he accepts his wife's suffering, rejection, faith, and love as an internal, integral part of himself

Angry energy, used like precious river water, facilitates growth. Release too little anger and one's self-assertion is but a trickle; release too much and a flood of self-righteousness threatens. Healthy anger makes us aware of imbalance. It can signal that something is threatening, frightening, hurtful. Something has gone wrong in our world. We must try to discover what needs readjusting in order to focus our life energy appropriately.

My youngest daughter, at age three, taught me the direct connection between hurt and anger. I heard her in her room screaming and throwing things. When I rushed in, demanding to know what was wrong and why she was so angry, she answered, as tears streamed down her cheeks, "You hurted my feelings!" I had been ignoring her requests for help dressing up her bunny family. In my haste to accomplish something in the kitchen, I turned off the positive, loving energy between us, and she felt it immediately. I suspect it was not what I did, but the fact that I cut her off, my failure to empathize, that hurt her and made her fly into a rage. What amazed me was that a three-year-old was able to connect her hurt with her anger.

Anger is our protest at being disconnected from a source of security. My daughter, like all two- and three-year-olds, was learning to express her needs, fears, and wants. By the time most of us reach adulthood, we may be unable to express anger effectively. And yet this assertive energy can help us stand up for our values, defend ourselves, protect others, and honor loss.

When my daughters were small and learning how to ski, I would follow behind them, ski poles ready to jab at any reckless speeding skier who might threaten to run them over. I could have been wearing a sandwich board reading, "Don't you *dare* invade this safe space!"

How many of us can easily channel aggressive energy into helping others or acknowledge anger over injustices to those we care about far more easily than we recognize and attend to slights and infractions on our own personal boundaries! We're taught that righteous indignation is healthy if we feel it when someone else is hurt. If it's our own hurt, we may well view it as self-centered. We're told, or we tell ourselves, to ignore the fear, get over it, forget it, and get on with it.

Many times anger erupts unbidden, like an uninvited visitor. Much of the anger between married partners is like that: a surprise lightning-like protest in response to a perception of love withdrawn. In my thirty-two-year marriage, the times when I have flown into a rage were always a result of feeling, like my three-year-old daughter, that love had suddenly disappeared, leaving me in a black hole of rejection, or indifference. Awareness is crucial at these times to access the observing ego (or the Higher Self) in order to establish the understanding that the wellspring of love is always within. Sophia, or Wisdom, would tell us that Father—Mother—God is eternally present, embracing and nurturing.

This knowledge can reinstate our balance. Wisdom says that anger is an expression of our fear, and there is no longer any need to be afraid. As adults, we recognize our anger as the natural drive to release tension, express fear, and ultimately to connect compassionately with all parts of ourselves and reconnect with the spirit of love, even though we may not be feeling very loving.

It is often a surprise to clients when I suggest, following a discussion of their life experiences, that their anger is a form of depression and that it represents unresolved grief. Reframing anger and depression into aspects of grieving can be a great relief since our feelings are then part of a normal process of recognizing deep-seated emotional pain. This insight has not only saved marriages, it has saved lives. Several of my clients who were physically and sexually abused in childhood had made suicide attempts or were contemplating suicide when they came in for consultation. They were distorting their angry energy into self-hate. At the end of their treatments, they told me that viewing their feelings within the context of a grief process made them feel that something about them was "normal" and gave them hope that they could change and eventually transform that energy into self-acceptance.

Hansel and Gretel

Fairy tales have been used through the centuries to teach children about watchful self-care and about the power of emotions. Psychologist Bruno Bettelheim, in his book *The Uses of Enchantment,* added to our understanding of how children benefit from fairy tales because they are metaphors for growth and development. Psychologist Clarissa Pinkola Estes more recently captured the interest and imagination of adults with her book, *Women Who Run with the Wolves*.[2] Through fairy tales and folk stories Estes points to the fact that within every woman there is "a wild and natural creature, a powerful force, filled with good instincts, passionate creativity, and ageless knowing."

The story of Hansel and Gretel describes how adversity can mobilize the energy of anger and use it for self-expression and survival. Brother and sister, Hansel and Gretel left their father's cottage after their mother died and their stepmother intended to let them starve. They stole away at night, wandering far into the woods. Eventually, after several days, desperately hungry, they saw a beautiful gingerbread house in a clearing. Delighted to find such lovely food, they broke off little pieces and began to eat. An old woman came out and invited the children inside where she fed them nourishing food. She invited them to stay.

What initially looked like a nurturing situation became an imprisonment. The old woman was actually a witch who wanted to cannibalize the children, literally and figuratively. Hansel was placed in a cage to be fattened up for cooking. Gretel was made the servant, to cook, to clean, and to prepare her brother to be devoured.

Gretel's angry energy toward the old witch began to build and a plan of action germinated. When she could no longer convince the witch that her brother was too skinny to be eaten, she did as the witch instructed her and fired up the oven. She then used her child-role to feign ignorance about how hot the oven should be. She suggested that the witch have a look in the oven to test the heat. When the witch leaned over to do so, Gretel summoned all her strength to shove the witch inside the oven and close the door. Gretel's outrage—her angry energy toward someone, or the part of herself, who would choose destruction over life—frees her (and her brother, the masculine part of herself) for further growth.

We are all Hansels and Gretels. We leave home and sometimes we get lost. We may find gingerbread houses in the form of jobs, lovers, friends, hobbies, or addictions, which give us the temporary illusion that we have arrived at wholeness. We have found a home. In terms of growth and transcendence, however, we have only arrived at an encampment, a place where we shed self-indulgence to learn and prepare for the next phase of our life experience. At some point, we recognize that what we starve for is love, an inner connection that nurtures and demands greater self-expression. We must leave the place where we are and, in so doing, aggression and great courage are required to "burn the witch" and continue on our journey.

Angry energy saved Hansel and Gretel and placed them on a path that safely returned them to love. The children were given a ride across a lake by a lovely white swan, back to their father. Without the stepmother now, their father had been waiting anxiously to be reunited with his children. This represents a reunion with one's expanded self, the part of oneself that has discovered a greater capacity for assertiveness, self-protection, morality, and love.

The fairy tale of Rumpelstiltskin teaches us that angry energy, when used to intimidate and manipulate others, eventually proves to be self-destructive. When the princess in the story outsmarted Rumpelstiltskin and learned his name, he flew into a temper tantrum, and jumped up and down on the floor so hard that the floor gave way and he crashed to his death. While Gretel directed her angry energy toward constructive action and maturation, Rumpelstiltskin stunted his growth by staying in anger until it literally killed him. For Hansel and Gretel, the grief and growth cycle resulted in an increase in awareness, self-acceptance, and intimacy. Successful living, including the constructive use of angry energy, became successful loving.

Life is not two-dimensional like the Grief and Growth Chart. One does not climb a great mountain by marching straight up to the top. Along the way, there are ascents to minor peaks, and descents into valleys. Sometimes storms trap climbers at their basecamp for long periods of time. So I ask that you imagine these grief and growth markers in three dimensions and place yourself there in space among all the levels, knowing that at times you are functioning in different places on each different level. For example, there are some losses that affect us so deeply that we have remained wrapped in our anger or depression as though it was down clothing on a climber waiting out a storm in a mountain tent.

Survivors of childhood torture, for example, have told me that allowing themselves to experience their feelings is the most difficult act of growth. They have learned to avoid falling into any grieving feelings by dissociating from them, functioning only on the creativity or transcendent levels. As long as they appeared to be productive adults, they could deny their outrage and anguish about the violations they had endured.

Until we acknowledge and live with our feelings, we cannot live the truth, feel whole, and connect deeply with others. Be aware of your personal truth and accept where you happen to be in your grief and growth. Honor what you are currently attempting to face and learn from. And be encouraged by the words of Sophia: "Drink the water of wisdom."

It is important to acknowledge the impact of socialization on one's ability to use aggressive energy effectively. Women in the United States, for example, are generally socialized not to express anger. It's more acceptable in our culture for girls to cry and boys to yell. Women friends who are attorneys and elected officials tell me that public expressions of anger or outrage from men are judged as assertiveness or amusing eccentricity, while the same types of angry expression from women are judged as "hysterical," "out of control," or "aggressive"—terms that diminish the women's credibility. Recall that after Job's wife expressed outrage over his denial of grief, she was completely dropped from one version of the Biblical story. In order to be effective people, both men and women require greater awareness of how to communicate consistently from the neutral position of self-assertiveness, not from the extremes of aggression or passivity.

When we are angry or passive, we are generally *reacting* to a situation rather than *responding* with self-assertion. Both genders suffer when they live the unconscious "lies of limitation" resulting from misguided socialization or what some call the "tribal consciousness." Women, in order to feel their "wholeness," need to have access to the powerful feelings that come from balanced aggression or assertiveness. Men, in order to feel their "wholeness," must know that empathy expands their capacity for inner strength and creative self-assertion.

Years ago, a woman psychiatrist from Latin America was speaking on this topic. She commented on how women in the United States are expected to suppress their anger. She thought it an outrageous violation of femininity. "Latin women are expected to be passionate!" she declared. "If a woman can't get angry, she's considered passionless. And that makes her boring and unattractive." To me, this was a fresh new concept.

While a consistent *over*-expression of anger is certainly not boring, it does not make us appealing. Awareness and balance are the key ingredients. Luce, a beautiful dark-eyed woman of mixed ancestry, came to my office for help with anger management. She was five months pregnant with her second child. "I've got to get my anger under control," she said, "or I'm going to hurt my children and lose my husband. Jack said I had to come, but I know I must do something."

As Luce let the story of her early life unfold, she readily acknowledged the fear and sadness she tried to compensate for with her anger. Her father was an angry, verbally abusive alcoholic who regularly told Luce that she was "puny and stupid." These types of rebukes became programmed in her mind and Luce came to believe these lies about herself. She married a well-educated man but didn't believe she herself could do college work. She became a mother but didn't believe she had the knowledge and control to raise healthy children. Her resentment fired off in adolescence as rebelliousness and an addiction to drugs, which she fought desperately to overcome before her marriage. Now her anger ricocheted off her husband and her home, threatening the security of her family.

As Luce learned to "grow her self-expression," the process of creating her true self, she discovered she enjoyed writing, in spite of the fact that she balked at doing it when I first suggested she keep a journal. When she overcame her fear of talking to her parents about hold-over behaviors from her childhood, she found her mother's receptivity encouraging. As she recognized she was capable of slowly building a bridge to her parents, her ability to put her feelings into words with her husband improved dramatically. The pride she felt was much more reinforcing than the self-hate she felt when her angry energy was uncontrolled. Now that she's handling motherhood with a second child, Luce is planning how to handle going to college.

Anger is the life energy that germinates constructive action and the drive to mend the fractures in our personalities. It may be expressed as the pain of recognizing childhood hurts, the intensity of protecting one's children, the insistence on respectful boundaries at work, the indignity of feeling the need to learn self-defense, the agony of coming to terms with death, the howling screams of reliving terrible trauma. From minor to major loss and life change, angry energy gives us the drive to heal the past.

My daughters and I attended a women's self-defense course. The focus of the class was self-assertiveness. We learned that women who are passive or women who are aggressive make easier targets for assault. Perpetrators look for someone to victimize. A woman who appears fearful or who acts angry is seen as provoking an attack. The offender can rationalize his assault by saying, "She gave in. She didn't fight it," or "She was a bitch. She tried to hit me." The safer middle ground of self-assertiveness was stressed repeatedly; when one clearly asserts the right to physical space, privacy, and personal boundaries, tension usually de-escalates. The message was to communicate clearly and hold the perpetrator accountable for any intrusive behavior.

The self-defense instructors, all women with black belts in karate, clarified that being assertive does not necessarily mean that aggression is not an option. It's simply not the first option. The immediate goal is to de-escalate and dissolve tension. At the end of a role-play situation in which the male attacker gave no sign of giving up after verbal assertiveness and the easier physical "hands-off" techniques were tried, one of the participants asked, "What would you do if the guy clearly intended to rape or kill you?"

The instructor answered, "I'd say, 'Make my day,' and I'd take the guy out."

After the nervous laughter died down, the instructor explained that she was not hesitant about protecting her life. She had been assaulted and raped in her teens and had spent many years resolving her grief, especially her anger. She then invested years in learning karate and other martial arts, training, competing, and teaching with men as well as women. She was quite aware of how to calmly hold her ground with others. Her angry energy had been converted to powerful, disciplined self-assertion, with a good deal of humor thrown in. For those in the course who would not consider killing an attacker, she taught disabling techniques for escape. Her consistent message was how to learn confidence and self-assertion.

᛫᠊ᢩ ᢌ᠊᛫

Angry energy became drive and determination when my friend was greeted years ago by her accounting professor with, "What are you doing here? This is a man's class." Betty had decided to become an accountant and his words merely fueled her fire. She not only proved she could do the work, she graduated first in the class!

My closest friend from childhood, Karen Karros, is the mother of Eric Karros, power hitter for the Los Angeles Dodgers. We were talking one day about Eric's drive to become a profes-sional ballplayer.

"From the time he was a boy," Karen told me, "he was always focused on improving his game. When he was playing in the minor leagues, a reporter wrote, 'It remains to be seen whether Eric Karros is major league material.' Eric enlarged that statement and put it on his bulletin board. It became a challenge that motivated him to work even harder."

While others may have been insulted and angered by such a comment, Eric used it to fuel his drive toward success. The antidote to anger, the grief relief for rage, is constructive drive. The drive may be self-focused toward personal success, or it may be altruistic, focused on helping others. Remembering that the definition of successful living is successful loving, we respect and champion those among us who work long and hard to overcome obstacles to achieve their dreams. We share their spotlights and learn from their examples. When one person succeeds, all succeed.

What happens when we never experience angry feelings? It may be that we are stalled in blocked anger and passivity, removed from our goal of creative self-expression. We haven't acknowledged our hurt. We may feel trapped in confusion and depression, as I did in college.

One day, I went to talk with one of my favorite professors, a sociologist. I asked whether I should go to see a counselor.

"What for?" he asked.

"I just always feel unhappy," I replied.

"What do you do with your anger?" he pressed.

"I never feel anger," I told him.

"That's the problem!" he said. "After graduate school, go into therapy."

When I followed his advice and entered therapy, I began to realize how my childhood fears and hurts had been tucked away inside me. I had denied them and my anger about them until I was safely grown.

Suppressed anger often breeds depression. Just as depression is a cover for anger, anger is a cover for hurt feelings. Two groups of people in our society are vulnerable to getting stalled in their anger: men and women who have unresolved sadness, confusion, and disappointment. The only difference may be that more of the men are stalled by over-expression of anger through aggression, and more of the women are stalled by under-expression of anger through passivity and depression. Both must seek the balanced middle ground of self-assertiveness.

Men and women who are intimidated or abused verbally or physically in childhood often grow up having difficulty modulating their anger and converting it to constructive drive. Barbara, the woman who suffered physical and sexual abuse within her family's satanism, as an adult occasionally became so angry with her daughter that she feared that she would attack her. She felt she was drowning in her anger and would pull her daughter down with her.

Like Luce, as Barbara processed her grief by recognizing all of her reactions to past events, she learned that she could make choices about her thoughts, and choices about her current behavior. While as a child she wasn't allowed to have personal boundaries, a buffer zone of safety, as an adult she had many ways to assert herself and maintain personal privacy. Many people who have angry outbursts have them because they had no security or sense of safety as children. They were intruded upon and assaulted at the whim of the adults they relied upon to protect them.

Andrew, the man who molested his stepdaughter, was totally unaware of harboring any angry feelings until he developed an awareness of his past. When he remembered the hurt and humiliation he suffered as a boy, he was able to recognize and work with his anger, obsession, and depression. Eventually, he was able to unblock his energy and transform it into clear expressions of his wishes and beautiful expressions of his creativity.

Remember, depression obscures anger and fear, and anger takes the front seat to fear and depression. Fear bubbles beneath the surface of both emotional states. Tom, a man who was beaten nearly every day after school, appeared neither depressed nor angry. Occasionally, however, if he perceived someone challenging him or being rude, he would have an angry outburst. These outbursts were often followed by illness and depression that necessitated a week's stay in bed. Tom and his wife worried that he was alienating his friends and coworkers. Anti-depressant medication helped for about a year, until he realized the cycle was continuing.

Once in psychotherapy, he began to understand that much of his unconscious rage was associated with the alternating neglect and physical abuse he experienced as a child.

Tom's growing awareness of his childhood pain—his reliving his memories and exploring his reactions to them—was a germination process. He gathered in the seeds of creativity that he had sown as a child. He began to remember boyhood chemistry experiments, wildlife adventures in the woods near his home, and imaginative attempts to communicate with his aloof parents. The more he embraced his grief and recognized the hurt withdrawn little boy inside, the more he uncovered his anger. Tom practiced being more playful, letting his "little boy" self (inner child) roam around, being more curious and spontaneous. Through dialoguing, he released his anger and reassured the frightened part of himself. This brought him tremendous relief. He no longer felt the impulsive urge to act out his anger and drive away those he loved with self-destructive behavior.

Tom metamorphosed from a reserved, occasionally sullen man who had angry outbursts to a lively, comfortably outgoing man with great energy. He was given more responsibility at work. He discovered he had a knack for manufacturing innovations, as well as personnel problem solving. His newfound inner drive led him to rediscover inventing, the area of creative expression he loved most. But what made his new life complete was the strengthened bond of love and connectedness that he felt toward his wife, whom he had periodically alienated with his angry behavior. He transformed himself from feeling fragmented in anger to feeling whole in his love.

Luce, Barbara, Andrew, and Tom portray the personal pain that results from child mistreatment. When children's privacy and personal space are violated, self-expression is sacrificed, resentment and anger are turned inward and grief and growth cycles are blocked. The child is not taught to be self-assertive and cannot learn to modulate angry feelings. As an adult, there may be little creative energy for work or for intimacy.

Balanced anger results in assertiveness, strong protective expressions, and the ability to stand up not only for ourselves but for others. This life energy fuels and manifests our values. If we are encouraged to "grow our self-expression" as children, we're more likely to be proactive adults, able to listen, process information, and act in useful, adaptive and productive ways. The over-expression or under-expression of anger usually signals that a person was emotionally hurt, neglected, or abused in some way in childhood. The hurt and outrage that person feels tends to either "flood" out over others or stagnate inside, breeding sadness, cynicism, and sometimes illness.

Remember how Job became ill from head to toe? Survivors of childhood trauma and those who, stalled in their grief, and unable to release the past, often have ongoing physical problems, and sometimes, symptoms that defy medical diagnosis. With repeated emotional and physical violation, a child not only fails to learn to express emotional strength, but the physical barrier to illness, the immune system, may fail as well. Whether or not we were abused as children, all of us suffered trials, occasional terrors, and a multitude of large and small disappointments. The energy of that fear and confusion can be trapped in the body as well as the mind.

A sense of physical safety is required in order to be self-assertive. Inner expectations of being helpless or invaded must be overcome in order to set aside learned passivity, reactivity, or conversion of energy to physical symptoms. Studies show, for example, that girls who were molested as children are three times as likely as other girls to be raped in adolescence or young adulthood. These girls have unknowingly learned to project a sense of helplessness and passivity.

It is crucial to respect and encourage children's expressions of hurt, anger, and upset. It is never too late for us to become aware of our own feelings so that we can process our grief, deposit the atrocities in the trash, and come to the end of a grief and growth cycle.

One way to get in the habit of doing this is by monitoring our level of self-assertiveness.

Anger is protest. It may be a protest against change, loss, or unfairness. Once we acknowledge rage and utilize it as self-assertiveness, the energy may be transformed into constructive drive. It's not a coincidence that parents of abducted children begin hotlines for other parents of missing children, or people with life-threatening illnesses begin support groups for other people with these illnesses. Constructive compassionate life purpose makes us feel whole and connects us with our community.

Muhammad

A man's true wealth is the good he does in the world.
— Muhammad

Muhammad (or Mohammed), the great prophet and leader of Islam born in 570 C.E., was able to transform his grief into constructive drive, which was necessary to lead his people out of ignorance and persecution and into a faith that brought monotheism, morality, and social order.

Muhammad's parents both died when he was small. He was raised by an affectionate uncle, and as a child Muhammad was described as sweet, gentle, and sensitive to all human suffering, although the culture he was brought up in was not supportive of these traits. Lawlessness and ignorance were rife. Outside of Mecca, where the nobility lived, poverty was the rule. Tribal solidarity was breaking up. Extended blood feuds were common.

Muhammad's ministry began after fifteen years of meditative preparation. Through his caravan business, he had met and married an older woman, a wealthy widow. The marriage was happy and companionable, and Khadija, his wife, was supportive of Muhammad's long periods of solitude, during which he sequestered himself in a hillside cave. During one of these vigils, as he pondered the mysteries of life and death, and good and evil, he experienced a presence which he believed to be an angel of God, revealing truths that he was told to proclaim to others. He at first protested that he could not be a prophet, but finally accepted it as his mission.

Like all great agents of change, Muhammad met with strong resistance. His teaching that there was only one god, Allah, upset those in power who were taking revenue from pilgrimages to more than 360 shrines honoring numerous deities. Directives requiring lawful governance of communities and charitable treatment of all citizens stirred the wrath of the leaders and led to Muhammad's violent persecution.

Muhammad escaped Mecca and relocated in Medina, a city where he had developed a following. By most accounts, Muhammad became a brilliant statesman, bringing together numerous tribes to form an orderly confederation and developing a spirit of cooperation never before known in the city's history. Gentle and merciful when conducting his administrative duties, he also led strategic raids on caravans from Mecca and survived two years of battles and a siege against Medina by an enemy force of ten thousand men. Muhammad put economic pressure on the Meccans instead of crushing them militarily, and finally reentered Mecca with his own force of ten thousand men, encountering no resistance.

By the time of his death, Muhammad had united virtually all of Arabia under the banner of Islam, which means "surrender to God." Muhammad's records of the words given to him by the angel Gabriel over a twenty-three year period were compiled into the Koran, the Islamic bible. The Koran is a legal guide for faith, religion, politics, and social roles. In seventh-century Arabia it opened the door to freedom and justice for everyone. Primogeniture, for example, was struck down, and it was required that inheritance be shared by all heirs, including daughters. Unlike Christians, who venerated celibacy, Muhammad believed that sexual union was one of the great joys of life. Marriage, he believed, protected men and women from irreligious activities. He insisted that his followers wed, but instituted divorce laws promoting harmony and kindness between the sexes.³ Infanticide was outlawed, interracial coexistence stressed, and religious tolerance mandated.

Professor of comparative religion Huston Smith calls the revolutionary changes in the culture of that time a "near-miracle: The difference between pre-and post-Islamic Arabia raises the question of whether history has ever witnessed a comparable moral advance among so many people in so short a time."⁴ It is difficult for us to imagine the amount of forceful expression required to make these changes, the amount of violence Muhammad had to be capable of. And yet, the early loss of his parents and the value he placed on a better life for his people gave Muhammad the angry life energy and the aggression necessary to create a more unified and just society.

Gandhi

As heat conserved is transmuted into energy, even so our anger controlled can be transmuted into a power which can move the world.

— Mohandas Gandhi

Six hundred years after Muhammad's time, on the other side of the Arabian Sea, a shy lawyer named Mohandas Gandhi also used angry energy to change the world. He taught the world that nonviolent civil disobedience could be every bit as powerful as military force. Quiet and unassertive as a boy and young man, Gandhi surprised even himself when he reacted with anger to the injustices he experienced while working in South Africa. He was reprimanded for wearing a turban, thrown off a train for riding in the first-class compartment, and barred from hotels reserved "for Europeans only." He was outraged over discrimination and determined that he would not accept it as part of any social order. He would defend people's dignity.

Gandhi overcame his shyness and transformed his anger into

constructive drive. He entered politics in India, organizing marches to secure rights for his people. He also encouraged massive civil disobedience and willing imprisonment. At one point, more than sixty thousand of his countrymen were jailed by the British. He himself spent years in prison and endured long periods of self-imposed fasting. His single-minded adherence to his purpose resulted in Britain's withdrawal from India and the beginning of the end of colonialism. Later, Albert Einstein was inspired by Gandhi's pacifism as a possible protest method against nuclear bombs, and Martin Luther King Jr. adopted Gandhi's nonviolent stance to further the civil rights movement in the United States.

Both Gandhi and Muhammad, two remarkable religious and social leaders, teach us the truth about angry energy: we each have the *capability* and the *choice* to transform it into a beneficial drive for achieving our goals.

Van Gogh

I tell you the more I think, the more I feel that there is nothing more truly artistic than to love people.
— Vincent van Gogh

Artist Vincent van Gogh suffered all his life with anger and attacks of rage. Retrospectively, he has been diagnosed as having more than one hundred and fifty types of psychological and organic illness. While we will never know the exact etiology of van Gogh's affliction, he left powerful evidence in over eight hundred works testifying to his drive to connect with others.

We know that his mother was depressed and distant, and his father was religious and distant. Van Gogh was sent off to boarding school at age twelve.

In a later letter to his brother, Theo, justifying his choice to live with an ill-tempered prostitute, he wrote, "I cannot, I will not live without love. I want to touch people." While he was never able to achieve a lasting intimate relationship, he touched many people through his paintings of brilliant yellow sunflowers and the dazzling lights of his "Starry Night." Of his work he wrote, "I want to do works that will touch people. So that they will see that inside this wretch of a man, cast out by everyone, there is a soul that is beautiful, that despite all, is motivated more by love than by anything else."[5]

If love can be the overriding drive for someone as tormented as van Gogh, love and connection with others can be our aim as well. Be aware of how you use your angry energy. Does it flow as life energy that provides the drive toward activities that please you and those around you? Do you notice it as an aid to self-protection, to making firm your personal safety and self-expression? Have you observed it as an expression of the anguish of unresolved grief? Have you ever used this energy as a defense against new knowledge? Do you use creative aggression to work toward personal goals?

Most of us have used our angry energy in all of these ways. Recognizing anger and putting it into words is necessary in order for us to achieve a sense of balance and harmony in the personality. We want to consistently move toward *acceptance* and *awareness* of how we're responding to every life event in order to achieve the wholeness of inner peace, life purpose, and expansive love.

Daily Creative Discipline
(Anger: The Drive to Wholeness)

1. Being aware that anger is one of the grieving feelings, make a list of the reasons for your upset. Write down your **crisis credentials,** the experiences or events that have hurt your feelings or frightened you into under-expressing or over-expressing your anger.

2. Honor the battlefield of your life experience by learning **creative cursing.** Catch the pain in your anger and transform it into creative energy by yelling as many "original" curse words as possible. Get warmed up by saying any words at all, but with strong feeling: "Hair! Dirt! Swamp! Chaos! Nails! Grease! Mud! Bolts!" This will remind you that your anger does not need to be destructive, but in fact is leading you through a crisis.

3. Notice **where your body feels anger.** Ask the energy why it lodges there. Give the anger a shape and give it a color. See the shape changing, becoming more smooth and flowing. See the color changing to a brighter, more joyful hue, or a soft relaxing blue. See the blue mixed with green and let it flow, like a gentle waterfall, right out of your body. (You can use this meditation with pain as well.)

4. Think of your favorite storybook character. What is it you like about the character? Identify those **positive traits** in yourself and be aware of consciously growing and expanding those traits.

5. Identify a historic figure whom you admire. As you transform your angry energy into the **constructive drive to accomplishment and wholeness,** create a **vision** of yourself achieving something important to you.

6.   Buy finger paints, spread newspapers on the kitchen table, and set to work being as messy as possible. (On a nice day, spread a tarp in the yard and use big sheets of paper.) Use both hands to squish the colors and spread them around with water. After you've made pictures of your angry curse words, do one design on a separate piece of paper with the one **color you love.** Dry and save your creations.

Chapter Five

Obsession: The Energy of
Passion and Personal Power

*If only I could go back to the old days, to the time when
God was watching over me...*
— Job (29:2)

Worry takes you into the past or the future.
— Sandra Ingerman, A Fall to Grace

Obsession, Bargaining, and Loss

We waved our sixteen-year-old daughter off at the airport as
she left with only a backpack for two months of public health service
in an isolated village in the Dominican Republic. My husband and I
could not sleep that night. Instead, we shared our worries.

"She left behind the bag of granola bars and instant chicken
soup," I said as I pulled the covers up under my chin and curled into
a fetal position.

My husband turned on one side and then the other. "That's
nothing. She forgot to take her medical insurance card and the
special water filter I got for her."

My stomach tightened. "She hasn't even finished high school
yet," I said. "Why did we let her go? She can't find things in her

own bedroom. How is she going to find her way around in a foreign country?"

"What if she gets that gastrointestinal disease from toxic reef fish? There's no medication for it," he said with an edge of panic.

And so on.

Obsession prevailed that night, as it does when we are caught up in fear. We marched each fear out, observed it, and shared our attraction to it in the darkness. We respected our obsession as part of processing our grief and we felt slightly better in the morning. But for me, meditation and prayer are my anchors through each life crisis, and this was no exception. I went to my meditation place earlier than usual that morning, relieved to give myself over to the routine of allowing my thoughts to come and allowing them to go.

My "meditation place" is the easy chair next to the desk in my study. While normally this chair is backed up to a sliding glass door, when I meditate I turn the chair around to face a view of the Rio Grande River, the forest of cottonwood trees on either side, the city of Albuquerque, and the Sandia Mountains in the distance. I light incense and sometimes candles to give me a sense of the sacred. On this morning I lit an extra candle, pulled my legs up into the lotus position and closed my eyes.

Repetitive fears fluttered through my mind and I noticed the tension in my body that seemed to accompany them. After awhile I shifted my attention to prayer. I concentrated on sending light and love to my daughter and asked for guardian angels to be with her throughout her trip. I envisioned her as healthy, happy, and powerful, floating in a bubble of white light. I asked for help to overcome my fear and gave thanks, a demonstration of faith that my requests would be manifested.

When I opened my eyes, I saw a graceful white bird flying downstream directly above the middle of the river. I smiled involuntarily as the remaining tension in my body turned to joy. I thanked the Great Spirit and that beautiful bird for giving me a sign that my daughter's journey would be a smooth and safe one.

Meditation has made me mindful that every living creature is a messenger, a connection to the Whole, and a symbol of security.

When I turn inward and become deeply relaxed, I go to a deep inner pool of calmness. I can see a larger picture of the future and sense possibilities for the present that I can only refer to as a sense of "spaciousness." Despite knowing there wouldn't be any phone contact with my daughter for those two months and that her letters would most likely arrive after her return home, I had no further fearful obsessions. I could now choose to think of my daughter as being on a soulful, gratifying adventure.

.د   د.

Obsession is what the mind does when it fears separation from a source of love. It provides a container for our anxiety, a structured way to process fearful thoughts. Obsession is a cognitive strategy to attempt to control the future.

Dr. Elisabeth Kübler-Ross used the term "bargaining" to describe the mental plans one devises in an attempt to delay the death experience. The desperate prayers from parents of terminally ill children convey the message that they will do anything "if only" their child is healed.

In Job's complaint to God, nine times he cries *if only* "...there were one to arbitrate between man and God, as between a man and his neighbor" (16:21). And, *if only* "...God might take his rod from my back" (9:33-34). Thirteen times he asks, Why is this happening to me? Why do I have to experience this pain when others less moral or less faithful do not?

Repetitious ruminations and "if only"s are attempts to master the experience of losing control over life events. It is also the way we wade through life change and begin to reorient ourselves, restoring our certainty that we are in charge of our responses to life, no one else. Pushing up the periscope on the Grief and Growth Chart, we can see that in venting each thought, each fear, we are healing the split within, the false belief that we are separated from our inner power. When we become mindful of every thought and the emotions attached to those thoughts, we can transform our fear into faith.

Like Job, all of us want to "go back to the old days" of innocence rather than face something frightening that must be dealt with emotionally. In the face of cataclysmic change, Job must look within and find "the lumber from which a new house of meaning can be built."[1] Initially, Job has no belief in his ability to do that: "Oh how shall I find help within myself...?" (6:13). He is completely hopeless: "I shall never again see good times" (7:7); "I have no desire to live" (7:16).

Three friends, Eliphaz, Bildad, and Zophar, come to offer Job their condolences. The obsessive thoughts the friends express represent Job's doubt and self-blame. We can view the friends as Job's obsessional states and find themes and reactions in his ruminations, themes that help him move from entrapment in fear and resistance to surrender, toward self-acceptance and personal power. One theme Job is confronted with is the orthodox teaching that one reaps what one sows. If Job is in misery, to some extent he brought it on by his own deeds. Another theme is that one must respect the teachings of one's elders, and yet another is that one simply cannot fathom the mystery of God's perfection and the workings of God's world.

The third speech, credited to Eliphaz, is one that contains enormous self-recrimination. Up until now, Job has portrayed himself as a completely upright and devout man, almost saintly. At this point, however, we glimpse a darker side, behaviors that suggest reasons why Job might feel guilty and be resorting to anger, obsession, and denying accountability for his life. In one speech, we hear that Job's "depravity passes all bounds. Without cause you exact pledges from your brothers, leaving them stripped of their clothes and naked. To the weary you give no water to drink and you withhold bread from the starving. Is the earth, then, the preserve of the strong, a domain for the favoured few?...No wonder there are pitfalls in your path, scares to fill you with sudden terror! No wonder light is turned to darkness..." (22:6-11).

Like most of us, Job found behaviors in his past that he was not proud of. Even early in the story, Job tells us that he had been living in fear, fretting about losing his possessions: "Every terror that haunted me has caught up with me; what I dreaded has overtaken me. There is no peace of mind...." (3:25).

There can be no peace of mind in the defensive throes of obsessional thinking. In obsession, we are trapped in our fear, our grief over life change. We are living in the hell of the past or the purgatory of the future. What we must do is to somehow plug into the present moment and discover that our personal power is here and now.

.⌣ ⌣.

Obsession can be transformed into careful, conscious planning so that it ceases to be a defense. Tending to each thought becomes a self-nurturing act. Repetitive thoughts are part of the process for overcoming obstacles, developing self-mastery, and putting forth a passionate plan.

Sarah Orne Jewett, a nineteenth-century novelist, describes this process in *A Country Doctor,* published in 1884. The protagonist, Nan Prince, decided to become a physician in an era when women were not welcomed into the professions. She repeatedly considered her reasons for wanting to be a doctor and weighed them against the loss of social acceptance and the inevitability of spinsterhood.

Her thoughts were busy enough, and though some reasons against the carrying out of her plan ventured to assert themselves, they had no hope of carrying the day, being in piteous minority, though she considered them one by one.

The process of appraising each thought surrounding her choice strengthened her determination and prepared her for the difficulties she would face. Using our obsessive energy in this way propels us toward planning and fulfilling our life purpose. Honoring each thought and choosing which ones to discard and which to retain or implement is the practice of creative self-expression. Self-expression is the invincible extension of the spirit that gradually manifests personal power and passion for life.

When we are at our best, our energy nourishes our minds and the mechanisms of our intelligence process each thought, emotion, and intuition, carrying us forward along our path of personal creativity. Thoughts are reflected upon, evaluated, released. Specific thoughts are chosen to aid us in making important decisions or plans. Some thoughts help us to accept a sense of inner peace about our life changes and new realities.

I wish there'd been someone to reassure me instead of shame me when my reaction to the death of our seventh-grade history teacher was embarrassed laughter and then obsessive guilt.

One spring morning, when lilacs were blooming in the school yard, the principal came into our second-period class instead of the teacher. He fidgeted with his keys and stared at his shoes and then lifted his chin and said, "Mrs. Briggs died last night." After several minutes of stunned silence, a giggle escaped me. Even with my hand over my mouth I hadn't been able to suppress it. I felt the heat rise in my face as my classmates and the principal looked at me in condemnation. They turned away when someone asked how Mrs. Briggs had died. The brief discussion of the teacher's heart attack seemed to take place in another room, apart from me. Their words were distant, covered by the sound of my own heart pounding: "Shame, shame, shame." I was completely confused by my behavior. I had liked Mrs. Briggs. What was wrong with me?

Most likely, my parents' divorce had left me adrift and vulnerable to change. I perceived myself as different from the others, tainted by a tragedy possibly worse than death, since divorce in 1949 was a rare and preventable event. I knew of no other child with divorced parents. Perhaps hearing of my teacher's death introduced the previously unacknowledged and overwhelming thought that not only could I lose my family through divorce, I could lose them through death as well. If the principal had been able to say that there are many ways to express grief, and embarrassed laughter might even be one of them, my behavior could have been placed reassuringly in the realm of the normal.

During times of loss, most of us move alone through uncharted territory, not quite certain what our emotions mean and whether we'll be better or worse after surviving the event. Usually we're convinced life will be worse. For many years I had the obsessive thought that the only thing my classmates would remember about me was that burst of inappropriate laughter.

.‿ ‿.

It is important to remember that obsessional thoughts and seemingly bizarre reactions are attempts to cope with, develop mastery over, and grow through a significant life change. My thirty-fifth high school reunion, a slumber party, was particularly stirring and remarkable because the life stories of fifteen fifty-three-year-old women contained every stress imaginable: alcoholism, divorce, incest, domestic violence, accidents, job loss, children's issues, death, and the psychic death of Alzheimer's. We sat in a circle on Marilyn's living room floor, taking turns telling our stories, passing Kleenex and coffee instead of the popcorn and Cokes we had gulped in high school. In high school we had discussed dates; now we discussed disasters.

It was after midnight when Mary Jo began telling us about her husband Sam's death. Mary Jo and Sam had a long and happy marriage, becoming closer companions each year as it became clear they would not be having children. Sam worked as an investment banker in San Francisco and Mary Jo had a long career with a major airline. They traveled extensively and had a wide circle of friends. Then Sam began showing symptoms that were eventually diagnosed as pancreatic cancer. In addition to traditional medical care, they also began attending groups at the Center for Attitudinal Healing.[2] By the time Sam died, he and Mary Jo had become closer than they ever thought possible.

"The morning of the day he died, our dearest friends came to the hospital," Mary Jo told us. "It was so strange that everyone was available. I called Jack, one of his friends, as he was on his way to the airport. 'This is more important,' he told me. 'I'm canceling my trip. I'll be right over.' Sam and I and these close friends had all come to believe that death is merely a transition to another plane of existence. We've all had contact with people who have had near-death experiences. And if you meditate as I have for many years, you simply know that the spiritual is every bit as real as the physical. Anyway, Jack came, my favorite nurse came, and we all sat around the bed quietly sharing stories about Sam. Late that afternoon, someone brought a bottle of wine and we drank toasts to him, honoring the joy he'd brought to our lives.

"When his breathing became more labored and I sensed he was dying, I began talking to him about how we were all with him, loving him. I encouraged him to go on now and leave his body. I told him I would be all right, even though I'd miss him. So if it was time, just let his spirit float out of his body toward the light." Mary Jo's voice broke, but her face looked smooth, peaceful. Her eyes glistened but contained the same joyous energy that made me want to be her friend in high school.

"I don't remember all that I said," she continued, "The words came easily and spontaneously. I think I said there would be family waiting for him and that he would be perfect and happy. All of this is so strange, but I actually felt I could see his spirit leaving his body and floating up and out of the room."

"I know it all sounds wonderful," Mary Jo said, quickly, "but let me tell you the next part. First, you need to realize that I haven't told you about all the emotional agony I went through during the year-and-a-half-long process of dealing with the cancer. Two months after Sam died, my father, my closest buddy, died suddenly. I was probably in shock for several months and then I began to feel strangely euphoric. I stopped eating and I kept going over and over in my mind those last hours with Sam and some of the special times with my dad. A girlfriend who was keeping tabs on me told me I had to eat, but I really wasn't hungry. I felt fine. After a week she said she was going to take me to the hospital. She thought I was depressed. I didn't agree, but I didn't object either. I had no idea what was happening. I was actually feeling better than I ever had in my life.

"At the hospital, a young psychiatrist talked to me about my symptoms and advised me to enter the hospital for evaluation. He apparently thought I was manic-depressive and was having a psychotic episode. I refused to enter the hospital. Before I knew what was happening, I was going through a forced admission to the hospital! I even broke away at one point and began to run out of the place, but two big attendants came after me and brought me back. I gave up and decided I would cooperate so I could be discharged quickly."

The psychologist in me spoke up. "Mary Jo, this is incredible. You've always been so stable, self-reliant, willing to help others. What diagnosis were you given, and did they realize you were having a grief reaction?"

"They eventually diagnosed me as having a major depressive episode, but the amazing part is that no one ever talked to me about Sam's death or my father's death. No one even asked questions about what might have precipitated my unusual behavior."

"You've got to be kidding! Are you sure of that?" I asked her. I couldn't imagine any mental health professional failing to explore such significant events as the recent deaths of a spouse and a parent. Counseling focused on bereavement can facilitate the obsessive need to review the details of such loss in order to integrate the experience and emerge with a greater sense of personal power.

"Oh, I'm sure no one asked about those life events. They just talked about my symptoms and which medications to prescribe. I think I was a helpful participant in the ward's daily group therapy sessions, but I just behaved myself so I could be discharged. Two weeks later, after my discharge, I tossed the medication and, of course, I've been fine without it. The fascinating part is that when I began yoga again, I told my instructor what had happened after Sam's death. She said I had received a 'kundalini experience,' basically a spiritual rebirth related to Sam's passing.[3] That really made sense to me. After that, I became a volunteer at the Center for Attitudinal Healing, leading support groups. It's very uplifting, actually, to be able to help others go through their own expressions of grief. I have no obsessive thoughts anymore about Sam or his process of dying. It took over a year to settle into this new person I've become, but I feel quite peaceful now."

None of us knew quite how to respond to Mary Jo's story. It seemed like such a blessing compared to Janet's earlier sad story of her husband's sudden death one Monday morning while lying in bed beside her. Janet's resulting fear of being out-of-control and losing yet another family member led to obsessive self-blame and worry about the safety of her teenage children. Janet seemed to sense that we were comparing her outcome to Mary Jo's.

"Okay," Janet said, "my experience was nothing like that, but you guys have to know that I'm fine now. It took some time, but here's what happened. I kept thinking that if only I'd been a better person, less irritable and less of a complainer, if only I hadn't been so strong-willed and was more appreciative of Joe, maybe he wouldn't have died. I know it doesn't make any sense, but the next part doesn't make sense either. I believe that somehow we choose when to die.

"So then I began to worry that someone else in my family might be unconsciously preparing to die and I wouldn't be able to handle another loss." Janet suddenly stopped and looked around the circle. "Is this too morbid? I don't think most of you expected to spend the night talking about death and dying."

Alise spoke for all of us, with her deep melodious voice. "Please go on. We want to know as much about your experience as you feel comfortable sharing."

Janet took a deep breath and continued. "After over a year of feeling anxious and worried, there was one week during which I fell three times. The last time I actually fell flat on my face on a huge rock in the garden. It hurt so badly that I was certain I had broken bones and would be black and blue. I realized the next morning, when I was not black and blue, and wasn't even sore, that there was some lesson I was supposed to learn. I knew there was a message, like in a recurring dream. Several days later I got it. The realization hit me that my obsessive thoughts represented a lifelong tendency to procrastinate, to stay put and not make decisions for fear of making the wrong ones. I'd facilitated my husband's life, I'd tried to control my kids' lives, and in the process I'd abdicated responsibility for my own life. I was afraid that if I tried to make a life of my own, I'd fall on my face. Ever since that insight came to me, I've been working hard to make responsible choices."

"And I'll bet you're more careful when you walk in your garden," Alise joked.

"How are you feeling now about yourself?" I asked Janet. I was having trouble connecting the wisdom and humility of her words with the always-smiling sixteen-year-old drum majorette of Hoover High School, class of 1959.

"I feel like I'm finally discovering who I am. I'm more active than I was when Joe was alive, and I think he'd be proud of me. My kids say they are."

"We're proud of you, too!" said Judi, the loquacious organizer of the get-together. She had explained earlier that in spite of being voted most likely to succeed and having received a full scholarship to Stanford, she managed to flunk out during her first year due to her addiction to the game of bridge. When she returned to San Diego and found her parents unwilling to support her, she went to work as a deck hand on a fishing boat. One morning, she woke up after a night of drunken debauchery to find herself married to one of the other deck hands, who didn't even speak English!

"What did you do?" we had all asked, laughing in amazement.

"I got it annulled, of course. But I didn't trust myself after that. I lived with Chuck, my current husband, for six years before I even considered marriage again. And the thought of having children struck terror in me. Luckily, Chuck had done that already."

Judi continued to speak of being proud. "I feel proud of being part of this group. Do you know how rare this must be? Fifteen women getting together after all these years and still caring about each other...I think it's wonderful!"

"There's so much grief we've all been through," I commented, "and yet no one here seems depressed." I spoke of the stages of grief I was studying and about the middle stage, obsession. "Do any of you feel that you're still caught up in obsessing about loss?"

"I don't," answered Mary Jo. "I think going over and over events in my mind is simply the way I get used to the change that's taken place. That's why it's so important for bereaved people to have a place or a person to hear their story. We just keep going over and over it until it's digested and we're ready to go on."

"I agree," said Janet, "but with a qualifier. I had to learn something before my obsessions could stop."

"I think I'm metaphysically disabled, or unwilling to learn any cosmic truths," Alise stated with a grin. She looked as though she'd just read the contents of a fortune cookie.

"I suspect you've learned many 'cosmic' truths through the years," I told her. "One of the sad truths I've learned about myself has to do with my intense capacity to obsess over arguments and hurtful comments from my husband."

"Oh, I am the grand master of that!" declared Jackie. "In fact, I think I got rid of several husbands by hanging onto every nasty thing they ever said to me. Of course, they were thoughtless jerks, so there were a lot of nasty comments to hang onto. I'm working on attracting a nice man now. Do you think it's possible?"

"Possible that nice men exist or possible for you to attract one?" Alise teased. Our joking and laughter alternated with contemplation of the meaning of suffering. As each woman related her most profound life-changing experience, it was easy to see how their journeys through grief took them through denial, anger, obsession, and depression. They all had occasional swirls and stops on their way to accepting a drastically changed reality. Obsession seems to be a back-eddy that catches and holds us for a time no matter how hard we struggle to get free. Maybe it holds us because we are flailing and resisting the freedom of the current.

After an early breakfast, we parted, but all of us promised to meet the following year to continue sharing our life experiences and discussing each woman's cycles through grief, growth, and creative self-expression.

Obsession and Compulsion

We cannot find our enlightened minds while continuing to be estranged from our neurotic ones.
— Mark Epstein, *Thoughts Without a Thinker*

In graduate school at the University of Southern California in 1964, I was looking forward to a course on abnormal psychology. A psychiatrist from the medical school, Dr. Edward Stainbrook, was to teach the course. The information circulating about him included his reputation as a profound intellect and an entertaining lecturer. But most intriguing was that he was one of Lewis Terman's subjects in the longitudinal studies of genius, which began in the 1920s. He was one of the original "whiz kids."

The descriptions of him proved correct; he was a stimulating and inspiring speaker. I remember waiting with poised pen when he said he wanted to give us a definition of mental health. After studying child development, theories of personality, numerous aspects of mental illness, and behavioral psychology, I eagerly awaited his wise integrative assessment of what constitutes mental health. Dr. Stainbrook stopped his pacing, looked up, and proclaimed: "Good mental health is the ability to think about anything without needing to act on it."

"That's it?" I thought. "That sounds much too simple." But after thirty years in the mental health field, I've decided it was a brilliant definition. It has helped me reassure many people struggling with life change.

Obsession is the state of having repetitive thoughts. Compulsion is the acting out of repetitive behaviors. "All I do is think of this problem over and over," a client might say. "Am I crazy? I can't just drop it."

"No," I can answer. "Our obsessions do not make us crazy. They pose questions for us to answer, lessons for us to learn, grief for us to cope with, fears for us to master. Our worries make us human."

Several years later, when I was married and living in New Mexico, my husband and I returned to Los Angeles for further medical training. Los Angeles hadn't grown that much; the freeways and intense traffic were the same. But I discovered fears within myself. I was no longer used to the high speeds. Images would flash across my mind of me crashing into the car in front of me during a sudden halt of traffic, or swerving to avoid a car and smashing into a concrete overpass. Was I sliding into madness? I remembered the definition of mental health—being able to think of anything without having to act on it—and reminded myself that the real fear that seized me was of acting on the thought. I was afraid that somehow the *thought* itself put me in danger.

As soon as I became aware of the connection between a thought and the compulsion to act, I could use my observing ego to distance myself from the impulse. The revelation that I could simply observe my thoughts led to my being curious about my thoughts, interested, delighted, even amused by them. Instead of needing to act on them in a dangerous way, I could play with them.

I began creating whimsical stories in my mind during those long glides or long halts on the freeway. When I was angry with other drivers, my car would become James Bond's, armed with fantastic gadgets that would slingshot cars off the road, gouge their tires, or make them disappear. I could imagine purposely smashing my car into a concrete bridge abutment and then pretend I was watching my funeral. Who would be there? What would they say about me?

Clearly, it is the sense of being in control of one's thoughts, one's mind, that is the key to feeling healthy and power-full. When we feel out of control of our thoughts, we feel anxious. We fear going crazy. Obsession is the area of grief and growth where anxiety lives, and anxiety is typically about future events. When we have fearful thoughts that cause anxiety, we feel compelled to do something about them. We either try to avoid the cause of our anxiety, like public speaking or the dentist's chair, or we embrace a desire, such as a lover, food, drink or exercise. We compulsively behave in ways we think will avert loss or abandonment. Compulsive behavior is an attempt to control or bind anxiety in order to assure that there will be no further hurt or loss in one's life.

.᠎ ᠎.

Sometimes when we make a choice we initially feel completely in control, certain of success, only to discover that this particular choice brings us face-to-face with a desperate problem. Brandon, a successful physician, became romantically involved with a much younger woman following his divorce. Initially, he felt powerful and proud. She was quite beautiful and in need of his financial help. She also provided the most exciting sexual experiences he'd ever had.

Soon he discovered that there was a huge price to pay for having Cindy in his life. She was insanely jealous. If she thought, as she frequently did, that he might be seeing another woman, she'd destroy his favorite possessions or steal his money. He'd given her a part-time job in his medical office, but she became so disruptive he had to ask her to leave. On two occasions, Cindy physically attacked Brandon, leaving him with cuts and bruises. She also objected to Brandon's spending time with his children and interfered with their visits. Just before he came for psychotherapy, she'd made a scene at an important medical gathering, leaving him humiliated and afraid of losing his hard-earned respect in the community. Brandon's friends couldn't understand why he tolerated Cindy. His old college football buddies told him to dump her. He couldn't.

"I feel crazy in this relationship," he said. "All I do is think about her. I think about sex with her. I think about how it feels when she stays away from me. I can't stand it when I think she's going to leave me. I can't sleep when she's not there. I'm addicted to her. I don't even like her and she's ruining my life!"

Brandon had to stop and take time to look at his lifelong pattern of working to please others. He reflected on the fact that his younger brother was his mother's favorite child. In fact, his mother had a habit of blaming Brandon for every misdeed that occurred in the house and in the neighborhood. He had decided, when quite young, that he must do everything in his power to try to please his mother—earn good grades, become a doctor, save lives, and rescue women.

Brandon requested that I hypnotize him and change this pattern immediately. I explained that that was not possible, but that hypnosis could help him learn more about his personality pattern so he could access his own inner strength in order to change. In a trance, Brandon relived an experience when he was six years old and his mother blamed him for an accident at his fort in which a playmate, a little girl, was injured. His brother had, in fact, been responsible, but his mother never listened to Brandon's side of the story.

When I brought him out of hypnosis, Brandon wiped the tears away from his eyes and explained that he'd wanted that fort so badly. He had asked repeatedly for it until his parents arranged to have it built. After the accident, for which he'd been held responsible, he never asked for another thing. As soon as he could, he began work as a paperboy and vowed to save and buy the things he wanted. "I never asked for a chocolate sundae, even though I wanted one so much. I finally bought one when I was thirteen," he said. "I guess I was never going to be dependent on a woman again."

"What happened?" I asked him. "How did you get to be so dependent on Cindy?"

"I don't know," he laughed. "But I sure got hooked on this one."

Brandon began to see that it was a perfect time, midlife, to become aware of the grief he'd experienced but never resolved in reaction to his mother's emotional distance and blaming. In another hypnosis session, he returned to when he was a toddler, just prior to his brother's birth, when his mother was holding and rocking him.

The feeling was one of rapture; he didn't want it to ever end. Back in his normal awake state, he associated the way he felt when his mother held him with the way he felt with Cindy.

"Oh my God. You mean I want my mother?" he asked plaintively.

"No," I answered. "You long for that same feeling of total acceptance, of merging with the feminine, of floating in bliss. Wouldn't anyone want that?"

As Brandon became familiar with his longings and his fears, he also came to know a feeling of inner strength and personal power. Brandon and I came to call it being in his Man Trance. Since he knew exactly how to summon that feeling at the office, teaching at the medical school, or presiding at meetings, he began to go into his Man Trance with Cindy as well.

Brandon felt the event that led to a permanent shift was when he decided he would take his daughter, instead of Cindy, to a meeting in the Bahamas. In the past, he would have waited until the last minute, told Cindy, endured her abuse, and then allowed her to come along. This time, we came up with a careful strategy outlining how to tell her, when to tell her, how to firmly maintain the travel plans, and ways to respond should she become violent.

On his return, Brandon looked tanned and pleased. "It worked," he said. "I was able to stick to my plan. She did throw a few things when it was clear I was really going. Also, when I was leaving to pick up my daughter and go to the airport, she began tearing up my mail and I suspected she'd get even more destructive. I arranged for a friend to come over and then I called the police and left. When my daughter and I were at the airport, Cindy showed up there. I never said a word as she yelled at us and called us names. Finally she left with her usual parting shot, 'You'll never see me again!' The little old lady in front of us in line turned and said, 'I think it's good riddance.'"

"It sounds as though you were able to stay in a place of quiet firmness and strength throughout the ordeal. What happened when you got home?" I asked.

"She was apologetic, said she'd never act like that again, she missed me, etc. She also told me she went to Vegas with some guy.

These are all ploys I expected. What's new is that my obsessions have stopped. I don't think about her at all in the old ways. I used to think I couldn't stand it if she left or slept with someone else; now I know I can live without her. Something else you said helped me a lot, too. It was that statement about letting her 'live in my mind without paying rent.' I decided I wouldn't allow her to do that."

Remembering that term helped Brandon to be more conscious about choosing to end the obsessive attachment. It took a few more months for Brandon to practice "living in his mind" with his own chosen thoughts, but the payoff was how much more comfortable he felt being in control of his life, or as he liked to say, "being the captain of my own ship." He was no longer afraid of his feelings, of loss, of change, or of asking for what he wanted. Cindy, being addicted to high drama in relationships, soon became bored and sought out someone who would be a better partner in an obsessive let's-take-turns-hurting-each-other relationship. Eventually, Brandon reported how pleased he was to be "attracted to 'normal women' for the first time in a long while. 'You know, women I can talk to, relax with, and just be myself with.'"

A Past-Life Compulsion

While Brandon resolved his obsession with a dangerous relationship using traditional therapy and hypnosis, Cecily had a striking abatement of symptoms in one surprising session.

It had been several years since I had seen Cecily. Her earlier therapy, when she was in her thirties, had been focused on reactions to her mother's cancer and eventual death. Cecily had learned a great deal about her family's dynamics. She was an average student in a family of college professors and felt inadequate intellectually. When she surpassed her brothers in size, she was teased and ridiculed. Her resulting self-image was of a stupid, awkward, and unattractive girl. By the end of therapy, she realized that actually, at this time in her life, she was the leader of the family. Her siblings looked to her to consolidate ideas and make important decisions.

It was good to see Cecily again. Her warm, outgoing nature was engaging, and I was pleased to hear that her personal life and her work had been going well. Cecily shared with me, though, that for the past six weeks she'd begun feeling anxious and uncomfortable around knives. In fact, she had developed an obsessive fear of seeing or using knives.

"As a nurse, this fear is definitely detrimental to my work!" she joked. "You know I've been anxious all my life, but it was never focused on one thing. I can't shake this. Now I've started having this fear that I'm going crazy! You've got to help me; I think hypnosis would be the fastest way."

I questioned Cecily about what she associated with knives and she answered, "suicide." Yet she had no family history of suicide and no experience with losing friends in this way. When I asked her what she associated with the word "crazy," she said, "I have no idea! There's no history of mental illness in my family that I know of." I also asked about anniversary dates: the date of her father's death, birthdays, the onset of her mother's cancer, her mother's death. Often we react unconsciously to dates of significant life events. And yet, we didn't find any connections between family events and her new obsessive fears. While Cecily had always endured a low level of chronic anxiety, she hadn't encountered an experience that caused overwhelming anxiety, hopelessness, or a wish to end her life.

Once in a trance, Cecily reviewed several incidents from adolescence and one from childhood. These events had damaged her self-esteem, deeply imprinting in her mind the notion that, compared to her family members, she was huge, gangling, and ugly. "I feel like Bigfoot," she said forlornly.

I then suggested that she move directly to the cause of the current problem. "Return to the experience or event that has caused these fears."

When she said, "I'm here," I asked her to describe where she was and what she was doing. She said she was standing in a field swatting flies away from her face. "I'm going crazy," she said. "I'm just going crazy."

"What is this place?" I asked.

"The war...the war between the states." Cecily had slipped into a past life drama as a Union soldier during the Civil War. Her name was "Jack," she said. "I put my gun up against the tree over there. I'm just standing here jumping from one foot to the other, swatting these flies. It's so hot. I can't stand the killing. It's so hot. I'm going crazy."

"What will you do?" I asked. "Will you leave?"

"No, no. I couldn't desert."

When I asked what happened next, "Jack" described how he was allowed to work in the field hospital, a converted brick building. He tried to stop the wounded soldiers' bleeding; he cleaned up their blood and bodies as much as he could. But it was a "living death." Following the war, he made his way back to his brother's home in Massachusetts. He had no family of his own and became more and more depressed and despondent until finally he took his life using some type of knife.

When she came out of the trance, Cecily was amazed that she had spontaneously moved into a past-life experience. It surprised us both. "Do you think it really happened?" she asked me.

"I don't know," I answered, "but every hypnotherapist occasionally has a client that moves to a past life in response to the suggestion to go to the root of a certain problem. I would think the most important issue is whether the symptoms are extinguished now."

"Isn't it interesting that I worked in a hospital in that life, and in this one I'm a nurse?" she mused.

Cecily called the next week to let me know, with great enthusiasm, that the knife obsessions were gone. "I feel great," she said, "and I may come back for more past-life hypnosis. It made me feel big in a good way...like timeless."

Six months later, Cecily came back for another appointment. I was looking forward to seeing her. When I went out to the waiting room, I looked around and was about to turn back when my secretary pointed to a woman and nodded her head that it was Cecily. I was stunned. Cecily was transformed. The weight she normally carried on her large frame was gone. Her hair was styled and her typical baggy clothing had been replaced with a sleek pantsuit. She looked elegant and I told her so.

"I don't know exactly what happened, but I got all this energy. Maybe the anxiety turned into energy. I found myself in all these exercise classes and I decided I wanted to wear those thong leotards and look outrageously good!"

"Well, you certainly accomplished that! What else is happening?"

Cecily went on to tell me that she'd decided, after all those years of believing she wasn't as smart as others in her family, that she was going to return to college to earn a master's degree. She also was interested in teaching, and she felt optimistic about overcoming her lifelong fear of public speaking.

Under hypnosis again, she explored another lifetime, this one as a woman, possibly following the Civil War. During this lifetime she had a happy and peaceful family experience and lived to an old age. Her encounter with death was merely an extension of love and support as she died surrounded by friends and family members. She went on to observe her spirit leaving her body. She watched those below as if in fond farewell and then floated on into the clouds, becoming completely absorbed with light and colors.

In another session, Cecily went directly to the spirit plane and discovered spirit guides and guardian angels. She asked one angel to pay special attention to her real-life son, who was in the army. The angel, who appeared to be a male entity, told Cecily he was already looking after Paul and would serve as his guide.

These experiences seemed to give Cecily a greater sense of command over her life. Like being stuck in an elevator and then finding the right button to push to open the door, Cecily felt she had given birth to a self she had long been incubating—a powerful, intelligent, beautiful woman.

Rarely have I seen such a dramatic change in a client in such a short time. The energy blocked by Cecily's obsessions from past lives was transformed into personal power in the present. When she faced her fears, anxiety melted away and she essentially detoxified the future. Cecily found her voice and developed the art of growing self-expression. She moved from crisis to a more fulfilled, creative life.[4]

.ᴗ ᴗ.

Freud spoke of the "repetition compulsion." This term refers to the unconscious, compelling need to repeat or reenact situations in life until we are desensitized to the fear of them and develop a sense of mastery over them. Brandon's relationship with a violent woman was a repetition of his unresolved relationship with his mother. Overcoming his obsession led him to transcend his false belief that he needed to be punished for merely enjoying himself. Cecily's story shows us that we may be compelled to repeat limiting feelings and beliefs from past lives. With awareness, we can seize opportunities to finally release our grief, embrace our present proactive choices, and express our personal power.

Obsession and Addiction

All addictions are ways to avoid unacceptable feelings.
                                        — John Bradshaw

Addictions are attempts to cope with frightening feelings. They are also misguided attempts to process childhood grief. There is no conscious connection between the behavior and the traumatic cause, however. In the grip of addiction, one feels utterly compelled to *have* the substance and *do* the behavior—the work, the eating, the exercise, the drink, the drug, the sex—thereby temporarily easing the uncontrollable inner anxiety and tension.

This tension typically can be traced to experienced fears of abandonment, annihilation, or any behavior signaling a withdrawal of love. In Brandon's case, for example, the reason for his attachment to a woman who could only give him grief was completely unconscious. It was only as he began making connections to his past that he could see the reasons for his compulsive clinging to a woman who was cyclically affectionate and then rejecting and attacking like his mother. As a boy, he had no choice but to try to preserve his lifeline to his mother by avoiding confrontation and attempting to please her, weathering her hurtful behavior as best he could. As a man, while his relationship with Cindy offered greater rewards in the arena of sexual pleasure, that was small comfort for feeling trapped, humiliated, out of control, and afraid of being abandoned.

Compulsive and addictive behaviors sometimes result from childhood sexual molestation. Loni is an example of a person who found herself carrying out compulsive actions that she could consciously justify but which made no sense to those around her. Her family felt she was "addicted to cleanliness." The driveway had to be swept every day in order to clear away the leaves that fell on it from a neighbor's tree. Her husband and children had to remove their shoes before coming into the house lest they get dirt on the carpet. No one could work with her in the kitchen because she had certain methods of cleaning and preparing the food. She had many other strict rules of maintaining cleanliness, which members of her family did their best to observe. But over the years, her behavior became increasingly annoying and baffling to them. Loni's most distressing symptoms were her feelings of panic at somehow becoming out of control. Her anger, which periodically erupted at her husband, also frightened her with its potential rage.

As Loni reviewed the events of her childhood, she felt her most profound experience of loss involved her parents' bitter divorce when she was seven. Loni felt that her mother blamed her, along with the new woman her father eventually married, for the disintegration of the family. She was not allowed to visit her father, and her mother doted on her younger brothers. When Loni was sexually molested by her maternal uncle, she felt it must have been her fault. Somehow the experience validated what her mother consistently conveyed to her: Loni had "messed things up" again. From that time forward she decided she must be completely neat, clean, and orderly.

During a reflective moment, she confessed that no matter how hard she worked to control her environment, she could not get rid of her inner feeling of "badness, of rot. It's like I'm an apple in a barrel of lovely just-picked apples. I look like the rest of them, but inside I'm dark and rotten."

As Loni grieved the loss of a secure childhood, she slowly found that she was able to drop the compulsive barriers she'd erected to try to protect herself from further hurt. Loni recovered from her addiction to cleaning as she discovered she was safe in the present. She used one affirmation, "I am safe in the present moment," as a daily reminder of where she was in the grief and growth process—incubating her creativity and growing her personal power. Today, Loni works outside of the home (something she never thought she'd be able to do), handling the books and personnel for a property management company. She's doubly amazed that she has pursued another dream: in her off hours, she caters social events, expressing her long-time love of being creative with food.

.⸻ ⸻.

Addictions are a tragic mask for the compulsive search for love. John Bradshaw defines addictive behavior as "a pathological relationship to any mood-altering experience that has life-damaging consequences."[5] Addictions, then, are not about craving the substance—alcohol, sex, drugs—but about the underlying belief that in that softened state of merger, the "rottenness," as Loni called it, can be dissolved. When lost in our addictions, we may experience the bliss of feeling loveable, sometimes for the first time. Or we can experience a reunion with a love that was lost.

Compulsive behaviors are also a way of keeping anxiety in check. Repetitive behavior covers up the fear that some dreadful experience will occur or reoccur, possibly in the very next moment. When terror is added to the initial or ongoing experience, drugs and alcohol are often used to numb the fear. Survivors of childhood abuse, for example, display significantly more drug addiction and alcoholism than other people.[6]

The connection between the perception of having lost control in the context of terror and resorting to drugs and alcohol is also confirmed by studies of combat groups and Vietnam veterans. Seventy-five to eighty-five percent of veterans with post-traumatic stress disorder developed serious drug and alcohol dependence *after* their return to civilian life, to numb their fearful memories and feelings. One study showed that soldiers' use of alcohol increased proportionately to their group's combat losses, as they apparently[7] attempted to diminish their growing sense of terror and helplessness.

Finding some way to reduce our overwhelming fear is a survival reaction. As with all of our defensive maneuvers, however, once we're grown or away from the threatening situation, we need to address the need for the symptom that temporarily protected us. We must step out of the prison of unresolved grief and find love.

Eating disorders such as compulsive eating appear to be unconscious attempts to feel safe, secure, and loved. The following is one woman's story.

Forty-two-year-old Tory had been forty-five to sixty pounds overweight since her teens. Her father was a minister who believed constant criticism was the way to keep his only daughter from being selfish and vain. Her mother was not only shy, but cold, and withheld affection. The one way Tory learned to feel physically comfortable and fulfilled was to eat, and eat. As an adult, when she came for therapy, she was struggling with an even more insidious problem, which was threatening to destroy her marriage: compulsive spending. She had topped out one credit card buying clothes and had begun on another.

As Tory evaluated the impact of her parents' messages, she realized she had taken to heart what they'd said, that she was sinful and vain. No amount of fancy clothing would cover her ugliness, she believed. But she continued to purchase clothes. Tory had busied herself over the years trying to feel loveable.

In psychotherapy, Tory explored the full range of her grief about the ways she had been treated as a girl. When she looked at her anger, she realized she had displaced rage toward her father onto her husband and was secretly enjoying his anguish over their financial predicament. When she inspected her addictive pattern of eating, she realized something: "This isn't about food, is it? It's about getting my 'love bucket' filled whenever I need it." She began to find new and simple ways to express love to herself and to others.

In addition to Tory's gradual weight loss and control of her spending, she made two other decisions that resulted in enhanced personal power. She decided to quit her job under a domineering boss and develop her own consulting business; she also requested past-life hypnosis to see if there were other traumatic experiences influencing her tendency to eat compulsively.

Under hypnosis, when Tory went to a past life, she was a twenty-one-year-old woman standing in a long line of people. She was frightened and disoriented.

"Up to this time I've had a very happy life. Now they're separating me from my family. I don't know why this is happening."

Tory went on to say that her name was Magrite, this place was Germany, and the men who took her away were called Nazis. She was placed in a large building where she acted as a secretary during the day and was used for the men's sexual pleasure at night. Often groups of men were there. "I learn to just go away. I can't stand what is happening to me. There is one man there who never touches me. He just sits. He is younger than the others and when they leave, he talks to me. He is kind, but he never tries to stop what the men are doing." Tory cried and held her hands up to cover her face. "I am so ashamed. Why doesn't he try to stop them?" When her sobs quieted, she said, "I am nothing but a skeleton." Tory went on to relate that in the second year of her captivity she contracted an illness that killed her. "I could not continue in that life."

Afterward, Tory looked calm and self-contained as she reviewed her past-life regression. "That was amazingly helpful, I think, not only because of the experience of starving and knowing that is part of the compulsive eating in this lifetime, but also because of the sexual part. I think the young man in that lifetime is now my husband, Peter. I've had trouble being relaxed about sex, even though Peter is a very gentle, considerate lover. Now it makes sense."[8]

Toward the end of Tory's psychotherapy she announced that she had decided to change her name. "I've always hated my name. My parents named me Torrance, which was a family surname. It also sounds like a boy's name. I'm naming myself Theodora, after my one grandfather whom I loved. And it will not be shortened either. I will be Theodora."

Tory (Theodora) had created a new sense of self. She told me that understanding the grief and growth process had given her hope throughout her therapeutic odyssey. She developed great respect for her feelings and behavioral reactions. She felt encouraged that by engaging her grief, learning to accept her feelings, and understanding her addictive patterns, she could take responsibility for re-creating her life. And that's exactly what she was able to do.

Addictions to destructive substances, and abusive people, paralyze us and we live the "lies of limitation" we've learned as children or possibly in past lives. Uncovering the truth often requires a number of supportive resources, such as psychotherapy, focused group therapy, bodywork such as therapeutic massage, hypnotherapy, a Twelve-Step program, or a spiritual study group. Using these resources individually or together provides a safety net of security, which reassures us while we do the work of grieving.

As false thoughts are faced and fearful feelings tended, the tension that has kept the obsession operating is released. The compulsive pattern collapses and that energy is now channeled into self-creation and transcendent living. Awareness gives way to the powerful possibilities inherent in change. Fear of the past and anxiety about the future give way to the power of living in the present.

Michelangelo—Obsession and Passion

Passion is the fire that drives us to express who we really are.
— Neale Donald Walsch, *Conversations With God,* Book 1

What often caused Michelangelo trouble was his inability to recognize he only had a certain amount of time and energy.
— Kay Goebel, *Creativity and Madness*

Time distortion is one of the aspects of being in the state of creativity. Time disappears when we are in this state. All else becomes secondary to the immediate production of ideas and images. The rest of the world disappears as well. There is only desire and the object of the desire. We do a slow dance with heart and soul, and entwined with our exhaustion is passion.

Michelangelo Buonarroti (1475-1564) was passionately immersed in the art of the Italian Renaissance. He endured beatings when he left school at the age of thirteen to become an apprentice to a painter, and in later years he endured physical pain, privation, and the quixotic disfavor of governing popes. While he always felt as though he didn't have enough time to complete projects—he often had to interrupt his favorite work of sculpting to work on a new commission—he lived to be nearly ninety and earned the esteemed title "Michelangelo, the Divine." He was recognized for his artistic genius in sculpture, painting, and architecture. Although the original contract for the Sistine Chapel called for twelve figures, he painted more than three hundred. He had enough time.

We too have enough time and must give ourselves the time to develop our creativity, our self-expression. We needn't aspire to be or despair of being creative geniuses. People are born with genius. The gift may be pure intelligence applied to science, as in the case of Einstein, or the artistic genius of a Michelangelo. No matter how hard we might study, practice, pray, or meditate, we probably will not grow that gift. When we read about the lives of outstanding people, however, we learn that they struggled to come to terms with real and perceived losses. The passion for their work expresses both the need and the choice to create mastery over a situation in which they previously had no control.

Michelangelo was taken from his mother at birth and sent to a wet nurse near Carrara, one of the finest marble quarries in Italy. He was returned to his mother's care at age two, but when he was six years of age his young mother died, leaving him with inconsistent care and attention. Biographers suggest that this profound loss is the reason that the theme of the mother prevailed throughout Michelangelo's life and that in his representations of Jesus and Mary, the mother, Mary, appears aloof and is looking away from Jesus.

Michelangelo said, "…I was born in the good mountains of Arezzo and suckled among chisels and hammers of stonecutters."[9] It may also be that in his expressions of the perfect male form, Michelangelo was seeking to create his perfect male self, of whom his neglectful father would finally approve. Michelangelo also wrote poetry. The basic theme in his more than three hundred preserved poems is that love is what is necessary for humans to ascend to the divine.

In the last thirty years of his life, Michelangelo seemed to be striving to resolve his grief and to accept his life as being complete with success and failure. In his sixties, he found a friend and companion in Vittoria Colonna, a younger woman who became his spiritual guide. Through that relationship, he came to have a deep faith in Jesus. He identified with Christ's suffering and believed in His redemptive power. Michelangelo's last sculpture, the Rondanini Pieta, contains the strong suggestion of a merging between Mary and Christ. It appears as though each is barely supporting and giving the other strength, and both are looking down as though returning to the unfinished stone—or returning home.

Michelangelo's life struggles, his anger about being controlled, his obsession with producing his art, his despair over his father's neglect, and his sadness about maternal abandonment all represent his cycles through grief, growth, and creativity.

Throughout his sufferings, new ideas, plans, and creations were always incubating and then being expressed. His obsession for art, his passion, became his personal power.

What is this power that we aspire to? It is certainly not what is called "attributed power," the influence and control over others that we associate with certain positions in society. The personal power we desire and seek to grow is the "intrinsic" power of inner security, confidence, and strength of expression. Obsessive thoughts that keep us focused on our self-expression, as Michelangelo's did, result in passionate purpose and powerful possibilities. In order to move through grief to creative growth, obsessive worries and self-doubt must be seen in this context. We must observe, digest, and integrate our feelings. In this way, we overcome fear; we choose the thoughts we wish to put into action. In rising above our obsession, we are decisive, determined, and effective.

Krishna

The Hindus "posit a self that threads successive lives in the way a single life threads successive moments."
— Huston Smith

Krishna, a widely revered East Indian divinity, has drawn a large number of devotional followers who over the centuries have produced a wealth of religious poetry, music, and painting. Worshiped as the eighth incarnation of the Hindu god Vishnu and also as a supreme god in his own right, Krishna represents a religious tradition that to the unschooled Westerner may appear fragmented and confusing. How can a belief system include hundreds of gods dancing, celebrating, seducing, and destroying, not to mention the gods who are many-headed and multiple-armed, and bedecked with bangles and gaudy colors? What appears to be a religion obsessed with multiple gods is actually a rich tradition overflowing with rituals that honor every act of living. Once initiated by experience or by reading, one can appreciate Hinduism as an ancient and respectful approach to the boundless variety of life. It is rich in symbolism and mythology, offering many paths that all lead to the same absolute, undifferentiated God, Brahman.

Krishna teaches, in the Bhagavad-Gita, the major devotional book of Hinduism, that there is no reason to fear death. The soul is eternal and one must develop a strong faith in a personal God. The following description of God could have come from any of the world's monotheistic religions:

Thou art the Imperishable, the supreme
Object of knowledge;
Thou art the ultimate resting-place of this universe;
Thou art the immortal guardian of the eternal right,
Thou art the everlasting Spirit, I hold.

Without beginning, middle, or end, of infinite power,
Of infinite arms, whose eyes are the moon and sun,
I see Thee, whose face is flaming fire,
Burning this whole universe with Thy radiance.[10]

Krishna, the myth or the man, was born three thousand years ago. The story says that his mother was the sister of a wicked king, Kamsa, who had been told in a prophecy that he would be killed by his sister's child. He killed all the boys in the family. However, the princess was pregnant with an eighth child, so the king had her and her husband shackled in a dungeon to ensure that this baby would die at birth. But just when the mother was ready to deliver the baby, the guard fell asleep, the shackles fell off the parents, and the husband caught the baby and proceeded to carry him out of the dungeon. As the father walked outside with the baby, all of the wild animals became tame. The father took Krishna across the Yamuna River and placed him with a cowherd and his wife to be raised.

The story calls to mind the survival of the baby Moses, who escaped the wrath of the Egyptian Pharaoh who ordered all Hebrew male infants killed. Krishna's story emphasizes that no evil, no obstacle, is so great that it has the power to prevent the birth of someone or some idea of immense value. While Kamsa, the immoral king, obsessed about how to maintain his attributed power, Krishna, with his intrinsic God-energy power, was unstoppable. His birth was meant to be and everything that was required to facilitate it took place. And so it is with each one of us. As long as we draw breath, we have reasons to be alive and there is no one who can block us from achieving our lives' purposes, our growing alignment with love.

Hindus believe God has three aspects that help them to accept grief and growth. The Hindu Trinity consists of Brahman, the Creator; Vishnu, the Sustainer; and Shiva, the Destroyer. In India it is believed that when the earth is in need, a special person is born to help fight evil and teach good. Krishna is thought to be such a person. Krishna, or God the loving Preserver, is known as the "Blue God of India." He made love instead of duty the primary element of Indian religion.[11]

Hindus recognize that all things are in the process of being created, sustained, or destroyed, and thus are cycling through endless forms of creative change. Every stage and aspect of life is seen as sacred and meaningful. When I visited Bali, a Hindu culture, I noticed that every beautiful or unusual place in nature is honored with a shrine. Both men and women are required to wear a sarong to visit these sacred sites. When our tour guide requested that we put on sarongs to visit a bat cave, I was incredulous. There we were honoring hundreds of thousands of bats hanging upside down! We tried to avoid stepping in their guano and were barely able to tolerate the stench. The holy men and the shrines, however, attested to the belief that this place was as important in the scheme of things as the breathtaking cloud-rimmed lakes or the shimmering white sand beaches.

Balinese babies are honored by not being allowed to touch the ground in their first months of life. They are also spoken to in High Balinese (after all, this may be the incarnation of a great spiritual teacher). At death, elaborate structures are built for the community celebration of the cremation, the send-off of the spirit into the next plane of existence. According to Hindu thought, the primary goal in each of the four areas of achievement—Pleasure, Success, Service, and Liberation—is simply "to be." While the first three aims relate to connecting to the body and to the physical world, the last, Liberation, relates to connecting with "infinite being, infinite awareness, and infinite bliss," liberation from everything that distances us from God.

As Krishna's birth could not be prevented, neither could his physical death. During Krishna's exemplary life, he was mourning the loss of his brother and son in battle when he was struck by an arrow in the heel and killed. In the West, we associate this story of inevitable vulnerability with the Greek mythology that came hundreds of years later. According to Homer, the great Trojan War hero Achilles was also killed by an arrow to the heel. In spite of his mother's attempt to make him invincible by dipping him into the River Styx, the part of his body she held him by was not protected.

Like Krishna and Achilles, we cannot be protected from the cycles of birth, pain, defeat, success, and death. The more we are able to simply "be" in these cycles, the less we struggle and resist the current, the more easily our life energy flows toward self-expression and creativity. The story of Krishna reminds us that there is no need for worry because our lives, our spirits, transcend every earthly problem. Hinduism inspires us to choose passion over obsessive grief, passion for the earth and its intricate web of life.

Obsession is fear of the future. When we act on the fear, attempting to maintain control, we find ourselves ironically out of control, our will displaced by compulsive behavior or addiction. The child parts of our personalities are at the helm trying to be in charge and not knowing how. In order to free ourselves of the inner terror, we must allow the adult parts of our personalities and our Higher or Transcendent Selves to take over, and trust.

A look at the Grief and Growth Chart tells us that as we wallow in obsession, if we look ahead we see we are close to achieving *acceptance* of life as it is right now, with great possibilities for inner peace. If we look up, we see we have been incubating new thoughts and plans, which will result in a greater sense of passion and personal power and love.

Daily Creative Discipline
(Obsession: The Energy of Passion and Personal Power)

1.   **Observe your thoughts** and notice what you think about most. Are your cogitations pleasant, or do you find yourself responding with anxiety, fear, and tension? What is the focus of the worry? Make a conscious choice to **shift your energy** to some wonderful desire. Each time you notice your obsessive thoughts, channel them toward the desired goal. Practice focusing on what you really wish to **manifest** and enjoy.

2.   **Consider your behavior** in light of your most important goals. Does your behavior support the achievement of your goals? If you compulsively avoid or procrastinate taking the steps toward your goal, write down one behavior that will move you out of this pattern and **do it.**

3.   **Notice any compulsive behavior** or thought pattern that interferes with your inner peace. Trace this fearful response to a childhood experience or to an adult experience involving loss or disappointment. Take a few minutes and allow yourself to feel the full impact of such a loss on your inner child. Make a small piece of art or find some object, like a lovely smooth stone, to represent the wounding/learning experience. Display it where you can see it every day to **honor your grief and growth.**

4.   **Be aware of the self-blame component** of obsession. "If only" tends to repeat itself when we're feeling anguish and guilt. If there has been a drastic change or loss in your life, **create a document** describing every detail of what happened. List all of your "if only"s and anything you would do differently if you could do it over. Now **create an affirmation** that you can repeat, instead of shooting

yourself with "blaming arrows." Silently chanting your affirmation each day will gradually focus your thoughts and energy on the possibilities for your life so you don't stay locked in limitation.

5.   **Ponder unlimited personal power.** Make a long, detailed list of every demand, large and small, on your life. Tear it into teeny, tiny pieces. Throw them into the air and release every bit of anxiety along with them. See how long you can leave them on the floor. **Think about floating in freedom.** See where these thoughts take you. Notice what goals you **feel passionate** about.

6.   With one crayon and a piece of white paper, make a small, repetitive pattern filling the lower left corner of the page. Now begin to **enlarge and overlap** the lines until the entire sheet is covered. On a second page, use two crayons at once as you **create a new expansive pattern,** then fill in with other colors. Date and save.

Chapter Six

Depression: The Dark Road to Discovery

Strictly speaking, every moment of our lives is a dying: the I of that moment dies, never to be reborn.

— Huston Smith

Depression and Loss

In his view, death, with its ancestral weight of Terrors, is merely the abandonment of an unserviceable shell at the time the spirit is reintegrated into the unified energy of the cosmos.

— Isabel Allende

Depression is when fear has won and even though the victory is only temporary, we believe it is final. We feel defeated. We may have been able to overcome our denial of a new reality and acknowledge a life change. We may have protested and felt anger about the loss and our subsequent disappointment. We may have obsessed over how to handle the change. Whether we are aware of it or not, we may have moved in and out of denial, anger, and obsession. Now, however, we collapse in a seeming void. We can't function normally.

The collapse may take the form of empty, "it's just no use" lethargy, or sleepless, hand-wringing agitation. An overwhelming blanket of sadness and loss covers us. We'd like to push a magic button and return to life as it was before the crisis, or be transported to a different, more benevolent world. Or we may simply wish not to exist. But what we're being moved toward, instead, is a return to life. This life. As Steinbeck said, "…the first rule of life is living."

It is useful to remember that we are part of the natural animal world and that each human body and mind has a limit to how much concentrated change it can adapt to before refusing to continue. Like any horse that is overworked, without rest and proper care, we sicken and die. And maybe since horses are not as self-protective and resolute as donkeys, we must learn to emulate the ass who refuses work that's too heavy.

Eighty-one-year-old Lydia refused to get well following brain surgery. Her grown daughter, Brooke, called me, distraught. "I have to fly back to Portland tomorrow," she told me, "but Mother, who has always been a fighter, has refused to cooperate with any rehabilitation since her surgery. The hospital is basically kicking her out. She's completely depressed. Please see if you can hypnotize her and motivate her to get well."

I was persuaded.

Lydia looked, as her rancher husband put it, as though she had "one foot in the grave and the other on a banana peel. And right now she wants to slide with the banana peel." She could barely keep her eyes open and it seemed to take her a great amount of time and effort to answer my questions. But I knew there was hope as soon as she answered the first one, "Do you have a nickname?"

She rolled her eyes toward me and said with slurred speech, "Yeah, Ornery."

Over the next hour, I learned why Lydia was lost in the depressive phase of grief: Her other daughter had been killed in an accident six months earlier; in addition, one month before her brain surgery, her adored younger brother had died suddenly. Lydia didn't have the energy to actively participate in her own physical convalescence. During her hypnosis session, I emphasized how natural it was for her to be resting and refusing to adapt to the healing schedule set for her by others. I suggested to her that it was time well spent to honor the love bonds between herself and her daughter and her brother by processing her grief in her own way. When she was completely ready, I said, she would begin to come out of her mourning and live life again. She would continue to share her love with Brooke, the daughter who was with us.

When I finished and turned off the tape recorder, she appeared to be sleeping peacefully. I had no idea if Lydia had taken in any of what I'd said. Brooke was weeping, however, and had obviously been touched by her mother's great losses and also her great capacity for love and connection.

Several months later I called to check on Lydia. I hesitated because I feared she had given up and died, choosing to slide into the spiritual plane in hopes of reuniting with her daughter and brother. I asked her husband if she was all right. He was exuberant.

"We've got her back!" he said. "She still has more physical rehab to do, but her mind is back. Her old beauty-shop friends come over and she's even got her fake fingernails on. That's a definite sign that she's back to herself."

People are capable of surviving great stress and enormous loss. When life as we know it changes radically, however, we have difficulty recognizing ourselves. All of our familiar signposts and mirrors disappear. We begin to feel that if the trend continues there will be nothing left of us. The love that shone on us and made us blossom turned dark and left us alone to wither.

I felt that way several years ago. I had written my first book, *Lessons in Evil, Lessons From the Light,* and was elated that a major publishing house was interested. They flew me to New York, where a panel of senior editors and publicists met with me and fired questions at me to assess my knowledge of psychology, trauma, and the sadistic abuses I described in the book. I knew this was also a test to see how I would handle myself with the media, particularly for television appearances. I apparently passed the test; they purchased the book.

The thrill of my first book not only being published, but being chosen as a Book-of-the-Month Club alternate selection, made it difficult for me to sleep or calmly proceed with my everyday life. I had been pried out of my comfort zone. I was provided with two publicists and had to be constantly available to respond to media requests. I was sent around the country to speak to reporters and be on television and radio shows. I felt as though I had been lifted out of my life and placed in someone else's, someone who was used to having a driver and staying in hotel rooms with marble bathrooms. My life had taken on a sense of unreality. When I received a letter from the Brandeis University National Women's Committee, the largest library-support group in the world, saying my book was selected to receive their Major Book Award, I thought it was a joke. I called my editor, who told me it was not a joke but a wonderful tribute. I was to be honored at the Beverly Wilshire Hotel along with Marianne Williamson, Isabel Allende, and several other writers.

Where is the grief in all this? How bad could this life change be? During this same time a former client filed a lawsuit against me. She alleged that I had damaged her by using a spirit-release-ment exercise with her and talking to her about past lives. She had read two books about these methods and had expressed interest in them, so I was completely shocked to read the allegations that I had recklessly disregarded her wishes concerning her therapy. She claimed I had harmed her terribly and that because of the past-life hypnosis described in my book, I clearly did this to her to write another book and profit from her experience. Her lawyer stated that my motive was greed. I felt my professional world crumble. Over the next two years, between the unreality of my book's notoriety and the unreality of being sued, I felt destabilized.

One summer was particularly devastating. I'd been in the process of answering endless questions that felt personal and unrelated to the case, questions this woman's lawyer hoped would produce evidence that I was indeed greedy. I was required to turn over all my book and agent contracts and income statements. The lawyer was particularly eager to learn that the woman I'd written about was excluded from the book's profits. The fact was, however, that Barbara, whom I think of as my heroine, wanted her story told and was included in every step of the book's preparation and remuneration. But I was sick with worry. I couldn't sleep and food didn't interest me. One day I received a notice that my insurance liability carrier would no longer handle my malpractice insurance. That same day, when I got home, I went to feed our pet ducks and found that they had been beaten to death. That was as deep as I could go with my grief. I became numb.

I was clearly at a turning point. While my husband cursed and yelled about what he would do to the killers and my youngest daughter sobbed, I felt dead, fixed to the ground. I noted that my mind was hard at work and moving very fast. I was thinking, "So, what next? Will they kill one of my daughters? Will they try to kill me?"

I had been warned about publicly disclosing information about criminal satanic cults. I had been shocked to learn about other therapists of survivors being harassed, finding their pets dead, and being the target of frivolous but wounding lawsuits. My book had been viciously attacked by colleagues who had organized to defend those who had been accused of pedophilia, incest, or sadistic abuse. A representative of the FBI had even come on the *Larry King Live* television show when I appeared on it, to refute the existence of satanic or sadistic cults. The backlash had emerged as the darling of the media. The truth was being obscured by special interest groups.

While my friends and family tried to tell me that the lawsuit was meaningless in the scheme of things, it didn't feel that way. When my lawyer said, "Look, this woman just finished suing her gynecologist! You're simply the next person on her list," it didn't matter. When my friend Lynn said, "She cannot destroy your integrity," I didn't believe her. I felt ashamed about being sued and I felt an even deeper shame about being depressed over a lawsuit instead of saving my deep grief for a family tragedy. Did I value my professional reputation over my loved ones? It was time for a decision and in that instant it became clear to me that I would let no one stand in the way of my values and my personal happiness. It was a choice that came with energetic resolve. "Let's bury the ducks," I said to my husband, "and then I'll fix dinner."

My depression did not disappear that moment, but the event was a turning point. It was my own *Aha!* realization that nothing, externally or internally, could destroy me unless I allowed it. It was the beginning of my discovery that developing my resilience to change would make me more capable of redirecting and self-creating my life in alignment with my values, with love. This gift of learning is every heart's homecoming. As I look back, it's clear to me that as soon as this awareness entered my life, as if it were a much-needed chiropractic adjustment, every problem began to clear and straighten out.

My meditation and prayer each morning became a time of solitude that I looked forward to, instead of just the part of my routine that forced me to get out of bed in the morning. I asked for guidance and strength and turned over the details of problem-solving to Divine Intelligence. I began noticing that every prayer was granted: my liability insurance company called immediately to say there was no problem with maintaining my policy and the lawyers involved in the lawsuit settled the case. While the ducks were gone and I missed them, I was able to be grateful to them for their part in helping me transform my depression into discovery. I could appreciate my finding that I have all of the resources within me to transcend fear.

.⌣ ⌣.

When author Isabel Allende lost her only daughter to a rare metabolic disease,[1] and when the daughter of my friend, author Lois Duncan, was murdered, the foundations of their lives were shaken. Mourning the death of a child, regardless of the cause, is what my mother called "impossible grief." For years after their losses, these women manifested an inner tension, pain and grief that Allende refers to as evidence of "extreme love." She feels that this kind of love puts one in touch with the sacred. The depth of such a love bond brings with it excruciating, almost unbearable, pain when the bond is broken by physical death. Then comes the slow realization that the capacity for such a bond represents the greatest affirmation of life. Depression, then, is the dark burial ground from which the soul emerges surprisingly intact and prepared to celebrate life. Through such experiences we discover that the energy of love is indestructible.

"The person can die but the love can't," my friend and colleague Adrianne said to me during a recent visit. Her sixteen-year-old son had died five months earlier in a sports accident. "Although the pain of this kind of grief is so unbearable I sometimes want to die too, very slowly I'm being filled with love. I talk with Colin all the time and ask what it is I'm supposed to learn from this. I know there's meaning in his death because he was such a nontrivial person. The week before his death, he was reflecting aloud about whether there was life after death. I think he was an old soul and that he had accomplished everything he needed to in this lifetime, so he went on to discover what happens next. At his memorial service, his classmates came up to me to say how much he had meant to them. One girl said she believed Colin had saved her life with his wise counsel.

"We went to a psychic who told us that Colin was in a place of learning and that he was happy and very busy absorbing many different kinds of knowledge. The next day, in meditation, I asked Colin again to tell me somehow what it is I'm supposed to learn from his death. I went to the kitchen and looked around and asked, 'Am I supposed to be doing something here?' Then I went to several different rooms and asked the same question. It was when I asked the question standing in my study that I got a sense of Colin's presence. I knew then that the thing I must do involves studying or teaching about death."

"Why is it that losing a child is so terrifying that we can't allow ourselves to even think about it?" I asked her.

"I've heard it said that when you lose a parent, you lose your past; when you lose a spouse or partner, you lose your present; but when you lose a child, you lose your future. Although I don't think that captures the full extent of the anguish, I do think there is a sense of futility, of your future being annihilated and, therefore, of you being annihilated. I also think that with a child, there's always some degree of guilt, some sense that you could have or should have protected him, that if you had been a better person you would have had more control over the situation, that maybe other parents are better protectors."

Adrianne dabbed at her brimming eyes and continued. "But that reminds me of a story I heard about a woman who felt she could not handle her son's death. She sought out a great spiritual teacher and when she was allowed to talk to him, she told him of her unbearable sorrow. He instructed her to go around the country-side gathering mustard seeds from families who have known no sorrow. Naturally, she was unable to find any mustard seeds because there are no families who have not known sorrow. What she found was that she was able to help others and herself by sharing her grief. New bonds of love were forged in the process. Maybe the transformation of grief comes from the discovery that, at some point, you are again able to give and receive love."

Whether the grief involves the death of a loved one, physical illness, or even job loss, it marks the death of the self as we know it at that time. That death is like winter, with all our life energy withered into grayness and covered by a blanket of cold snow. We find it impossible to believe that spring will come or that new life is incubating beneath the hard crust of our hiding place. Creative energy warms us slowly, urging us to grow again and to notice the sun, the moon, and all of life illumined.

Depression and Suicide

Although the inadvisability of suicide is spoken of, it is all right. There is no punishment in God. There is only eternal love and understanding. No one acts alone. No one acts in a vacuum. No one kills himself without leaving a legacy of growth behind.

— Emmanuel

Are all of our lights visible from above at every moment? Or is it just when the wind of life threatens us that we truly shine bright? The only goal is to increase the glow and sustain it."

— Jeff Winberg

Jeff Winberg could not sustain his glow. Six weeks after his thirtieth birthday, he drove his truck into the tiny garage attached to the house he lived in with our daughter Niki, turned on the engine, lay down in the truck bed on his camping mat, looked at pictures of Niki, wrote a last love note to her, and died of carbon monoxide poisoning in less than an hour.

The previous year, I visited with a psychic friend who told me I would be learning a great deal from Jeff. Hearing that pleased me; I had already learned much about the outdoors from this beautiful man, my oldest daughter's great love. It was difficult but comforting to comprehend that I would now learn from him about death and despair.

On the surface, Jeff, like my friend Robert who suicided six years earlier, looked as though he had everything to live for. He was tall, blond, blue-eyed, and accomplished at every outdoor sport. Through his work at Recreational Equipment Inc. (REI), he became known as an expert mountain guide and rock climbing instructor. His climbing and skiing were nearly legendary. His skill at ski-tuning led to a video, "The Expert's Edge," and in the last two years he was involved in film production. He was the one people always relied on for rigging the stunt scenes but was also so handsome that the directors thought he should be the "talent" too. Jeff always seemed to see the possibilities, the solutions to every problem, the directions to take. He was at home in every wilderness. What wind could blow him off course?

"I think Jeff is depressed," Niki told me on several occasions.

"Don't you think it's a natural reaction to his knee injury?" I answered. "He's missing most of ski season this year because of the surgery and probably will miss out on climbing for all of this year, too."

"I guess. But he's drinking a lot, too. Just beer, but he drinks a lot of beer. It seems like every day. And I think he's obsessed with his lack of money, all his bills. My biggest problem is that he won't talk to me about it. I can tell when he's worried, but he won't talk to me."

"That tends to be a problem for some men," I told her. "Let me know if there's something I can do." I dismissed the notion that anything could be seriously wrong.

No one noticed anything wrong on the outside. Jeff worked long, hard hours on film "shoots," took excellent care of the yard, made improvements on the house, and socialized attentively with guests. Niki, however, was noticing symptoms signaling inner pain.

As I look back, I see that he fit perfectly into the four areas of suicidal risk described by researchers.[2] The first risk is having exceedingly high expectations of success. In this mind-set, we can never achieve enough and therefore are constantly vulnerable to feeling like a failure. The second risk is feeling that we cannot have an enduring relationship that anchors us in life. We feel essentially unloveable, apart from our achievements. It is only a matter of time, we think, before we are found lacking and then abandoned. The third risk is that death comes to be seen as the solution to our problems, the only solution. The fourth suicidal risk is not being able to communicate these painful thoughts and feelings. In this state, we feel that it is shameful and weak to hurt inside, and so we remain silent or minimize the life issues that feel so overwhelming.

With people like Jeff, who are not outwardly suicidal and have never injured themselves in any way, suicide comes as a shock. It's difficult to comprehend that the tremendous love you feel for this person was not felt by them, was not believed by them, was not able to be internalized by them. That helplessness, that inability to save your loved one with a lifeline of love, causes deep anguish during the depression phase of grief. Our family, along with hundreds of mourners at Jeff's memorial, felt our hearts had been crushed. Each morning I was awake at five, feeling an enormous pressure on my chest, as though a huge metal weight was on top of me. Niki said she felt like there was a black hole inside of her, and sometimes she felt as though she were sinking into it.

We talked constantly about what we could or should have done. I would have tried to talk to Jeff about his emotional pain and encouraged him to enter psychotherapy. My husband would have tried to talk to Jeff about his money worries and helped him make a plan for retiring his debts. We all agree we would have organized a "carefrontation," enlisting the help of substance-abuse counselors to help him with his growing addiction to alcohol. His close friends would have called more often. One of his childhood friends, Kevin, summed it up by saying, "We have to learn to love each other better."

Soon after Niki first met Jeff, our family took a trip to Israel. Niki was lovesick throughout our travels, constantly writing notes to Jeff and calling him long distance. The next-to-last day of our stay, we were on top of Massada, the monolithic sandstone fortress overlooking the Dead Sea. It was an unusually nice day in December, the expected cold replaced by sharp sunlight, warm and comfortable. A young woman rabbi, Gaylia, held a brief service during which she read this poem by Richard Allen:[3]

When you love give it everything you've got,
and when you've reached your limit give it more.
And forget the pain of it.
Because as you face your death
it is only the love you have given and received
which will count.
All the rest, the struggles, the success, the fights,
will be forgotten in your reflection.
And if you have loved well
it will have been worth it,
and the joy of it will last you to the end.
But if you have not,
death will always come too soon
and be too terrible to face.

We have to learn to love each other better. We also have to learn to be aware of the various manifestations of death in order to become more comfortable with death. Suicidologist Ronald Maris states it well: "The salient fact about us is that we are born, live, and die."[4] While we know a great deal about birth and life, it appears to me that we know much less, and do not wish to know, about death.

Jeff's death certificate intrigued me. I had never seen one. Under "Cause of Death" was typed in, "asphyxiation; carbon-monoxide poisoning." The reference books tell us that there are over one hundred specific causes of death, but only four *modes* of death: accident, suicide, homicide, and natural.[5] While that sounds quite simple, selecting "the final ordering into which each of us must be classified" can be complicated by psychological factors. For example, how many individual highway deaths called "accidents" may actually be caused by suicidal motivation, unconscious or conscious? Are there other types of "accidental deaths" that are precipitated by dangerous, risk-taking activities?

How many illnesses are exacerbated by psychic factors? We now know that the immune system is exceedingly sensitive to stress. Research has shown that the higher the level of psychological stress, the higher the rate of infection and clinical colds.[6] Ken Pelletier, in his book *Sound Mind, Sound Body,* offers page after page of research documenting the relationship between how the mind perceives life events and how the body responds accordingly. Dr. Pelletier provides an entire chapter on the importance of friendships, warm connections with others that sustain us through difficult life change.

Physician Larry Dossey tells us that the best predictor of survival across the next decade of a person's life is what the person *thinks* about his health! Family, health history, and risk factors play a less important role. Smokers, for example, double their risk of dying in the next ten years, but a negative response to the question, "What do you *think* about your health?" produces a seven-fold risk of dying![7] Jeff thought he wouldn't heal from his surgery. He took extreme action based on false beliefs.

There are some children and adults who tend to think negatively about every aspect of healing and see no hope for the future. These people have little resiliency to handle change. One mother of a young man who made numerous suicide attempts, and succeeded in killing himself at age twenty-two, said that from the time of infancy her son could not tolerate the slightest change in his environment. When his fears and sleep disturbance continued, his parents took him to the finest psychiatric facilities. The many years of therapy and hospitalization did not seem to alter this boy's neuropsychological makeup. In his suicide note, he said he was just too tired to go on.

We learned that Jeff had told his mother two years previously that he was going to kill himself. Perhaps meeting Niki and falling in love with her nurtured his commitment to life that much longer. In a note to her, he wrote, "Being with you has been like pulling a huge, lofty down comforter over my head." The "down comforter" of love can prolong life.

In a study of women with breast cancer, it was found that just attending support-group therapy doubled the life expectancies of the women.[8] Caring and understanding friendships sustained them in their grief. We also know that married people are healthier than single people, and that men who have weak social ties have a death rate two to three times higher than those with strong ties.[9]

Love prolongs life and enriches life. But our love cannot necessarily prevent death. In Jeff's note, he wrote, "I have no energy left. I've lost myself."

The mothers of young people who have died in accidents or suicided have told me that the only activity that proved beneficial to them was participation in a support group with others who had lived through the same experience. My friend Adrianne said, "Just to see that there are other mothers who understand and have been able to go on and continue to exist with their grief helped me more than anything else."

While learning to intensely love our children, ourselves, and each other is the antidote to isolation and hopelessness, Niki discovered another aspect of Jeff's suicide that was very comforting for her—a spiritual viewpoint that places full responsibility for his death with him. She visited with a friend who channels a spiritual entity called Jared. Following this meeting,

Niki looked radiant for the first time since the suicide as she told us about Jared's message.

"Jared told me that we all have a 'soul cluster.' Before we incarnate, we decide with our soul cluster what the lessons of this particular lifetime will be. Jared said that Jeff had fulfilled every part of his agreement and had managed to give and receive more love than would be expected under the circumstances. He said that Jeff's death is teaching the hundreds of people close to him about the value of love and friendship, and that many of them will be inspired now to influence the changes that must occur in order to save the planet from destruction."[10]

We sat in silence, listening to our daughter teach us about concepts we knew little about, pondering the idea that Jeff's life and death were entirely directed by him and were more meaningful than we had realized.

"Jared also said that Jeff is very proud of me," Niki added with her soft smile. "And he's still here with us for awhile. Jared said that when someone leaves great pain in those he loves, he stays around longer before going into the light. He said Jeff would be going into the light very soon now."

Depression and Trauma

Protracted depression is the most common finding in virtually all clinical studies of chronically traumatized people.

— Judith Lewis Herman, M.D.

You cannot oppress a person when they are in touch with something sacred within them. You cannot oppress them at the soul level.

— Jean Shinoda Bolen, M.D.

Several years ago, I broke my shoulder in five places. I was skiing at Taos with Niki, who was working on the Ski Patrol. But the first thing I broke was the family rule about stopping at 3:00 P.M. It was snowing lightly and we were having such a wonderful day. Niki said to me, "Let's do Castor one more time!" Castor is a steep, very expert "chute," one of several chutes we had skied that particular day.

I was tired, but I said, "Fine!"

About ten feet after dropping down through the trees onto Castor, I snagged my ski on something. Because the slope was so steep, I began to somersault in the air and landed full-weight on my shoulder. I felt incredible pain, but I had heard that dislocating a shoulder was very painful so I decided that's what I had done. Niki was at the bottom of the run and couldn't possibly hike back to me. When I couldn't seem to answer her query as to whether I was okay, she realized I was hurt. She was prepared to go for the Ski Patrol, but the last thing I wanted was to wait for them and then be tied onto a sled and bounced down the mountain.

I slowly inched my way down the slope, holding my ski poles in my right hand. Any weight on the left side of my body was nearly unbearable, but I managed to ski to the Mountain Medicine building at the base of the mountain, moaning loudly all the way. The medical personnel were astounded. I was clearly in a state of shock. I felt almost euphoric and kept chattering with the other injured skiers. The doctor took x-rays and showed me the different fracture sites. He gave me pain medication and said to go see an orthopedist the next morning.

As Niki began to drive us home, the snowfall increased, making visibility difficult. When we finally got to Santa Fe, with another hour before Albuquerque and home, I suggested we stop to get something to eat. I had no appetite, but I knew Niki must be starving. As we walked into the restaurant, I felt unstable. As soon as I sat down, I passed out. That was the end of the first episode of denial.

I had been grateful for a shoulder, rather than a knee injury. Since I could walk, I reasoned, I would be back to work in a week. After all, my work as a psychotherapist consists of sitting in my office chair all day. No problem.

But I learned how incredibly complicated the human shoulder is, with its many muscle and tendon groups overlapping one another. In my acrobatic flip, reaching for the ground and attempting to prevent myself from hitting a tree, I had twisted and caused whiplash in my neck. In the process, I tore most of the muscles in my neck and upper back. The soft tissue damage would take much longer to heal than my bones.

My trauma doesn't compare to that of people I've treated for sexual abuse, torture, or war trauma, or those who've been in automobile accidents where parts of their bodies were crushed. The reason I tell my story is to show how we learn about our own personal healers, our human souls or our Higher Selves, and their connection with the realm of Spirit.

I was not allowed to sleep lying down. I had to sit up for weeks, surrounded by pillows and ice packs. I had a colleague make a hypnosis tape for me with visualization and other techniques to facilitate sleep and pain management. I was on various types of medication. But I was not sleeping. I could not imagine ever being pain free again or having a peaceful night's rest.

One night, after taking my medication, positioning my ice packs, and listening to my tape, I was sitting there in the dark completely awake, wondering what to do, when I thought of asking for spiritual help. I had read about guardian angels and I was desperate. The worst thing that could happen, I thought, was nothing.

I focused all my concentration on receiving help of some kind. After several minutes, a beautiful woman in a white, filmy dress seemed to be floating before my mind. She also seemed to be giggling at me. Only an angel could get away with laughing at me in the shape I'm in, I thought. She never spoke words, but communicated with me psychically. Her message was, "How silly of you to take this so seriously. You're going to be fine. Come with me." And immediately, we were floating over huge ice floes, in a land I think of as Antarctica. An icy wind was blowing over me, numbing my entire body. As it blew, I began to feel so comfortable I drifted off to sleep.

In the morning, I wondered, "Who was that woman?" Later that day, I realized she was someone I had met several years before during a workshop in Santa Fe led by the surgeon Bernie Siegel.[11] Bernie did a guided meditation intended to introduce us to a spirit guide. He told us to imagine a very beautiful garden with a winding path. Way in the distance, someone was coming toward us. When he or she finally got close, we were to ask the person's name. I now remembered the approach along the path of this beautiful brunette woman in a white flowing dress with a deep-red rose brooch on the bodice of her dress. She smiled at me and told me her name was Aimee. Since I thought it was a sweet encounter, I asked a friend who knew French the meaning of that name. It means "a friend who is close to your heart, a beloved friend," I was told. I promptly forgot about the entire event until three years later.

Aimee came for me every night during my recovery and took me to float in the icy breeze that put me to sleep. For many months, we floated and drifted, Aimee always gentle but lighthearted in her amusement that I took my pain so seriously. I believe she was trying to communicate to me that this was just one of those physical experiences from which we learn that on the spiritual plane, nothing is ever broken or sick. Our bodies might be damaged or maimed, but at the soul level, we can never be destroyed. The spiritual body is always perfect.

The other lesson I learned is that we have all of the resources within for our healing. What that means is that we can trust our intuition (Higher Self, God, or Spirit) in order to find just the right help for the body. I used physical therapy and acupuncture. I used a neighbor's pool and swam every morning for more than a year. There were two junctures in my rehabilitation when I had to trust intuition. The first was when my shoulder joint became frozen and I had to decide on a course of action. I chose to go to an orthopedic specialist in California who works with a chiropractor.

I had met "Caren the Chiropractor," as I call her, at meetings in Florida, along with psychiatrist and author Brian Weiss, and Dr. Elisabeth Kübler-Ross. I had never been to a chiropractor and I'd been afraid of them ever since one of my clients described being injured by one. But I felt an immediate bond with Caren, as well as a sense of deep comfort with Brian and Elisabeth. (I find that great healers, particularly those who've spent many years working with children, are comfortable with and even prefer being called by their first names. Facing suffering children and confronting patients' fears of annihilation tend to strip away protective defenses and professional arrogance.)

Caren could tell with one look that I was "guarding" my shoulder and that most of the muscles in my upper body were in spasm. She insisted she would come to my hotel room to fix the problem. I never expected her to really come, but that afternoon she called my room and said she was on her way. She was bringing Brian and Elisabeth, too. I couldn't believe it. Why would these famous people come along with Caren to help an unknown colleague? I think I found out.

Since I was terrified of having my neck broken, Brian was there to use hypnosis to help me relax. Caren, like my angel, laughed at my anxiety and fear. "I've never hurt anyone," she said, "I've only helped." After carefully positioning me, she cracked my neck so loudly and with such force that I flew up off the bed. I had instant relief from my neck pain. Then she told me to lie on the floor where she would have more leverage as she worked to reposition two rib bones in my upper back that had become dislodged during my fall. After my therapeutic adjustments, she worked on Brian, and then very gently on Elisabeth, who was recovering from a stroke.

I didn't have any medication, as my luggage had been lost somewhere between Albuquerque and Miami. Brian reacted to this with alarm, saying I could not do without my prescribed drugs. He quickly set out to replace them. Elisabeth wanted to discuss the topic of my book, *Lessons in Evil, Lessons From the Light,* as the effects of ritual abuse were appearing in her workshops. The actual time we spent together was less than one hour, yet the joy and laughter and love felt timeless. We had had a healing party.

So it was natural that months later I would choose to go to Los Angeles to have Caren's colleague inject the shoulder with lidocaine and steroids so that Caren could break the adhesions and give me complete range of motion. She spent the entire day with me, restoring flexibility to my injured shoulder. Once back in Albuquerque, I returned to physical therapy to do the required exercises. Aimee had taught me about the power of my mind to facilitate healing, so that during every session with the physical therapist I focused my mind completely on allowing my body to achieve the intended movement. Often the therapist was amazed at my progress.

The next time I had to trust intuition was when the therapist and I noticed that if I put my arm out to the side, I could not raise it above shoulder level. When I shared this with my orthopedist, he pointed to the place on the x-ray where the tip of the humerus impinged against the acromium process of the scapula. He, of course, recommended surgery. To him, it was a "simple" arthroscopic surgery in which he would file down the tip of the scapula, allowing the humerus to slide past and up, as it was supposed to.

"Do I have any other option?" I queried. I was just beginning, after six months, to regain some strength and to feel that I might someday recover. Surgery, my physical therapist had said, would set my rehabilitation back nearly to the beginning. The doctor must have seen the pleading look in my eyes. He said, "Well, there is this woman who does something with muscles. I'll give you her name, but don't tell any of my colleagues I gave it to you."

Laura was a massage therapist trained in physical therapy. She asked me to stand in front of her and watched as I moved my arm in various ways. Then she asked me to lie down on her massage table. I couldn't imagine how massaging my body could help my shoulder. To my surprise, she did nothing I could think of as massage. She cradled my head in her hands and I fell asleep. One hour later, when she was finished, I woke up and left. This was repeated, session after session over the next two months, except that I noticed that she would hold my arm out in an extended position and gently stroke it. I finally asked exactly what she was doing.

Laura explained that the name of the method was "craniosacral therapy" and that she was working in two ways: one was to communicate to the muscles that had permanently contracted following the trauma that it was safe to relax now, so that the arm could extend. The other was to communicate to the nerves that they too could relax. I decided that I would again use what I had learned from Aimee and focus my concentration at the beginning of the session, before I fell asleep, on giving my muscles and nerves the same message: "It's time now for you to relax and heal. You are in a safe and loving environment."

Within several months, another level of healing had occurred and the impingement was gone. I was back to even more challenging exercises at physical therapy and knew that before too long I'd be able to do jumping jacks again in my aerobics class.

We must learn to facilitate our own healing from trauma, past or present. We can do so emotionally, by allowing our grief to come out, and spiritually, by finding our inner resources and connecting soul to Spirit. Now that I've shared about Aimee, I'll tell about my grief. Many times, early on after my accident, I used denial to minimize the difficult healing process I would face. How much I appreciate that defense now! I would have given up in despair if I had realized it would take two to three years before I would be completely recovered and pain free.

I was angry with myself for not ending the ski day at 3:00 P.M., as we had done as a family for longer than I could remember. I also found myself angry with my daughter for suggesting that we ski another expert run at the end of the day. She should have been more thoughtful, I told myself, more respectful of my—my what? Feebleness? I've never been feeble. She should have known. Known that I would fall? The anger was never satisfying, but I realized it was a natural part of grief. It was healthy life energy, and I would use that energy to heal and to learn a lesson about sticking to my rules and never allowing myself to feel intimidated or fearful.

Many times I found myself in the obsessive part of grief. If only I hadn't gone that day, if only I had quit at three o'clock, if only I'd done weightlifting exercises to strengthen my upper body, maybe it wouldn't have happened.

And when the obsession melts into depression, thoughts run wild with fear. One time, weeks after the accident, my husband found me sitting in the dark around midnight in my study. "What are you doing up?" he asked. I told him sleep was impossible, but that wasn't the problem. I thought I was dying.

Fortunately for both of us, Bruce is a sensitive physician. He asked what it was I thought I could be dying from. I replied that I thought I was bleeding internally and the doctors just hadn't picked it up. (The entire left side of my body was swollen and blue from blood leaking internally from the site of the breaks and muscle tears.) He assured me that if there was any more internal bleeding, I would have very obvious symptoms. If it were in my abdomen, I'd have severe pain; if it were in my lungs, I'd have increasing shortness of breath. He helped me back to bed, my fear relinquished for that night.

A few weeks later, I got a cold. He found me again in the middle of the night, feeling completely miserable. This time I tried to distance myself from the obsessive fear. "I know this is probably unreasonable, but I think I have that virus that acts like a cold but goes quickly to your heart and kills you. Didn't that happen to Jim Hensen, the Muppet man?"

"Sweetheart," my husband said, "You're thinking of the virulent form of streptococcus that causes congestive heart failure. You do not have that. You have a simple cold virus and you're going to be fine. Your entire body is going to heal. Now come to bed."

No amount of learning can equal experience. Many of my physical-trauma patients have the same kind of obsessive fears, which snowball into fantastic beliefs about paralysis, loss of limbs, or death. Observing my own grief reactions of denial, anger, obsession, and depression will forever aid me in being a better therapist and a better teacher. And every bit as important as that knowledge was my growing awareness that my healing was in my own hands. At the very least, I would have to be a partner in my medical treatments. I was gaining confidence that my mind, in conjunction with faith, had the power to heal my fear and mend my body.

Believing that our inner resources can heal us may be the crucial first step to resolving the depressive grief reaction to trauma. Marvin, a Vietnam veteran, came for hypnosis when his tinnitus (ear-ringing), which had developed following an explosion during his army service, worsened after a sonic boom occurred over his home. He explained that over the years, a number of problems had sprung up, one after another, involving pain in his jaw and chronic discomfort in other parts of his face due to referred pain from tooth extractions. He was feeling desperate for a sense of hope, some belief that he could learn to control the discomfort and irritation.

When I asked him what he most wanted to accomplish during this first session, he answered, "I just have to find some strength." During that first brief hypnosis session, I encouraged him to go within and to find a symbol, some representation of his own Inner Strength. Marvin found a tree, a tree he'd forgotten about all these years. It was a place of hiding when he was a boy. Marvin would often go to his tree to find a sense of protection, safety from his abusive stepfather, and solitude.

It would be this symbol of connection with life beyond his family, of the sacredness of spirit, of the strength and endurance of trees to withstand storms, that would help Marvin to learn more and more about his inner abilities to grieve the past and cope with the present. Marvin had to focus consistently to release the "unfinished business," as Elisabeth Kübler-Ross calls it, of his lost childhood and his painful experiences in Vietnam.[12] As he did his grief work, his physical pain slowly diminished and he found he had greater control. He could distract himself by focusing on pleasurable events, or "turn down" the ear-ringing just as he turns down awareness of other sounds in his environment.

Marvin also began daily meditation. A visualization that came naturally was his tree. He became that tree for twenty minutes every day, learning to feel deeply connected to the earth, strong enough to withstand the cold of winter, loving enough to provide a home for birds, joyous enough to offer a play space for squirrels and little boys, content enough to feel the soft warm air of summer.

I also suggested to Marvin that he keep a daily journal. "Write down a little each day about how you're feeling, what you're thinking, and detailed memories from childhood.[13] You've had a very interesting and adventure-filled life. If you don't end up with a book, you'll have a touching document for your children and grandchildren."

When we honor ourselves for surviving difficult experiences, we release the inner tension and fear that was bound up with the events. Our inner child may still be trapped in that time. That part of us may believe that the trauma is sure to happen again, that it was our fault, that grieving and moving on, which implies self-forgiveness, is impossible. Taking time to listen to these inner voices through meditation, self-hypnosis, journal-writing, or any number of other therapeutic contexts prepares the ground for inner reassurance, the sense of safety necessary to allow feelings to rise to the surface, and for us to pay our respects.

If we were traumatized as children, and especially if we were hurt by those whom we trusted to take care of us, their betrayal is confusing and impossible to understand. Much effort is required to deny the threatening aspects of the experience, to diminish the significance of the offending adult's behavior in order to keep growing. Self-nurturing has no ground in which to grow. The mind tells us that if those in charge treated us badly, that must be what we deserve.

Learning to hold those who hurt us accountable for their behavior allows us to hold ourselves accountable for healing. We can then be responsible for learning how to feel our reactions and metabolize our grief.[14] Survivors of abuse must discover the truth—that those who torture the body and mind can not destroy the soul. That discovery catalyzes healing.

Frida Kahlo

And you know that love is the only reason for living.
— Frida Kahlo

The life of Frida Kahlo, the renowned Mexican painter and the wife of renowned Mexican muralist Diego Rivera, stands as a monument to the transformative cycles of crisis and creativity. Her work reminds us of the powerful self-expression that can emerge from trauma. Frida was born in Mexico City in the summer of 1907, three years before the Mexican Revolution broke out. When she was six years old, Frida contracted polio. She was a bright, mischievous, outgoing child, who had to be quarantined in her room for nine months. It was during this time that she created an imaginary friend, an alter self, who continued to play, dance, be understanding and supportive, and live with gayness and laughter. This persistent alternate self would be essential for Frida's later survival of an accident of monstrous proportions.

Frida's zestful energy enabled her to cope with her polio-withered right leg by wearing long skirts and thick socks, cursing the children who teased her, and exercising with dedication.

There was no similar equation for coping with the next trauma. When she was eighteen, a two-car train ran into and through a wooden bus Frida was riding on. Although she was one of the survivors, her injuries were so extreme she was not expected to live. Her spinal column was broken in three places, her collar-bone was broken, as were her third and fourth ribs. Her right leg had eleven fractures and her right foot was dislocated and crushed. Her left shoulder was dislocated and her pelvis was broken in three places. A steel handrail had pierced through her body, entering at the level of the abdomen and exiting through the vagina. "I lost my virginity," she said.[15]

Throughout the rest of her life, until her death at age forty-seven, Frida fought to transcend constant pain and disability. She endured more than thirty operations, one of them to amputate her right leg after it became gangrenous. For much of her life, she was confined to bed or encased in special corsets in order to stand or sit up. Her biographer wrote: "Painting was part of Frida Kahlo's battle for life. It was also very much a part of her self-creation; in her art, as in her life, a theatrical self-presentation was a means to control her world. As she recovered, relapsed, recovered again, she reinvented herself. She created a person who could be mobile and make mischief in her imagination rather than with her legs."[16]

Notice the terms "self-creation," and "reinvented herself." Many of her more than two hundred paintings are self-portraits, the first one painted for her boyfriend, Alejandro, as she convalesced following the bus accident. After every trauma, she painted a vivid portrait of herself as if to say, "I did not die. I am here and this is how I look. Nothing can stop my self-expression."

The importance of reframing depression in terms of grief cannot be stressed enough. It provides a starting place for understanding our moods and focusing our energy on healing. Everyone has known sorrow and disappointment; some, like the woman looking for mustard seeds, or like Frida Kahlo, to an overwhelming degree. Frida had to mourn, not only her life of pain and loss of physical activity, but also her inability to have children. She wanted children very much, but was never able to carry a pregnancy to term. She called Diego her "child."

Depression causes certain brain chemicals to change, but we don't know which comes first, the altered level of neurotransmitters or the depressive response. Could antidepressant medication have helped Frida Kahlo cope with her tremendous physical pain and disability? We will never know. We do know that she became addicted to massive doses of pain medication and alcohol. The slow decay of her body due to osteomyelitis and poor circulation, along with her accompanying physical and emotional torment, resulted in her death on July 13, 1954.

Although the cause of death was designated as "pulmonary embolism," the last words in her diary suggest a completed suicide: "I hope the exit is joyful—and I hope never to come back—Frida." One of her last comments to a friend leaves a more representative and touching memory of Frida Kahlo: "And you know that love is the only reason for living," she said. Her illness so diminished her ability to give and receive love that she could not continue living in physical form.

Frida Kahlo's life is an extreme example of the deep depressive reactions that may occur as a part of grieving trauma. Her life also teaches us that intense pain can fuel a fierce creativity, and that loss can highlight the importance of love. We owe ourselves the same kindness and respect we would give to Frida Kahlo. By paying attention to our disconsolate feelings, connecting them to physical or emotional trauma or disappointment, and then expressing them in some consistent and persistent way, we allow for learning and self-discovery.

Depression and Everyday Life

Depression is a major health problem that is estimated to affect more than forty million U.S. adults.
— The American Institute of Stress

Tears that have no reason, fall in my sorry heart.
What, there was no treason? This grief hath no reason.
Nay, the more desolate, because I know not why...
— Verlaine, *Romances sans paroles*

Life is a mystery to be lived, not a problem to be solved.
— W. B. Yeats

For more than two thousand years, depression, or melancholia, has been recognized as a major source of suffering. Four hundred years before Christ, Hippocrates, the Greek physician known as the Father of Medicine, listed melancholia as one of the major forms of mental disease. Robert Burton, an English clergyman and scholar, published a book in 1621, *The Anatomy of Melancholy,* that remained famous for several hundred years for describing the nature and experience of depressive disorders. By the nineteenth century, depression had become a pervasive concern of Western medicine and psychology.

What is this disorder we call "depression"? Could it be that in actuality it is the manner in which we physically and emotionally adapt or fail to adapt to life change? In the American Psychiatric Association's diagnostic manual, there are five categories of depressive symptoms: Major Depression, Dysthymia, Adjustment Disorder with Depressed Mood, Post-Traumatic Stress Disorder, and Bereavement. The category of Bereavement was included in the last edition of the manual as a "condition that may be the focus of clinical attention." Previously it was listed as "Uncomplicated Bereavement, a condition not attributed to a mental disorder," and therefore excluded from health insurance coverage.

There are common symptoms across these clinical categories, including sleep disturbance, low energy, poor concentration, under- or overeating, diminished ability for enjoyment, and constriction in our ability to give and receive love. If we look closely at the manifestations of anxiety in panic or obsessive-compulsive worries, we see a hyper-arousal, rather than the slowing or retardation of the nervous system that occurs in depression, but with the same result—inability to sleep well, work well, and love well. We basically feel that something is missing; something has happened, is about to happen, or will happen again, and we can't possibly cope with this change. Our confidence is impaired. Our mentality has become focused on the fear of life rather than the joy of it.

Whenever I reframe depression into grief, someone invariably says, "That makes sense. It's wonderful to know that I'm not crazy, but how do I grieve? What should I do?" The first answer is to make ourselves consistently *aware* of this new knowledge and respect ourselves for being in grief, which is a time of powerful transition. The next step is for us to look at our particular situations. Write a clear description of lost dreams and deep disappointments, and consider what needs to happen in order to process them.

For the first month after Jeff's death, my daughter had a small table devoted to pictures of him, with votive candles that she kept lit around the clock. She made a book of pictures, poems, and letters written by the two of them. She documented her dreams each morning, noting that some contained direct references to Jeff, including two with images of Jeff giving her messages of regret and also of encouragement.

Because we live in a culture that has lost much in the way of rituals and ceremonies to mark our passages, we must create our own. When we are in emotional crisis, we need structure in our lives, a more "holding environment" to make us feel secure. Designing rituals and schedules helps us to feel in control of time at a time when we very much need to feel in control of something.

Vonda, whose husband died suddenly, needed to return to Alcoholics Anonymous meetings, not because she was in danger of drinking again, but because she needed the structure and group support. Jack, a businessman who felt overwhelmed by lawsuits, needed to join a gym, not because he wasn't fit, but because he needed to look forward to the mindfulness of lifting weights and moving through the aerobic workouts. Lettie, a teenager whose divorced father made only a small pretense of caring for her, needed to keep a diary expressing her thoughts and feelings about his abandonment in preparation for a later time when she thought she might want to visit with him and share the impact of his behavior. Thomas, an elderly man coping with terminal cancer, needed to establish regular meetings with a priest in order to fulfill his lifelong desire to have philosophical discussions about theology. The rituals you add to your life help you to process your grief and represent your creative self-expression in action.

Depression and Medication

To my mind, psychotherapy remains the single most helpful technology for the treatment of minor depression and anxiety.

— Peter Kramer M.D.

Turning to medication for relief from depression is not a choice we tend to view as creative or empowering. Because of our pull-yourself-up-by-your-bootstraps culture, it still feels like a failure of courage for us to put our emotions in the hands of a medical doctor. The more distressed we are, however, the more resources we must explore and the more help we must ask for. After all, few people balk at taking antibiotics. Since the mid-1940s, the discovery of penicillin, streptomycin, and related drugs has essentially arrested death by tuberculosis, pneumonia, and many other diseases. Medications can be just as effective at helping to control certain psychological disorders.

Chlorpromazine (Thorazine), introduced in the 1950s, completely changed the nature of mental treatment with its ability to mitigate delusions and hallucinations, and reduce agitation and violent behavior. In the past, episodically psychotic family members were permanently institutionalized. Now, with medication maintenance, these people can live in the outside world, with more internal peace and increased ability to think rationally and to utilize conventional psychotherapy.

With the introduction in the 1960's of imipramine, an effective mood-elevator, or antidepressant medication, became available. Drugs such as Tofranil, Elavil, and Norpramine caused marked improvement in mood without having stimulant effects. Research demonstrated that in depressed patients the medication worked specifically on norepinephrine and serotonin, the brain chemicals related to depressed mood. In normals, mood was not affected—the medication simply caused sedation.

After thirty years of research seeking a medication to work specifically on facilitating the brain's use of serotonin, fluoxetine oxalate (Prozac) was discovered. According to psychiatrist Peter Kramer, "Whereas drugs like imipramine are more effective in major depression, drugs like Prozac have a special role in the treatment of minor depressive illness."[17]

For clients in the depressive phase of grief, part of our brainstorming involves listing resources and creative rituals, always including the possibility of an evaluation for antidepressant treatment. Five or more months, or longer for some, of being on medication can effectively lift us out of the deepest part of the grief cycle, and help plant us firmly on the road to discovering emotional strength—to discovering, as Kramer says, a self that feels "normal, whole, and authentic."

There are cases where I believe that medications for depression, anxiety, and manic-depressive illness have saved people's lives. Elisabeth Kübler-Ross believes that many suicides could be prevented by diagnosing the early signs of manic-depressive illness and placing the person on lithium.[18]

Enough suffering is inherent in a grief and growth cycle without placing the body and immune system at even greater risk for breakdown. When BJ's grandson died of AIDS, he became so depressed that he couldn't sleep, spent a great deal of time crying, and had no wish to live. BJ told me that his grandson's death had brought up all his grief again over his wife's death and the accidental death of their first daughter, forty years earlier. BJ said that his wife had come to him in a dream and said she was worried about his health. He felt incapable of making any decisions to further his recovery. Antidepressant medication helped BJ to get more rest. With more rest, he could tolerate the pain of his grief. Eventually, BJ volunteered his time at a residential AIDS facility and began to feel a sense of purpose in his life.

An accident at school caused teacher Lucy Madrid to gradually slide into depression; she feared she would remain there. Her arm was closed in a metal door, crushing the bones. Following several surgeries, from which she emerged with pins in her arm and a guarded prognosis for recovering strength and effective use of the arm, she felt completely depleted of energy. Her resentment, anger, and finally depression, stemmed from feeling that the school administrators consistently placed obstacles in her way instead of facilitating her smooth return to teaching. Medication enabled her to recover her energy, rise above her fear, and assert herself calmly and competently. Continuing psychotherapy helped her to reclaim her sense of self and to discover an important metaphor for learning from the accident: Lucy felt her family had tended to "crush" her attempts to open doors into the world beyond their Hispanic culture. It was clearly time, she felt, to recognize her ability to be successful in whatever areas she chose, even if her dreams were beyond the sphere of her family.

Psychiatrist Peter Kramer maintains that psychotherapy is the single most helpful method for treating minor depression and anxiety. It is important to add that recent research has confirmed that psychotherapy is as effective as medication in treating depression, and that if medication is used, psychotherapy should be utilized along with it to prevent a high rate of relapse, "as much as 60% with medication alone."[19]

Only we can decide when depression is no longer "minor" but has become an affliction that makes us feel lost and without the energy to love ourselves or others. At that point, we should first consider psychotherapy. Then we can consider an evaluation for antidepressant medication or a trial on natural herbs. The herb Saint John's wort, or Hypericum, is fast becoming recognized as an effective antidepressant. In one study of 3,250 patients, eighty percent improved or became symptom free in four weeks.[20]

As surgeon Bernie Siegel says, "If you lose your health, go and find it." Seek to rediscover your "self," the unique feelings, attitudes, and self-expressions that are your personal creativity, your way of "being in the world" that feels right.

Depression and Discovery

The Barbie doll, created by Ruth Handler, brought five hundred million dollars to Mrs. Handler's company, Mattel Inc., during the first eight years it was on the market. Financial success was incidental to her wish to provide little girls with toys other than baby dolls. She and her husband and high school sweetheart, Elliot, created furniture together, then dollhouse furniture, and toys, and then the first teenage dolls with accessories. Barbie was named after their daughter. Ken, the boyfriend doll, was named after their son. Barbies were created by Ruth Handler because she observed that little girls longed to play out fantasies about their futures that involved more than mothering babies. Up to that time, the only older dolls were paper cut-outs. Later, another observation by Ruth Handler resulted in a very special accessory for women with cancer.

Mrs. Handler was vice president of Mattel from 1948 to 1967 and president from 1967 to 1973. In addition to having an active life in the business world, she was "a founding member of the Los Angeles Music Center, a member of the National Business Council for Consumer Affairs, a director of the Federal Reserve Bank of San Francisco, a member of the Presidential Advisory Committee on the Economic Role of Women, and a guest professor at UCLA and USC."[21]

In the early 1970s, when Mattel was experiencing financial difficulty, Mrs. Handler faced an additional stress—breast cancer. Following a radical mastectomy of her left breast, she felt depressed, disfigured, and "unwomanized." This woman, who had revolutionized the world of dolls, who was a leader among women executives, was grieving. What helped her emerge from her grief cycle was the same intuition and sensitivity that made her victorious in toy manufacturing—discovering her creative purpose.

When Ruth Handler was recovering from breast surgery, she was unable to find a comfortable, natural-feeling breast prosthesis. She began working with a prosthetic designer and several retired Mattel technicians. Eventually, she offered the Nearly Me line of breast replacements and specially designed swimwear to breast cancer survivors around the country. Out of loss and grief, Ruth Handler created a new career, a new company (Ruthton, Inc.), and a contribution that would enhance the lives of many women.

Depression and Relationships

Depression and grief typically reflect some aspect of a relationship lost or gone awry. It may even be our relationship to our own bodies, as with illness, or our self-esteem, as in perceived personal failure. In my thirty years of work as a psychotherapist, I have never consulted with anyone who didn't view some relationship, past or present, internal or external, as a stimulus for sadness, anger, disappointment, or regret. In my experience, the most common reason for psychiatric consultation is marital distress, the challenge of long-term love.

Our ambivalence about our basic dependency on others fuels a full range of behaviors and emotions during our life span. How is it possible to balance our deep longing for love and connection with our sometimes deeper fear of rejection and abandonment? How can we pursue independence and personal power and, at the same time, invest our souls in loving others? These complex interconnections are part of the mystery we all live.

In order to transform depression into acceptance and inner peace, we must always follow our intuition and look more deeply within. Terri, thirty-nine, a spunky lawyer on the road to a career in politics, dropped her briefcase and coat on the floor of my office and sighed heavily as she sat down on the sofa. "I've got a new problem," she said, "and I've got to solve it quickly, before I ruin my life!"

Terri had been in therapy with me a number of years earlier with her husband, John. Both had worked to correct marital patterns of hurtful behavior that each discovered they had learned unconsciously from their own parents. This time, Terri burst out, "I don't have time to do the traditional therapy thing. I have this intense attachment to a colleague and I thought I could control it, but I can't. I'm losing weight and sleep, not that I care about the weight. But I recognize anxious depression and I don't want to fall into it any deeper. I've known this man for a long time and the pull has been there all along. I was trying to ignore it. What can we do?"

First, we evaluated Terri's marriage, children, work, and social relations, looking for any significant contribution to the present problem. Finding none, Terri chose to use regression hypnosis to see if there was some connection to this man from a previous lifetime that might explain the attraction.

In the past life that Terri moved into under hypnosis, she was extremely poor and living in the Middle Ages in the region of Macedonia. Her mother had died when she was eight and she didn't know her father or his whereabouts. Her older brother had been caring for her as best he could for the past five years. She adored him. But then, when she was thirteen, he went to sea and never returned. As Terri relived this experience in hypnosis, she twisted her hands and cried until her hair and the pillow were wet. She sobbed her protest over and over, "He can't be dead! He can't be dead!" But she never saw him again. And she despaired over his absence for the remaining years of that unhappy lifetime. The brother, she said, was now her male colleague.

Whether or not that experience had actually happened did not interest Terri. The truth of the story was that it projected the intensity of her grief in a manner she recognized. It provided an explanation for her fierce attraction to a man whom she simply wanted to be with, not necessarily have an affair with. "And that seemed bizarre to me! Usually it's a sexual attraction I can chalk up to galloping hormones."

"So how can you use this information?" I asked Terri.

"It's a real relief. Understanding that he was my brother means that I can feel that way for him. I can love him like a brother or like a friend. The stunning awareness is that I can use these feelings to enhance my life rather than atomize it. Whew! I think I can do it!" she declared, smiling. And she did.

Illicit attractions are a common source of depression. The exquisite ambivalence about the attraction and the compelling impulse to act on it is cause to turn inward for understanding. Without self-reflection, as Terri intuitively knew, she risked losing her marriage, family, and hard-earned reputation.

Anthony, an internationally renowned researcher, approached me at a large professional meeting in San Francisco. I was surprised he remembered me from a dinner party several years earlier. I was also surprised that he seemed to want to talk privately. We found a corner table in the hotel dining room and caught up on our families and our writing projects. Then there were a few moments of silence while Anthony inspected the corners of his napkin. He looked up and said, "I am having a hard time with something in my life. I have a powerful attraction to a woman researcher at another university. I have no intention of leaving my wife, and yet I can't seem to stop thinking about this other woman and surreptitiously planning ways to see her. It's causing depression and an interruption in my productivity."

"Are there any other problems of any kind that you haven't told me about?" I asked.

"There's nothing at all wrong in my life that I would be looking to a love affair to distract me from. In fact, I'm at the top of my career. I can work for as long as I choose, or I can retire whenever I like. My marriage is solid and companionable." Anthony looked reflective. "I guess that leaves 'mid-life crisis' as the issue. I can't say I'm too keen on getting old."

I looked directly at him and said, "To anyone else I would make a referral to a good psychiatrist or psychologist. All of us have to grieve over losing our youth." He immediately made a face indicating he would not consider psychotherapy. "But since that's obviously out of the question, I'll ask you to think about the following idea.

"Whenever we find ourselves drawn to someone, as though a powerful magnetic force were pulling us, I believe we need to look closely at the admirable qualities of that person. What is the lure? When we're young, we think we need a partner that will supply us with traits we lack, someone whose intelligence or daring will help make our own lives a success. Even then, trying to acquire personality characteristics from someone else often leads to disaster. But now, in middle age, it may simply be a signal that we need to change something about ourselves. The pitfall is that we usually compare this new person with our spouse and find the spouse lacking. It is we who are lacking."

Anthony nodded knowingly, "I think I've known that all along."

"Ask yourself," I suggested, "Is this woman more adventurous, intellectual, literary, loving than you perceive yourself to be? Whatever it is that tugs at your heartstrings, find ways to develop those qualities in yourself. It's probably time for some expansion in your life."

"I know exactly what it is," declared Anthony with a broad smile. "She's an 'outdoors' woman, and I spend too much time at my research. And now I know what I have to do." He thanked me in his dignified way, planting a kiss on my hand as we left the restaurant.[22]

Terri, too, had benefited from pondering the qualities in her colleague that attracted her to him, but found none that appealed to her sense of self. For Terri, it was the past-life connection that solved her heart's puzzle. The longing for this other man was the longing to love a kindred soul. She had simply confused this impulse with romantic physical attraction. With that clarified, she could not only maintain all the loves in her life, she could infuse them with more joy and energy. Anthony, on the other hand, needed to infuse himself with new interests and greater love.

.⁀ ‿⸜

Paul, an inventor and computer engineer, moved from a lifelong struggle with depression to the awareness that it was time to focus more love and appreciation upon himself. His wife had encouraged him to come for regression hypnosis, he told me. He had been depressed for as long as he could remember. He had been in traditional psychotherapy three different times on two different continents. Antidepressive medication helped some, but after twelve years, he knew he did not want to be dependent on medication for the rest of his life.

Paul was raised in South Africa in a middle-class family. He was a brilliant child, the first and only son. While they were not wealthy, Paul's education was guaranteed by his father and grandfather.

No unusual information arose during the history-taking. Paul didn't have any medical problems, serious childhood illnesses, or physical traumas. He had been told his depression was biological, although there was no history of depression or mental illness in his family. He had felt close to his mother growing up, he told me, while his father was more distant, the family power holder and disciplinarian.

Even when a client comes specifically for past-life hypnosis, I routinely spend the first part of the trance exploring the past in this lifetime. When I suggested that Paul go back to a significant childhood experience that would shed light on his current problem, he found himself hiding under the covers in his bed. He was nine years old. He was shivering with fear and could hardly speak. His father would be home soon, he whispered. If he could pretend he was asleep, maybe his father wouldn't beat him.

"Why would you be beaten?" I asked.

"I took his radio apart, and I did not have time to put it back together," he whispered in his little-boy voice.

"Has he beaten you before?" I asked.

"Oh, yes. Many times. I don't live up to my responsibilities, he says."

"Tell me what happens when your father comes."

Paul was very quiet for a few minutes, then he whispered, "He came into my room and thought I was sleeping, so he left." Paul's breathing began to return to normal. I suggested that he let those images fade away and that he go even deeper into relaxation and total comfort. As we moved back further in time to a previous life, I suggested that he select a lifetime that would help him to understand more about his difficulties in this one.

Paul found himself on the high seas in a storm. He was a Norwegian sailor, in fact the captain of the ship. There was much action aboard trying to ensure the ship's survival. In the next scene, Paul was on land visiting with the leader of his community. The year was somewhere in the mid-1600s. The leader, a grey-haired bear of an older man, had been like a father to Paul. It was widely believed that Paul would inherit his title. While the leader commended him on his safe return with the ship and cargo, Paul sensed that the mantle of leadership was to be withheld from him. He felt a deep sorrow and confusion about this.

"Did you feel angry about it?" I wondered aloud.

"No, just very sad."

Out of hypnosis, Paul rubbed his eyes and looked contemplative.

"Which experience seemed more real or important for you," I asked, "the past life or this life when you were a boy?"

"The boyhood time I felt very strongly. I didn't remember being that afraid of my father. I knew he was strict, but the beatings...the beatings I hadn't realized affected me so much."

"Could the man in Norway have been your father in that previous lifetime?"

"I don't know. And while that experience seemed real, I don't know that it was. I felt I was living in a story, or creating a story because I knew that was expected."

"Is it possible that you could use that story in the same way that you might use a dream?" I asked. "Since you created it, the fact that you chose a story about an older man betraying you might be a way that your unconscious mind is trying to communicate your unresolved grief over the harshness and sadness of your relationships with father figures."

Paul felt he had unearthed the reason for his many years of depression. Hiding under the covers as a boy was a useful metaphor for his pattern of hiding his feelings and keeping his grief under wraps. He wasn't sure how the insight would change him, but the discovery gave him hope.

Three days later, Paul's wife called from their home in another city. Since Paul was out of town regularly on business, she said, she hadn't known when his appointment with me was scheduled. But she noticed that when Paul returned home that evening he looked different, lighter in step and in mood. The tension that seemed to shadow Paul was gone. The next day she asked him if something had happened and he told her about his hypnosis. Paul's wife felt as though her husband was on his way to becoming the man she had seen flashes of when they had fallen in love so many years ago, a man who could be expressive, comfortable, and "just himself."

.⸱ ⸱.

Another striking example of someone who used regression hypnosis to overcome a lifelong depression is Marlis, a woman in her early forties who was referred to me by her physician. She had become so seriously depressed, she rarely left her rural home. The doctor had tried several antidepressant medications with no change in her mood or her levels of fear. Marlis had also utilized psychotherapy when she had lived near Denver, and although she learned a good deal about her early childhood family dynamics, the fear that had made her home a retreat now turned it into a prison.

I greeted Marlis in the office waiting room, noting immediately how reticent and shy she seemed. During the entire first session, she rocked in her chair, jiggled her right foot, and repeatedly pressed her hands together, feeling each finger on one hand and then the other. I never saw her eyes.

Marlis told me she had been depressed and anxious since she was a small child, but her family history was unremarkable. She told me in her quiet voice that she hoped hypnosis, and specifically regression hypnosis, might help her. The expense and the three-hour drive to reach my office precluded ongoing weekly therapy sessions, but she could manage to come three or four times, she said.

Marlis brought her own blanket to wrap around her during the hypnosis session. She lay on the sofa, unable to stop her nervous movements. When I began the hypnotic induction, she began to cry. "I can't do this," she sobbed.

"Of course you can," I assured her. "You'll do it in your own way. Just let the tears keep coming if they need to."

After what seemed like a long time of weeping, Marlis quieted and through her sobs said, "Okay, let's try again."

As part of the induction, I suggested that she follow her tears, just follow the feelings attached to the tears and see where they led. Eventually, Marlis found herself in the body of a twelve-year-old girl. This girl was living in an asylum during the 1800s. She was not able to communicate with me, so I called on Marlis's Higher Self to observe and tell me about her. The girl was born blind, deaf, and mute, she said. She had been placed in the institution by her parents when she was five. She was dragged, pushed, and pulled from place to place and abused in many ways. She died of a contagious illness at the age of fifteen. As Marlis described this heart-wrenching experience, I noticed her hands carrying out the ritualized behavior of feeling each finger, trying to know her body and prove her existence.

At the end of the session, I gave Marlis some positive suggestions. Important learning had accrued from that life. It was all there in her unconscious mind. I added that now was the time to leave behind all of the sadness and depression, and any guilt she may have had from the mistaken belief that she had done something wrong to have suffered that way. Marlis said she would listen to the tape, but left the office with the same nervous and downcast manner she had come in with.

The next week when I greeted Marlis, she smiled at me. Once inside the office, she looked at me several times as if experimenting with making eye contact. I told her how striking her bright blue eyes were, and her smile turned into a giggle. She giggled and laughed throughout most of the session and the ones remaining. It was as though she had been released from a spell. Marlis agreed that she had been living this life as though she were still in that institution, with no way out and no way to express herself.

Once she was consciously aware that she had been needlessly reliving past trauma, Marlis awakened to this life with great energy. She began "attacking" the overgrown landscape around her house, cutting back, pruning, and mowing. She reinstated her license to do massage, work she had trained for but never felt confident enough to perform. How fascinating, I told her, that she had chosen to use her hands in this lifetime in order to help others feel better in their bodies.

During one of the last sessions, she asked shyly but with a smile, "Do you suppose I could have sex someday and enjoy it?" So we used that hypnosis session to help her feel comfortable with her body and feel delighted about the prospect of choosing when and where and with whom to share her body.

Some time later, she called to say, "It worked!" All of Marlis's nervous habits disappeared, along with her depression, as she grieved her past and moved comfortably and joyfully into the present.

The people I have described shed their grief and grew their self-understanding in order to lead more self-expressed, creative lives. Others need to move in the opposite direction, from the "creative" life to one more conservative, interactive, or worldly.

Gabriel was trained as an opera singer. She had never questioned this path since her mother was a voice teacher and recognized Gabriel's ability when she was young. As an adolescent, she was given voice lessons with a highly respected vocal coach. Just as she accepted her mother's direction for her career, when it was time for marriage, she accepted the proposal of a man she admired, a successful businessman who also liked to sing, but just for fun. Over the years, Gabriel grew disenchanted with her demanding rehearsal and concert schedule. As she looked for ways to escape her life of music, Baldwin, her husband, became increasingly interested in singing and appearing in musicals. Gabriel's unconscious way of bringing focus to her problem was to have an affair.

When knowledge that she had a lover spread like a time-lapse photo of a flower opening, Gabriel felt exposed and humiliated. When she came for therapy, she was "completely depressed." She felt she couldn't cope with Baldwin's rage or her lover's allegiance.

Within several months she was able to make some decisions. She chose to separate from her husband, work part time as an office "temp," and return to school. What would she study in school?

Counseling appealed to her. Four years later, Gabriel had a master's degree in counseling and a job that had evolved from one of her internships. She had extricated herself from her lover and was completely surprised to find that she enjoyed being with Baldwin again and that he wanted her to move back in with him.

Several years later, Gabriel told me she finally felt like a fully grown woman. She was a recognized expert in the field of domestic violence and was director of a women's shelter. While Baldwin continued to sing occasionally, she felt free to express her creativity through social service.

"Years ago," Gabriel said, "I heard Joseph Campbell talking in television interviews with Bill Moyers about 'following your bliss.' I thought that must mean something magical and creative, like opera. Now I've learned that it simply means to follow your heart. I've left my depression behind with all my other misconceptions. Now that I'm teaching others to grow in personal strength, I feel more creative than I ever did in the past."

Many others have happily made the move from "creative" careers to those often categorized as mundane. Depression, or what some call "burnout," motivated the life change.

Rosalie was sent to performing arts schools from the age of nine in order to nurture her gift as a dancer. In her teens, she worked with New York ballet companies during the season and studied with other companies throughout the summer. By the age of twenty, an eating disorder and depression had sapped her energy. Her interest in dance had died. She enrolled in her hometown college and, with the help of psychotherapy, her life was revitalized through elementary-school teaching.

Helen was a well-educated writer who had worked as an editor, journalist, and creative-writing instructor. It was when she redirected her career to hospital administration, however, that she felt she reached the pinnacle of her creativity. She found her true voice expressed through the caring management of hospital personnel.

As we live longer and healthier lives, we are able to enjoy numerous careers, not just jobs, throughout the life span. But there is only one career, or highest calling, that applies to every human being—that of growing one's self-expression in order to be the embodiment of one's values. If the definition of "career" is "the progress or general course of action of a person through life," then to become successful at living and loving, we must make our "general course of action" the transforming of grief and defensiveness into the discovery of our true selves, the selves of powerful possibilities.

Become accustomed to viewing depression as unresolved grief, a defense mechanism that, if tolerated too long, can make us victims. Use feelings of depression as a signal that it's time to leave the "lies of limitation" where they belong, in the past. Choose instead, not only to survive, but to thrive. One woman came to my office wearing a T-shirt declaring "Compost Happens!" Yes, it does. We can use the depressive part of grief and growth as compost to nourish the rediscovery of ourselves in each new life experience.

I like to think of Job wearing that "Compost Happens" T-shirt following his awakening from depression. During his depression, every complaint Job makes expresses his "anguish of spirit." Deep depression darkens his words, whether they are words of numb denial, outrageous anger, half-crazed obsession or tedious rationalization. He can't sleep, but when he dozes nightmares and frightening visions take over. Depression ravages his body—Job becomes ill from head to toe with running sores and ceaseless pain. "My body is infested with worms, and scabs cover my skin; it is cracked and discharging. My days…come to an end as the thread of life runs out" (Job 7:5-6). Job is dying to the past, to limiting beliefs in God as a controlling, punitive patriarch, and to behavior that represents his moral parochialism.

Job is having a rebirth, the pains of labor forcing him to listen to a smaller, but more powerful voice. When Job's friends, his obsessive voices, finally give up, the young man Elihu cannot contain himself any longer. Elihu, Job's Higher Self, speaks with the innocence of youth and the wisdom of age. He says: "It is a spirit in a human being, the breath of the Almighty, that gives him understanding..." (Job 32:8).

This connection with the Higher Self prepares the way for Job to move out of his depression and his illusion of isolation to a powerful awareness of the presence of God. When Divine Energy speaks to Job from the whirlwind, dazzling him with stories of creation, Job leaves his depression and dark defenses in the past. Rooted in his inner strength, he accepts the energy of God and becomes enlightened.

Heighten your awareness of any past experiences that have caused depression. Feel the pain and let it go. You may have to do this repeatedly, feeling the pain and expressing and releasing it, until you develop an awareness of the future goals and dreams you've been incubating all along. It is time now to discover newness in your life. It is time to accept the present, embrace change, unplug and drain your energy from the past, and be transformed. As Oliver Wendell Holmes once said, "What lies behind us and what lies before us are tiny matters compared to what lies within us." And Joan Anglund reminds us, "It is in our Choice that all power lies. For that idea to which we cling...becomes our center...and creates a new world around us."

Daily Creative Discipline
(Depression: The Dark Road to Discovery)

1. Place the concept of "depression" gently within a beautiful, gilt-edged frame bearing the words "Grief, Growth, and **Capacity for Love.**" See yourself in that frame with someone who loves you.

2. Internalize the definition of depression as "the manner in which we physically and emotionally adapt or become arrested, as we adapt to life change." Resolve to consistently recognize that the time is coming when you will be ready to complete this **adaptation to a new reality** and be at peace.

3. **Take charge of your life** by scheduling every hour of your day. If you are severely depressed, schedule every minute. Begin with special attention to morning and evening, as those are the transition times between dark and light. Carefully **organize** these times of the day, in writing, beginning with the time you wake up. Be sure to schedule in some form of **exercise,** even if you are bed-bound.

4. Since the depression phase of grief confines us in our "emotional basement," look to the mental and spiritual aspects of your personality for strength. **Take charge of your mind** by catching every negative thought and change it to the positive message that you are safe and secure. What you think will affect your emotions, so **feed yourself abundant, uplifting thoughts.** Positive thoughts will help you **discover your Transcendent Self.** Meditate and pray every day.

5. **Ask for help.** Never expect yourself to handle depression alone. Isolation will aggravate the feelings that you are ill,

unloveable, or defective. Use this time to **strengthen your bridges to others.** Your confidence will be strengthened through discovery that **others want to help.** Your self-esteem will grow as you desensitize yourself to fears of self-disclosure and self-expression. You will **discover your own personal creativity.**

6.   Be like Frida Kahlo and do a self portrait, a bold represen-tation of your face. Using your crayons and white paper, make your picture as abstract or surreal as you like—no holding back on colors, images, and symbols. You will **be amazed** at the meanings that will speak to you from that work. Date it and save it in your file.

Chapter Seven

Acceptance: Embracing Success

There is only the love and understanding of instant acceptance...
— John Steinbeck

The greatest creation is the creation of one's self in the world.
— Brian Grodner

Acceptance is the point where we finally overcome our fear and transform our grief into awareness and self-expression. Accepting and overcoming the fear of life change requires trust, the kind of trust we could recover quickly as children. Five-year-old Kelly was in my office just after she'd been told her family would be moving, again. She sat scrunched up, with her arms folded and a stiff pout distorting her normally sweet mouth. I encouraged her to put her feelings into words. As she slowly spoke of her anger and disappointment, I suggested that she might need to put her feelings into loud crying and wailing, which she did. I coached and encouraged more and more expression until her grief bounced loudly off the walls of the office and her tears washed all over her face. Eventually, she became quiet. She raised herself up from where she had collapsed on the sofa and slowly a big, bright smile broadened her face.

"I feel really good inside," she said. "My heart is smiling. Maybe I'll like Montana. Dad says we might get horses in our family."

After Kelly expressed her fear and her grief, she could place herself back in the world with a smile in her heart and trust in her future. She could align herself with love, looking forward to life's possibilities instead of living with the fear of loss. "Getting horses" might serve as a metaphor, a reminder to us as adults to look at life's changes as opportunities for joy and the successful adaptation of loving life.

The stage of acceptance represents the celebration of life at the end of an exhausting inner battle of resistance. We emerge from the darkness feeling peaceful and renewed. We have embraced the present. Or perhaps simultaneously we embrace the present, forgive the past, and trust in the future. This success is the success of loving life again...loving ourselves, others, and even challenging circumstances. Inner peace is the result of reaching the last stage of grieving by accepting a new reality. With this achievement, profound prayer is answered, desired dreams come true.

Inner peace is proof that we have aligned ourselves with love energy, we have grown through our grief. The grief may have resulted from serious loss, a moderate life change, or defensive behaviors that kept us in "paradigm paralysis" and "lies of limitation." With acceptance comes the manifestation of dreams, a feeling that we have been delivered into a gentler world, one in which we can breathe more easily and move with less effort.

Earlier I told of couples who, after adopting babies, were able to create one; of inventors who, after struggling for years, dreamed how to complete a project; of artists who, out of grief, expressed their creativity in startling, vivid, new ways. Accepting grief and growth cycles as being as inevitable as the changing seasons allows us to be where we need to be and feel what we need to feel, for whatever time is required in order to make the next self-expressive move.

Artist Constance DeJong recognizes the growth cycles inherent in expressions of the inner self. She calls art "the tangible evidence of an inner life." After experiencing several periods of sustained production and then loss of focus, she can accept this process and use the meditative mind to observe where she is in her growth. "I've been through enough to know that I'm always incubating new work and that I'll be guided to do what is to come next. All I must do is be still and allow for that direction to come."

There is paradox here. Acceptance of reality does not mean passivity. It is an attitude and a mental practice that allows for peaceful observance of life's ups and downs. It is this capacity to observe without fear that gives the mind a neutral playing field where it can make effective decisions. In order to float through our grief and growth cycles and be in *acceptance* of the process, it helps to "be still and allow for direction to come." And when the direction manifests itself, our life energy will drive us to success.

Harvard physician Herbert Benson, who has been researching the "relaxation response" for twenty years,[1] teaches us a simple truth: For maximum physical and mental health, the "fight-or-flight" reaction must be *balanced* physiologically by relaxation, by taking the time to lower our heart rate, respiration, and the release of stress hormones. When we provide this balance in our lives, we are giving our bodies and minds the deep rest they need in order to incubate and grow.

What is happening when we are being creative, expressing ourselves in such a superb, natural way that we are surprised and amazed at the results? Five phenomena are taking place.

1. First, we are in a state of relaxation or "alert relaxation."[2] While the body is in deep relaxation, the mind becomes focused, concentrating. At once, we are deeply relaxed and yet intensely focused, as during sleeping and dreaming. Some artists experience this as "excitement."

2. Time disappears. Time distortion occurs when we're deeply absorbed in taking in or putting together a creative idea.

Focused concentration, including daydreaming (a time when we are germinating and incubating self-expression), works just as sleep does. When we "awake," we are surprised that so little time or so much time has elapsed. When people come out of hypnosis, they are invariably startled to discover how much time has passed. Two hours feels like ten minutes to someone who has been completely absorbed in exploring his or her inner world.

3.   Heightened imagery takes place when we are deeply relaxed and outside of time. Even scientists and engineers who consider themselves "noncreative" visualize answers to questions, dream discoveries, or mentally construct projects. Skilled hypnotists sometimes ask subjects who believe they cannot use mental imagery to pretend they're calling in someone to clean their windows. In order to get estimates, they must mentally count the windows in their homes. Most people are able to do this.

4.   Next comes a suspension of critical thinking. When we are relaxed and able to be, think, and feel whatever we like, we open up to being spontaneous. We might even be "outrageous," unconventional. Our minds are free to roam this way and that to explore space and juxtapose relationships. We might call this "brainstorming" although it's more than problem-solving. "Brainplaying" might be a better term for what can happen when we temporarily withhold judgment and unleash the full range of our thoughts and emotions.

5.   We now experience associational flow, receiving our thoughts in whatever way they come to us. Thoughts and images flow because there is no physical resistance, time pressure, or internal criticism. This is our "creative mode."

When we can cycle smoothly through life's disappointments, we can focus on living in life's possibilities. We are able to "get horses" because we can accept reality, rise above our fears, and experience these five aspects of creativity. We find peace, life purpose, and overriding love.

Resilient Adults

Joy does not come from outside, for whatever happens
to us it is within. Light does not come to us from without.
Light is in us, even if we have no eyes.
— Jacques Lusseyran

Jacques Lusseyran (1924–1971) had no sight to see the outside world. He was blinded completely at the age of seven. And yet he always saw, not only light, but color, objects, nature, movement, and people. Lusseyran credited his loving parents and his relationship with light for his resilience. From the time he was very small, he had a passion for light and for colors. Even in the dark, he could see shades of light and distinct colors, so that even after losing his eyesight, he insisted, "Nothing entered my mind without being bathed in a certain amount of light....In a few months my personal world had turned into a painter's studio."[3]

Also remarkable was his ability to move comfortably in the world, avoiding obstacles. Fear, he said, was the only thing that ever made him blind, and it happened when he was being interrogated by the Gestapo. For a brief moment, he became "stone blind." Another of his mysterious powers, along with being able to walk in the world without running into things, involved sound: "I seemed to hear people speak before they began talking. Sounds had the same individuality as light."[4] "Inside me every sound, every scent, and every shape was forever changing into light, and light itself changing into color to make a kaleidoscope of my blindness."[5]

Lusseyran discovered that his capacity for learning and memorization was limitless. He visualized a scrolling screen in his mind on which he could list the entire history of many countries, foreign languages, and thousands of names, addresses, and phone numbers. The "chalk" for his inner blackboard he called "spirit."

He also saw truth. When I say he saw truth, I mean he was clear about the pre-eminent values of peace, purpose, and love. In fact, he devoted his life to fighting for these freedoms.

How could a blind man fight? Lusseyran was fifteen when the Nazis occupied France. At his home in Paris, a case of measles "catalyzed a pack of fears and desires, intentions and irritations." Purging his system of these poisons, he was left with a "torrent of energy" he called "resolve." With this moral resolve, Jacques Lusseyran organized a resistance movement against the Nazis. When he called his first meeting, he expected ten boys to show up. Instead, fifty-two boys crammed into his small room. He was a natural leader, admired by everyone. Within one year, The Volunteers of Liberty had over six hundred boys hard at work printing and distributing news of the war to the citizens of France (the Nazis had closed down or outlawed all outside sources of news). The morale of the French people was at stake.

Lusseyran was encouraged to lead the group, not only because of his courage and intelligence (keeping all records in his mind instead of written down was an obvious asset), but also because of his ability to recruit the right men. Just as he had always had deep, intuitive insights from nature, Lusseyran had immediate intuitive impressions about the morals and trustworthiness of people. He could "read" a man by the tone of his voice.

Two years later, in 1943, The Volunteers of Liberty merged with another underground group, *Defense de la France,* which printed a newspaper and distributed ten thousand copies per month. These papers gave the people news of the war and hope for liberation, ways to spread passive resistance, and awareness of the atrocities being committed in the concentration camps. Within two months, the number of those in charge of circulating the paper grew to five thousand. Before Lusseyran's arrest by the Gestapo, 250,000 copies of the paper were printed. But "a country in disaster is swarming with traitors." After six weeks in a prison in Paris, where he was interrogated sometimes for twelve hours a day, Lusseyran was sent to Buchenwald.

Of the two thousand men who were shipped to Buchenwald, thirty, including Jacques Lusseyran, survived. How was it possible that a blind boy still in his teens had the strength to outlive the Nazi terrors? He said it was his "love of life." In fact, his definition of God was "life." He stated, "I have maintained this love of life through everything."

As we discover the power of acceptance, we can learn from Lusseyran's attitude that accepting reality, instead of falling into denial and remaining in grief, gives us the courage to participate in history, in our community. Lusseyran's love for his fellow countrymen made him acutely aware of what was happening in Europe, even before the German Occupation. Lusseyran's "Inner Voice," or Higher or Transcendent Self, told him to prepare, to learn German, because he was to do "great things." Accepting even a cruel reality came naturally to Lusseyran because of his belief in the "oneness of the world." Regarding this reality, he said, "Don't be afraid to lose your soul there, for God is in it."

Lusseyran almost died in the concentration camp. He developed a high fever and dysentery, and was taken to the "hospital" where prisoners were left to die. He observed himself through that sickness until he came back to life. "Life...broke into my cage...came toward me like a shimmering wave, like the caress of light. I could see it beyond my eyes and my forehead and above my head. It touched me and filled me to overflowing. I let myself float upon it...I was not going to leave that celestial stream...the Life that sustained the life in me."[6]

⁖ ⸴

Jacques Lusseyran made a blessing of his blindness. He not only accepted it, he embraced it as another world, "a world closer to myself." His personality displays the attributes of resilience listed by psychiatrist Frederic Flach, from his research on this topic.[7] The traits of a resilient person are:

1. strong *self-esteem*
2. *independence* of thought and action

3. a strong network of *friends*
4. *discipline* and *responsibility*
5. the ability to recognize and *develop gifts and talents*
6. *openmindedness*
7. willingness to *dream*
8. a wide range of *interests*
9. a keen sense of *humor*
10. *insight* into one's own and others' *feelings,* and the *ability to communicate* them
11. a high *tolerance for distress*
12. focus and a *commitment to life,* including a philosophy for *meaning* and *hope,* even under the worst circumstances

Through his work, Dr. Flach has found that resilient people are able to adapt well to the "challenges of change." He sees creativity expressed through the unique ways people adapt to stressful situations. Creativity is an essential part of resilience.

While Jacques Lusseyran's resilience, physically, mentally, emotionally, and spiritually, was facilitated by loving parents, most adults and children who have been studied for their resilience have been betrayed by those who were expected to care for them. In years past, we referred to children who overcame neglect and abuse in childhood as "invulnerables."[8] Studies found that among these children from severely dysfunctional homes, six to twelve percent become outstanding individuals in terms of coping, confidence, and creativity. In my experience with survivors of various types of abuse, the courage to face the past and feel the pain of the loss is the process that propels resilient people through grief to acceptance. They accept the past as a fact of life, accept the present as a gift of growth, and see the future as bestowing plentiful possibilities.

Harvard psychologist Gina O'Connell Higgins studied forty adults who had been severely traumatized in childhood but had become highly successful adults in terms of work and their capacity to love.[9] She identified important traits that these *resilient survivors* share. They believe they can *choose* their own paths, "choose how to *see,* how to *be,* and how *not to be.*" (As children, we often know what we do not want before we know exactly what we do want.) Resilient survivors believe in the importance of human relationships, of a bond that gives hope for the future during personal traumas and life crises. They have faith in their ability to surmount problems through transcendent vision. Their faith enables them to create meaning from suffering and find pattern, order, and significance in the whole of life. Successful survivors of trauma feel an ethical responsibility to help others.

Choice, strong ties, personal faith, and a clear sense of responsibility are all embedded in the characteristics of resilient adults described by Dr. Flach. Most likely, if you stop to think about it, anyone you admire as a role model for successful living most likely displays these traits.

I am constantly impressed by survivors who *choose* to be thrivers. Anya, one of Dr. Higgins's resilient subjects, reminds me of Barbara, the woman who inspired my book *Lessons in Evil, Lessons From the Light.* Both women were raised in families that practiced satanic/sadistic abuse. Both women had strong values that supported their "determined overcoming" of cruelty. They chose to be different from their families. Both of them bonded with someone who gave them *hope.* The bonds may seem unusual to those of us who had caring, or at least "good enough" parents. In Anya's case, it was a gentle pedophile in the cult. This man was the only person who was kind to Anya in childhood. Because of his attempts to help rather than hurt her, this man was murdered.

Barbara's bond, like Jacques Lusseyran's, was with light. From the time Barbara was a baby, she could remember light coming to her and calming her when she was ill, surrounding and comforting her when she had been placed in isolation, bathing her in reassurance when she was being physically tormented or attacked. Sometimes she felt the Light was Jesus, other times she called the Light her Spiritual Mother. The Light was Barbara's lifeline and her hope that some day she would get away from the cult. Her greatest learning, she told me at the end of her therapy, was that the Light is always there. "I would turn my back when I was angry or wanted to die, but the Light was with me all along. I believe it has been my guiding force."[10]

The other bond that Barbara recognized through her therapeutic work was the bond to her own soul. Maybe that's what the light represented, the connection to her own soul. Or as Lusseyran might have said, the light always reminds us of the oneness of the Life force, of God. The turning point in Barbara's therapy was a regression hypnosis during which she re-experienced a previous life and viewed her death in that lifetime. She was amazed to discover that she had a soul that left her body as her Spiritual Mother called her away from that lifetime. Barbara had believed she was a "lost soul...that the clan had taken my soul...[but] I learned that my soul will never die. My soul is eternal. Also, I learned that I wasn't alone. I'm connected to all of the other souls."[11]

I believe the greater the distress we experience, the greater the possibility that there's a spiritual intervention to save us from turning our backs on life and giving up hope. However, most of us would not choose to be a Jacques Lusseyran, or a Barbara, or any of the thousands of people increasingly written about who have near-death experiences that give them astonishing knowledge of the afterlife.[12] Most of us will simply practice the attributes of resilience: choice, faith, hope, and responsibility. In so doing, we might even begin to recognize the telltale signs of Divine guidance in small or great miracles.

Confucius

Do unto others as your heart prompts you. Do not do to others what you do not want done to yourself.
— Confucius (551–479 B.C.E.)

The miraculous nature of life is often ignored. We are reminded of existence as a miracle when we observe lives of "determined overcoming," or the lives of remarkable people like

Confucius, who overcame difficult circumstances and also changed history. Such stories remind us that it only takes one person strong enough to grieve and grow, accept difficult social realities, and use his or her unique self-expression or personal creativity to change the world forever.

Like Muhammad in the Middle East one thousand years later, Confucius was born at a time of social chaos in China. Confucius the man, the teacher, the scholar, the philosopher, the reformer, brought a personal ethic to Chinese culture and to the world that remains to this day. Some refer to him as the most influential man of all time. He appeared to have had little influence during his lifetime, however, and his mission to be the first political consultant, to teach better methods of governing, seemed to fail. His resilience and his creativity lay in his ability to transcend the grief of personal and national crises. Confucius observed and accepted harsh realities, and aligning himself with his values, with love and with personal responsibility, used his energy to reaffirm life.

At the time of Confucius's birth about five hundred years before the common era, anarchy ruled. The ethico-political system of guiding rituals that had been developed during the Chou Dynasty, five hundred years earlier, deteriorated from the eighth to the third century B.C.E. That golden age of peace and harmony changed into a clash of rival barons, a period of Chinese history labeled The Period of the Warring States. Mass executions took place and entire populations were mutilated and beheaded, including the aged, women, and children.[13]

Also like Muhammad, Confucius was a child of loss. Confucius' father died when he was three, leaving him to be raised by an "impoverished mother." After his mother died, Confucius dreamed of a prominent figure of the Chou Dynasty. This vision of the Duke of Chou, the first ruler to be called "The Son of Heaven," may have opened Confucius to the awareness that "If he couldn't rule men, he would teach men" to "look into the past to understand the future."[14]

Confucius worked for the rest of his life to bring back the traditions and group-consciousness of the past to reestablish social order in the present. He was convinced of the power of tradition to civilize, to provide a structure for social behavior that would be advantageous for all. Since the Chinese character for "mind" also designates "heart," much of what Confucius taught included the recognition that emotions and learned attitudes affect the way we reason and relate to others. He taught a social ethic that became the foundation for the education of Asian youth for more than two thousand years. Perhaps what counts him among the great revolutionaries was his emphasis on the responsibility of all men, regardless of class, to have personal integrity focused on service. Recognition of this duty, to be part of "one world, one family," led eventually to the downfall of hereditary aristocracy in China.

"Human beings are by nature good" was the first sentence every Chinese child was taught to read for nearly two thousand years. This statement embodies the five ideals or themes of Confucius's thought:

1. The first, the "virtue of virtues," is that "all men are brothers." The Chinese concept of *jen* describes *ideal relationships* as those based on empathy and human-heartedness, the ability to "measure the feelings of others by one's own."

2. The second ideal, *chen tzu,* describes the *mature or wise person* as one who is poised and capable in all situations. This person has so much self-respect that respecting others comes naturally. To the "superior" person, kindly accommodating another is not only socially appropriate, but personally gratifying. According to Confucius, it is this loving, accommodating nature that can create peaceful civilizations. "If there is righteousness in the heart, there will be beauty in the character. If there is beauty in the character, there will be harmony in the home. If there be harmony in the home, there will be order in the nation. If there be order in the nation, there will be peace in the world."[15]

3.   The third ideal involves propriety, or *proper behavior* and conduct. With anecdotes, maxims, and stories, Confucius sought to teach people how to be in the world and share the world comfortably. The Chinese concept of *li* describes "right conduct" and the rituals which nourish the spirit and inform the soul that our movement in the world is creating harmony and not discord. The outstanding doctrines in this category are Constant Relationships, the commitment to honor all ongoing relationships; Rectification of Names, building expectations for behavior into every title and social role, such as father, friend, ruler, teacher; and the Doctrine of the Mean, "nothing in excess." This latter is the one most Westerners are familiar with, probably because it was underscored several hundred years later by Aristotle.

The importance of balance in life was taught with a powerful metaphor. Confucius observed a hanging vessel and showed his students that when empty, the vessel hung slanting; if filled to the top, it overturned; but, if half-filled, it hung straight.[16] What a clear illustration of a fact of life—that excess will not bring peace, and that "Everything has its limits." The metaphor reminds us that when we believe the lie that there is not enough wealth, success, or love in our lives, we are left off balance, just as when we act out the lie, obsessively bringing in more and more until we overturn what stability there was. We must accept the fact that we grow in assertiveness in the middle ground, not through passivity (too little of ourselves) or through aggression (too much of ourselves). Accepting this balance leads to an ability for true creative self-expression.

4.   The fourth ideal, *te,* means *power.* Confucius was trying to bring order to his world. There were two primary schools of thought during his time regarding governance: the Realists prescribed brute force, the *Mo Ti* prescribed love. Confucius balanced the two by bringing back traditions that provided social structure and a collective ethos. He was healing the

wound, the separation in the community, by prescribing intrinsic power, a shared power of cooperation for the common good. Confucius believed in the power of moral example. "He who governs by *te* is like the north star. It keeps its place and other stars turn toward it."[17]

5.   *"The arts of peace,"* or *wen,* is the fifth ideal. Confucius believed that art ennobles the human spirit and that it affects the international political success of a people. He taught that the most successful nation-state is the one with the highest culture. Among the recognized arts in ancient China were charioteering, archery, history, numbers, music, rituals, and poetry. Confucius loved music and was familiar with the eight different classes of instruments: the bells, the stones, the string instruments (zithers), the drums and timbrels, the mouth organs, the wooden boxes, and the bamboo flute-like instruments.[18] Music was so important in Confucius's teachings that one of his students, who was later placed in a management position, made music his first principle of government!

During the short time that Confucius was in public office, he introduced a system of uniform weights and measures, as well as uniform prices on goods. Promoted to Minister of Crime, he declared that moral education was the most effective way to combat crime. "In hearing litigation," he said, "the best thing to do is to make litigations unnecessary." It was said that in the area he governed, all crime ended.[19]

As Confucius suggests, "When you see an admirable person, think of emulating him; when you see someone who is not so, turn inward and examine yourself."[20] He lived the principle that "it is in one's own heart, not in the external world, that one must seek for happiness."[21] He was more successful than he ever knew in bringing positive social change to China. By accepting things as they were, he modeled a peaceful heart. Through constant focus on self-expression, he lived his life purpose. As he practiced awareness of his highest values, his life energy flowed into love.

.⌣ ⌣.

Remember, in the grief and growth process acceptance leads to success and inner peace. Confucius was able to accept social disorder and personal setbacks as facts of life. Being able to accept changing realities, harsh though they may be, allows us to transcend the current chaos of the community and follow our heart's true path. Ironically, in so doing we find ourselves also contributing to positive social change.

Biblical scholar Stephen Mitchell describes this paradox of being "separate from" and "one with" the world in a beautiful way: "Shalom, the word for 'peace' in Hebrew, comes from a root that means 'wholeness.' When we make peace in our own heart, we make peace for the whole world."[22] Getting to acceptance of life's problems places us in the powerful position of choosing inner peace. Resolving our crises, our grief, results in the creation of peace within and promotes peace without. Acceptance of change is like the naturalness of the sea to calm after a storm.

Jesus

Treat others as you would like them to treat you. If you love only those who love you, what credit is that to you?
— Jesus of Nazareth (Luke 6:31-32)

Prominent teachers throughout history are examples of transcendental living and are "artists" of social change. The world's eminent teachers, such as Buddha, Muhammad, Krishna, Confucius, and Jesus, emerged at crisis points in human history with the passionate purpose of uniting people in peace. They are called "masters," as the title denotes one who has both ability and intrinsic power. They were able to transcend fear and transform the energy of resistance and defense into the unrestrained vitality of creative leadership that still inspires us today.

Jesus of Nazareth was so inspiring that his words created a new world religion. The historical Jesus entered the world during desperate times, as did most of the world's great teachers. Jesus's people, the Jews, had been enslaved by Rome for nearly a century. Their land was occupied by Roman soldiers and government agents, and the people were taxed beyond reason. It was a world of oppression, violence, and intrigue. Tax collectors were essentially local traitors, collaborators with Rome, who were given license to use whatever means necessary to extract money from the farmers and tradesmen.

Over the years, political terrorists known as Zealots were actively engaged in armed struggle against the Romans. Many of these freedom fighters were Galileans. The historian Josephus tells of another group of patriots who were actually assassins. The *sicarii* stabbed their opponents with concealed daggers during festivals in Jerusalem and then melted into the crowd.[23] The Galileans were a rough bunch, described as "fighters from the cradle."[24]

There were frequent uprisings against Rome from the year 6 C.E. until the great revolt culminating in the total destruction of Jerusalem from 66 to 70 C.E. There were ongoing class wars, civil struggles, and economic grievances between the rich and poor, the city and country dwellers.[25]

Society was split on to how to deal with the enemy occupation, as well as those locals whose behavior brought bloody reprisals against the Jews. The conservative upper class, the Sadducees, traditionally the High Priests, wished to integrate the Hellenizing influence of the Romans. Greek was the language of much of the Roman Empire and during the time of Caesar, knowledge of Greek literature and philosophy was considered the mark of education and sophistication. On the other hand, in terms of the Hebrew teachings, the Sadducees were adamant that only the Written Law of the Torah (the first five books of the Old Testament) be used to conduct religious and social life. They were willing to interpret the Law literally and concretely. For example, the Jewish historian Josephus reported an incident where the Sadducees wished to have a man put to death for speaking against the High Priest, based on their interpretation of Leviticus 24:15, "He who blasphemes the Lord shall be put to death."[26] The Sadducees' literal reading of the scriptures, their small numbers and greater wealth, plus their belief in a God that held little regard for the individual and allowed the soul to perish with the body, set them apart from the masses.

The Pharisees were the educated, popular leaders of the day, a large association of scholars who not only knew the Written Law (the Torah) but also the Oral Laws of the Prophets. They were in open conflict with the Sadducees, perceiving them as unjust. The Pharisees were the champions of the disadvantaged and were not afraid to stand up for them. Their large popular following may have been a result of their efforts to adapt and democratize the Jewish religion to meet the problems of their time. This is just the way Moses had responded to the advice of his father-in-law Jethro more than one thousand years earlier, regarding the importance of delegating and sharing responsibility for evaluating and resolving societal disputes.[27]

The Pharisees were teachers of justice, admired for their simple life and emulated by the lower class. The respect they received was natural, given that they were descendants of the Maccabees, who won freedom for the Jews from the Syrians around 160 B.C.E. The Pharisees believed that God cared for every individual and, further, that souls are immortal, people being punished or rewarded in the afterlife according to their deeds.[28]

A third group in the Jewish population was the Essenes, a group of mystics who believed that God would destroy the Romans in their lifetime. They withdrew from the world and lived in communes, strictly observing the Jewish calendar of Feasts and Fasts. They took to heart the commandment of Isaiah 40:3, "in the wilderness, prepare the way of the Lord." They believed purification and repentance were necessary for membership in the true Israel. It is thought that John the Baptist, who baptized Jesus, came from this community of mystics, who called themselves "the children of light."[29]

Through this society of political factions, religious extremists, economic and physical oppression, and resistance fighters walked Jesus of Nazareth, along one of the busiest trade routes of the ancient world. He was one of the many holy men the Jews were accustomed to, and was referred to by the common name Joshua, which means "Savior" in Hebrew. Translated into Greek, Joshua becomes "Jesus."[30]

What was different about this particular Jewish teacher, and why did his teachings not only touch the hearts of his countrymen but also inspire his disciples to spread the word far beyond Israel following his death? In order to understand the impact of Jesus's teachings, they must be set in the context of his spiritual tradition, which began eight hundred years before Confucius in the time of Moses. Remember that the Golden Rule—"Do unto others as you would have them do unto you"—is an edict that we in the West associate with Jesus. Yet, more than five hundred years before Jesus, Confucius taught the same principle in the East, and hundreds of years before Confucius, Moses delivered the Ten Commandments on Mount Sinai. These ethical principles would bind people together, helping them to contain behavioral impulses that, if acted upon, would be dangerous for the community. "Judaism laid the groundwork for the social conscience that has been a hallmark of Western civilization."[31]

In the Jewish tradition, Jesus was a monotheist with unquestioning belief in Yahweh. This God of Judaism was unique at that time for several reasons. While other gods were amoral and unconcerned about humans, Yahweh commanded human adherence to a moral code and affirmed that his creation was "good." He became a personal God who gave meaning to suffering through social justice.

In the turmoil of the early part of the first millennium of the common era, Jesus gathered around him a group of twelve followers, representing the twelve tribes of Israel established by Moses: Simon, whom he renamed Peter; Simon's brother Andrew;

James and John, the sons of the Galilean fisherman Zebedee, whom he nicknamed the Sons of Thunder; Philip and Bartholomew; Matthew and Thomas; James and Thaddaeus; Simon the Zealot; and Judas Iscariot.

The presence of these last two disciples signaled to Jesus's countrymen, and later to the Roman authorities, that he was involved with serious resistance fighters, since Simon, as his name implies, was part of the historical armed struggle against Rome, and Judas was said to be one of the *sicarii*, or political assassins.[32] Why would Jesus associate with dangerous men, traitors (tax collectors and collaborators with the Romans), disreputable women, and the insane? When he was asked that question, he answered, "It isn't the healthy who need a doctor, but the sick."[33] His reputation spread, as a miracle-working healer and a compelling speaker, whose words drew the attention of huge crowds. Jesus's words seemed to add a richness of *compassion* to the Laws of Moses, teaching his people to heal their physical and emotional crises through traditional faith in the power of God. He said, "I come not to destroy the Law, but to fulfill it" and "Do not suppose that I have come to abolish the law and the prophets; I did not come to abolish, but to complete" (Matt. 5:17). He stated his dedication to the Jewish laws and his expectation that everyone in society would abide by them.

When Jesus said, "unless you show yourselves far better than the scribes [lawyers] and Pharisees, you can never enter the kingdom of Heaven," I believe he is referring to authorities in any age or culture who, as they try to interpret civil codes and become attached to their power, may apply laws unevenly and unjustly and fail to monitor their own behavior. How creative this declaration of Jesus's was, to suggest to the common person that he or she could be even more worthy in God's eyes than these educated, esteemed men who governed their daily lives!

Jesus has been viewed as an Essene, probably because John the Baptist may have been his cousin, and because he would have been influenced by these mystics to some degree. Since he obviously lived and worked in the world, he was not a member of one of the ascetic cults. It is more likely that he was closer to the Pharisees, if not a Pharisee himself.

For those singularly familiar with New Testament accounts of Jesus's conflicts with the Pharisees, there are two reasons why the idea of his affiliation with them should not be shocking: first, anyone who understands Jewish culture knows that heated intellectual argument reflects a passionate dedication to scholarship and its application to social life. Thunderous debates and strong assertions are routine exercises in secular and religious Jewish life. If Jesus were a Pharisee, there would have been frequent intense discussions of both the Written and Oral Law. Pointing out hypocrisy within his own group would be expected. Second, it is important to remember that the New Testament accounts of Jesus's ministry were written for non-Jews. Paul, the urbane, Hellenized Jew from Tarsus, also claimed to be a Pharisee. The Biblical texts state that he came to know Jesus's teachings through his conversion, which took place after the crucifixion. He was eager to separate Jesus from the Jewish world in order to draw Roman converts.[34] The means to this end was to place Jesus in complete opposition to his own culture. That deed led to the anti-Semitism that has lasted to this day.

I would like to think that Jesus, like Confucius, walked a middle road between the conservatives and the liberals of his day, one which he hoped would bring about the "kingdom of Heaven" on earth, a unification of his people in God's love. The many parables and metaphors Jesus used in his teaching tell us that he was prodding people to think abstractly and to take personal responsibility for their every action. He was encouraging the masses, the most disheartened Jews, not only to hear God's Law, but to remember His love as the central force in their lives. And Jesus did not talk down to them; he spoke to their highest capacity for understanding. In terms of ego states, he was not only speaking to the inner child, the internalized parent, or even the "adult," but to the Transcendent or Higher Self, the soul. And the people were "amazed."

Just as Confucius urged the Chinese to return to an earlier age of peace, order, and creativity, Jesus urged the Jews to reinstate in their own lives the earlier teachings of Moses and the prophets. In his well-known Sermon on the Mount, Jesus refers to the Mosaic Laws in Leviticus and extends them as though stretching his listeners' hearts to understand even more deeply the concepts of compassion and forgiveness.

He tells his fellow Jews not to murder, adding that they should not even hate; he tells them not to commit adultery, but also not to spend time in lust. He reminds them that "an eye for an eye" has been interpreted literally, but urges them not to obsess about revenge, and instead to practice "turning the other cheek" and allowing the evil to pass by.[35] He makes the "outrageous" assertion that not only should his kinsmen love their neighbors, but that they should love their enemies as well: "Therefore be merciful, just as your Father is merciful," and "There must be no limit to your goodness, as your heavenly Father's goodness knows no bounds."[36]

In a time so desperate and full of despair that many believed the end of the world was approaching, Jesus preached a radical pacifism. He encouraged a total focus on "righteousness" in preparation for the next world when souls return to God, the Source of their energy. Biblical scholar Stephen Mitchell says of Jesus, "By a righteous man, he means a man whose whole being is illuminated in God's light, and who therefore naturally acts with justice and compassion."[37]

Jesus's teaching about illumination is made more clear in the Gnostic Gospels, the early Christian writings thought by Harvard professor Elaine Pagels to predate the New Testament Gospels.[38] In the Gnostic (Greek for "intuitive knowledge") Gospels, Jesus sounds like the wisest of psychologists. And if we remember that "psyche" actually refers to the soul, then he is truly trying to instruct his followers on how to care for their souls. In the Gospel According to Thomas, for example, Jesus says, "If you bring forth what is within you, what you bring forth will save you. If you do not bring forth what is within you what you do not bring forth will destroy you."[39]

For these early Christians, as for the followers of Buddha, ignorance was as much a sin, or mistake, as other misconduct because self-ignorance was seen as self-destructive. Jesus encouraged self-awareness in many ways. He warns that "if one does not understand how the fire came to be, he will burn in it…" and the unconscious person is likened to "…a loose horse which has no rider. For this [one] needed the rider, which is reason…before everything else…know yourself."[40] As Jesus said in Luke, "The kingdom of God is within you." The gnostic Christians taught that liberation would come, not because of historical events, but because of self-discovery, internal transformation: "When you come to know yourselves, then you will be known, and you will realize that you are the sons of the living Father. But if you will not know yourselves, then you dwell in poverty, and it is you who are that poverty."[41]

We come to acceptance of who we are by acknowledging where we are in our grieving and growing, by learning to be aware of our attitudes and our feelings, and by being cognizant of where we tend to get stuck in our resistance and defenses. As Stephen Mitchell says in *The Gospel According to Jesus,* "The first step in becoming perfect is to accept your imperfection, just as the first step in becoming merciful is to treat yourself with mercy."[42]

Jesus seemed to understand how difficult this grief, growth, creativity and self-renewal process truly is when he said, "Let him who seeks continue seeking until he finds. When he finds, he will become troubled. When he becomes troubled, he will be astonished, and he will rule over all things."[43] Anyone who has faced a crisis head on can never forget how painful this learning is. When Jesus says that through this process we will "rule over all things," I believe he's designating all of the dysfunctional defenses arising from our fear.

The compassion Jesus extends through the Beatitudes suggests to me that, here again, he is recognizing how painful all of our grief is: "Blessed are the poor in spirit…Blessed are the sorrowful…Blessed are the gentle…Blessed are those who hunger and thirst to see right prevail…Blessed are those who show mercy…Blessed are those whose hearts are pure…Blessed are the peacemakers…Blessed are those who are persecuted…" He tells us, "The kingdom of Heaven is theirs."[44]

The history of humankind, the history of culture and religion, is a history of crisis and of grief. The tradition in which Jesus was nurtured taught the love of God through prayer, just action, and organized conflict resolution. The contribution of the Jewish people is twofold: (1) an example of insistent survival through faith, and (2) the illumination of the One within, the "internalized God."[45]

A third contribution of Judaism is the tradition's emphasis on education. Great value is placed on learning because study is viewed as one of the three forms of prayer. The other two forms of prayer are the articulation of hopes and aspirations, and doing good deeds.[46]

As the curtains close on this millennium, we must find ways to bring back and integrate various ancient traditions of peace through ethical teachings. The pacifism of the early Christians was quite soon disregarded. "When Christianity became the official religion of the Roman Empire in the fourth century, the doctrine of absolute pacifism, already receding, was pushed far into the background."[47] We must bring to the foreground the essential nature of Jesus's teachings: that during times of change, it is time to look to the internalized God, the God within, the Light that guides us to the other side of grief, to acceptance and peace.

This inner Light, traditionally viewed by Judeo-Christian-Islamic cultures as God and by Buddhists as Mind,[48] was seen by Jesus as both God and Mind, as we learn from the Gnostic Gospels. In the Dialogue of the Savior, Jesus says, "the lamp of the body is the mind,"[49] and "whoever has known himself has seen pure light."[50] In Matthew, Jesus urges his listeners to "Let your light shine." He says in the Gospel of Thomas, "There is light within a man of light, and it lights up the whole world. If he does not shine, he is darkness."[51] Jesus does not say, "he is in darkness," but that he *is* darkness. Jesus's words confront us with choice; that we must choose the light of God and life, or the darkness of ignorance and death. I do not mean death literally, but the death of the human soul.

Thich Nhat Hanh, the Vietnamese monk nominated by Dr. Martin Luther King Jr. for the Nobel Peace Prize, has written twenty-five books. In *Living Buddha, Living Christ,* he finds common ground in all spiritual traditions through the concept of the Holy Spirit. "All of us have the seed of the Holy Spirit in us, the capacity of healing, transforming, and loving." He reminds us that "the very word 'spirit' means 'breath,' and to breathe means to live." For those of us who need reassurance that this Spirit is not patriarchal, we're told that the Spirit of God has always been feminine.[52]

Sophia, the name of Wisdom and the feminine aspect of God in the Old Testament and the Apocrypha (Wisdom of Solomon), is recognized in depth by Carl Jung in his 1958 monograph, "Answer to Job."[53] Sophia describes herself in the following way:

> *I came out of the mouth of the most High,*
> *and covered the earth as a cloud.*
> *I dwelt in high places,*
> *and my throne is in a cloudy pillar.*
> *I alone encompassed the circuit of heaven,*
> *and walked in the bottom of the deep.*
> *I had power over the waves of the sea,*
> *and over all the earth,*
> *and over every people and nation.*[54]

Wisdom, Sophia, is seen as "the breath of the power of God," and "the brightness of the everlasting light."[55] I believe that we are all being called to recognize our own sacred internal light.

Sculptor Michael Naranjo

Cry and live.

— Michael Naranjo

How is it possible to be blind and be an artist who uses knives, power tools, and other implements for carving wood and stone, and making models for bronze statues? Santa Clara Pueblo

Indian Michael Naranjo defied the impossible. He was driven by an internal light to create and maintain the beauty and spirit of the gentle world he knew before Vietnam.

In 1968, Michael was with the Ninth Infantry in the Mekong Delta. On Christmas Day, the old French fort where they were housed was hit by mortar fire. A week later they were shelled again. Michael's squad was sent out and dropped off by helicopters to find and destroy the enemy mortars.

"We were in a rice field when the Viet Cong opened fire and six guys were killed immediately. In the movies they call them 'men,' but it's boys who fight wars. Babies, really. Several of us had run off to the right, into the jungle where some of the gunfire was coming from. A medic had just been shot trying to get to two of the guys. I'd dropped to my belly two or three times. Every time we stood, someone was shot. I crawled as far as I could and took off my pack. I took out two grenades and threw one. When I looked up, only a few yards away I could see a Viet Cong soldier in a 'spider hole.' I fired, then let go of my rifle with my right hand to reach for another grenade. My sergeant yelled, but I couldn't hear what he was trying to say. He'd seen another VC throw a grenade. It rolled right into my right hand. I turned to my right to look as I began to throw it, and it went off.

"After the blast, I was suspended in space and time. I wasn't sure if I was dead or not. If not, I was waiting to die and see what that would be like. My one thought was, 'Oh, God, don't let it be too hard on my parents.' As I waited to die, all I could see was a red dot with a thin red line going clockwise around it. Then I heard my friend say, 'Baby, are you okay?' I knew I was alive. At that moment I knew I wanted to live. I made the choice. 'Just get me out of here,' I told him. Then I tried to stand up and fell over backwards into the mud.

"I must have been a horrible sight, bleeding everywhere, one eye enucleated, my right arm and hand mangled. Shrapnel was in my face and my body. My friend rolled me onto a poncho and dragged me to a clearing where the medevac copters were coming in behind several gunships. They had to make several passes before they could drop down, and even then they could only hover for a few minutes while four men flung me up and into the helicopter. I remember talking to the medevac team, asking them questions, afraid to stop talking for fear that if I stopped talking, I'd lose consciousness and die. If I talked, I knew I was alive, I was in this world. Then someone gave me a shot and said, 'You're going out now,' and I was 'out' for about two days.

"When I woke, I heard Vietnamese, so I thought I'd been captured. But then I realized I was in an American hospital. Then I was taken to a hospital in Japan. There were rows and rows of us in a large space like a gymnasium. On one side of me was a man who had lost his ears and was deaf. On the other side was a man who did nothing but babble. He was brain-injured and had lost his mind. I had my mind and I had one good hand, so I was in great shape. I came to appreciate what I did have, rather than what I didn't have."

Michael Naranjo has a deep appreciation for the healing process, for the slowly evolving readiness to reach a true acceptance of frightening life reversals. At first, like the Biblical Job, it appeared as though he was completely accepting of his dreadful physical loss. And yet, "extreme denial of the situation is imperative, because if you had to deal with the extreme emotions at that time, you couldn't survive," Michael told me. "You'd be overwhelmed and unable to cope."

Anger came in the form of frustration at having to learn new ways to do "everything" now that he was completely sightless, and at the unfairness of "being blind when the fly buzzing around me in the hospital could see. Rabbits and other animals can see, I thought, but I can't. I cried a lot."

Obsession came in the form of repetitive dreams of running in the jungle and being shot, getting up and running again and being shot down again.

Depression shifted forms like vapor assuming ghostly shapes, one day tears and self-pity, another, self-hate from remembering certain actions during the war. "I noticed the day I became what I had been trained to be, detached and cold. I walked into a thatched hut looking for Viet Cong. There was a very old man with long white hair sitting with a pot of tea. He smiled at me and offered me tea. I had the barrel of my M16 pointing at him. I simply pointed my rifle to the tea and to his mouth, indicating, 'You drink.' He did, and I calmly and coldly walked away, feeling so sad and thinking, 'What's happened to me? I've lost the innocence of common decency.'"

The energy of his grieving feelings gave Michael the will to live and propelled him through his hospital stays in Japan and Denver and at the Veterans' School for the Blind in Palo Alto, California. Beginning in Japan, he was so bored and restless, he asked a volunteer for some clay. He immediately began making small figures with his left hand, often doing this in the middle of the night. In Denver, he once was so absorbed by his creations that he refused to leave his room. "The doctor had to come and chew me out, and then I got my cane and went off to therapy."

The defining moment of declaring his intention to be a sculptor again, just as he had been before the war, came in Palo Alto, after he had been informed that such an aim was completely unrealistic.

"The VA called it a 'Workshop,' but I called it, 'The Basement.' I was sent there to learn a skill. I found the place I was to go to, a room where I sat and was instructed on how to make a leather wallet. I laced the leather strings through the holes for about three inches and then told the instructor, 'I can't do this. I'm not going to make wallets.'"

"What do you want to do?" he asked me.

"I want to do woodworking."

"Well, you can't do that, and besides, if we let you do that, the next person who comes here may decide that they don't want to do this either."

"I'm sorry, but that's your problem," I told him. He said he'd have to go talk to his supervisor. When he returned, he said, "You can go to the next workshop area."

"When I got there, I was shown a loom and was handed cloth and told that I could weave a rug of all one color or I could weave one with a stripe. I said I would not weave a rug. I wanted to do woodworking. The instructor said he'd have to talk to his supervisor. When he returned, he said I could go to the wood-working area.

"When I got there, they showed me around and gave me two pieces of lumber. They said the first thing I would make would be a bench. I told them I didn't want to make a bench. On the table, I had felt a smooth piece of carving out of walnut, like a bowl. It felt so good, so soft. I wanted a piece of wood like that. So I was given one and I worked on a bear. I didn't get too far, but it was a beginning.

"I had always been a sculptor. My mother was a potter, and I grew up fashioning clay figures while she worked, first at Santa Clara, then at Taos Pueblo where we moved when I was nine. My father was a Baptist minister and a skilled carpenter. He built the first Protestant church in any pueblo."

"So, you were working as a sculptor before the war," I stated.

"Yes, but not with the clear focus and motivation that I later developed. I was raised with the expectation of attending college. Most of my nine brothers and sisters completed college and some are professionals, but I couldn't tolerate that structure. I attended Highlands University for awhile, and even the Institute of American Indian Art in Santa Fe, taking drawing, design, and sculpture. I'd end up back home, though, where I could be outdoors. As an adolescent, I spent summers working on a ranch owned by family friends."

Michael told me about his ongoing love for the Taos mountains, the forest images that filled his eyes as a boy, the fishing trips that resulted in pockets filled with tiny, wriggling cutthroat trout. "Not too long ago, I went for a hike in the mountains with a friend. It was a lovely day and my friend could see, but I was the man who knew the way," he said.

"Back there, I would hunt and fish in the mountains as I had since I was a child with my older brother, Tito, my best friend. Tito is my idol, my model for unconditional love. My parents were absorbed with work and family, but Tito was always there, ready to love me no matter what. We've never argued. He simply affirms me."

Michael Naranjo affirms life through his art and through his love for his family, his wife, Laurie, and their two daughters. His home, north of Santa Fe, feels like a place of peace. Being with Michael gives one the sense of being with a holy man, a man who reveres and accepts every aspect of life. His sculptures, with their gleaming bronze or alabaster surfaces, appear to be moving through every room of the house—an eagle being released to fly; a "Spirit Maiden" dancing in graceful motion, holding feathers in her hands; Grey Fox, from Taos Pueblo, skillfully performing the Hoop Dance; a nude female figure, "Joy," extending both hands upward as though greeting the morning sun. Both the front and back yards of the adobe home designed by Michael and Laurie have welcoming fountains with large bronze female figures. There is "Spirit Mother," with her digging stick for medicinal herbs and water flowing out of her pottery bowl, and a mother pouring water over the head of her little boy sitting below her in a pond.

"Disability is destroyed by doing something you love, something you're excited about," says Michael. "I forget that I'm blind until I run into a wall. Of course it's a challenge. Life is a challenge, a game. If you accept it, though, it's a gift and the inspiration and the dreams you have can come true.

"I had a dream—I often have colorful, vivid dreams—a dream that I could see and touch Michelangelo's sculptures. Not too long after that, I was invited to Rome to have an audience with the Pope. Following the Papal audience, I was taken to a chapel and allowed to examine the Moses. I crawled all over him for about a half hour, and for days after I would have flashes of feeling the softness of that flesh. Two years later, I went back to Italy and was allowed to see the David. On top of scaffolding, I felt the beauty of the eyes, the tear ducts hiding in the corners, the pupils like hearts. I cried. My dream had come true. I felt the lips, so soft you could feel the heart beating and pumping blood to them…the veins in his neck, the tension of the hands. It was amazing to feel the flesh and feelings of a man eighteen feet tall.

"Afterward, I had a new sense of stone. I knew there was life and warmth in these pieces. I had new life in my hands. I could see twice as much."

Each of us knows the way to acceptance of life just the way that it is and just the way that it is not. "Right now is what we make of it," Michael states. "What we put out there is what we get back. But sometimes we simply can't understand our suffering." Using the sculptor's metaphor, he says, "We just have to keep chipping away and feeling, finding what's inside. Love makes the difference. What you love and nourish gets better. We get better and better at creating."

Michael's exhibitions, awards and honors are vast. His sculpture is found in many collections, including those of The Vatican in Rome and The White House in Washington, D.C.

"My blindness is a gift," he insists. "It has given me a new way of looking at life."

Accepting Miracles

The world of spirit is not closed, your consciousness is closed...

— Goethe

Michael Naranjo's work as a blind sculptor could be considered a miracle. At the very least, he proves that creativity can emerge from the worst crisis. When we affirm life through transformation, our faith can manifest miracles even when we are unaware of them.

Once a man told his minister he didn't believe in miracles because when he was lost in the Arctic, he prayed for God to save him and He didn't come. "How did you live to tell about this?" asked the minister.

"Well, some Eskimo came along and took me back to town." Without conscious awareness, we will be ignorant of the many miracles in our lives.

My sister, Judy, with whom I'm extremely close, has four daughters and five grandsons. One day she called me in a state of shock to tell me that Lucas, her five-year-old grandson, had been run over by the back wheels of a truck. I said I would come immediately. The first miracle was that Lucas was alive. He had five broken ribs and both lungs were collapsed. His heart was bruised and his liver was lacerated. He was in intensive care at San Diego Children's Hospital; the doctors were guarded in their prognosis.

Upon arrival, Lucas had immediately been placed in an induced coma so that he could not move. He was in a coma, attached to a life-support system, for six days. There were several prayer groups praying for him regularly and, except for times when medical personnel asked the family to leave his bedside, there was always someone with him. When we weren't with him, we were camped in the intensive care unit waiting room.

My sister married into a large Italian family and Lucas's mother married into a large French family, so the waiting room looked like a Gypsy camp, colorful, filled with food, and loud, even when some were in tears. At one point, when everyone was particularly noisy in lamenting this terrible event, my niece Gayle yelled, "Shut up! Everyone just shut up! Lucas is fine. He's just fine in this coma."

I looked at her, and in the silence that followed her directive, asked, "Do you know something we should know?"

She answered, "Yes." Ten years earlier, Gayle had been in an accident that left her in a coma for several weeks. Gayle, too, was never left alone in the hospital, day or night. Family members took turns talking to her and massaging her feet and hands.

"Gayle, you've never talked about your coma or the hospital experience," I said.

"I've never talked about it with anyone. But you all need to know that I just know Lucas is having an important experience. During my coma, I floated outside of my body sometimes, and other times I had truly amazing travels. I saw God, and I saw Satan."

"What do you mean? What was that like?" I asked on behalf of everyone in the room.

"Like everybody says, God was Light. Satan was darkness. Somehow I knew that I was being exposed to both sides of my spiritual nature so that I could make a choice. I didn't like the feel of the darkness, so I chose the light."

"Did you choose to come back and be in your body?"

"Yes, I was able to choose. I didn't want to come back, though. Being in spirit alone was so peaceful, but I knew the family could not let me go, and I knew I had more work to do in this lifetime."

"Can you tell us what work you needed to do?"

"I'm not sure of the full implications yet, but before the accident I had been praying for months, asking God to change my life. I don't know if you remember my boyfriend at the time, but he was involved with drugs and it really scared me. I couldn't seem to break it off with him. I hated my life."

"Well, I guess God answered your prayer with a big whack in the head!" I laughed. All of us laughed together with such relief, such a release of built-up tension.

"You're right," Gayle said, giggling. "The accident really was an answer to my prayers because it turned my life around. And the spiritual experience was a big bonus. Remember what I'm telling you. Lucas is fine. He's safe. He's being looked after."

That Lucas lived is the first miracle; that he healed so quickly is another. As far as I'm concerned modern medicine's incredible life-saving technology is another miracle. We should be thankful for every "Eskimo." It wasn't until many weeks after Lucas gained consciousness that the medical staff discovered he'd also had a head injury that affected the optic nerve. For many months, Lucas only had partial vision. Now that, too, has healed.

The following year, I enjoyed sitting next to Lucas at his Aunt Gayle's wedding. As we waited for the procession to begin, I asked Lucas how he felt about the Catholic school he was attending. He told me it was all right, but that he sometimes felt annoyed at being told how to think about God. "Nobody can tell anybody else what to think about God," he declared.

"I certainly agree with you," I answered. "Can you tell me what you think about God?"

"No. I can't put it into words."

"What about angels? Do you believe they exist?"

"Oh, I know they exist!" he said, as if such a question shouldn't even be raised. "They're everywhere!"

I've come to share Lucas' belief that angels are everywhere. I also believe that "God is our immediate mirror: what we give, we receive, as we judge, we are judged, when we forgive, we are forgiven."[56] And I think our behavior is being reflected more and more quickly because of our collective need at this time in history to come together as a true Family.

One winter night, I stopped for gas during a windy rainstorm. It was about 10:30 and I was exhausted; it had been a very long workday followed by an evening meeting. As I returned to my car after paying the attendant, a young man stopped me and asked if I had jumper cables. Two men had already refused him, he said, but he had to get to his night job and he knew his car would start if he had cables. He really needed my help.

I did have jumper cables, but I instantly considered saying I didn't. I was wearing only a light jacket and it was freezing. Knowing I would get soaked in the process, I pulled my car around to where he needed it to be, got out the cables and helped him start his car. We were both drenched when we were done. As I drove home shivering, I berated myself for being such a sucker. "You'll just never learn how to say 'No,' will you?" I castigated myself. "Now you'll probably catch pneumonia."

The next morning, my daughter called me at work. "Mom, you won't believe what happened to me this morning. It was 6:45 and I had a flat tire on the way to school! I knew I couldn't change it in this storm, and I knew I'd be late to school. I was frantic, when suddenly this really nice young man came over to me—I don't even know where he came from—and offered to fix my tire. And he did it so quickly that I wasn't even late. Can you believe that?"

"Yes, I can!" I told her. As the Jerusalem Bible says, "She [Wisdom] deploys her strength from one end of the earth to the other, ordering all things for good" (Wis. 8:1).

Accepting Responsibility

Freedom is "the will to be responsible to ourselves."
— Nietzsche

I believe that miracles happen to make us more aware of our wholeness, our connectedness to every part of ourselves and every part of the world. It is as we learn to grieve and grow our acceptance of each event in our lives that we become more compassionate, responsible, and wise. It may sound paradoxical, but when we are most connected to others, we are actually the most free. We are free from fear.

Roger Fisher, who teaches negotiation at Harvard Law School, told a story during one of his talks that highlights the idea that we are all interdependent and therefore responsible to one another for our very lives.[57]

During a weather-reconnaissance mission during World War II, the pilot began to test one of the new engines just installed in a B-17. At about fourteen thousand feet, he feathered two engines, then a third, leaving only the new engine running. The pilot then became so enthusiastic that he turned off the single remaining engine. The plane floated for several seconds as the crew held their breaths. He then pushed the button to restart the engine and nothing happened. He frantically pushed several buttons, but it quickly became apparent that there was no way to restart the engines. As the crew began buckling on their parachutes, the co-pilot laughed and said to his pilot, "Boy, have *you* got a problem!"

The co-pilot's humorous comment reveals how pointless it is to blame people, even ourselves, in a crisis situation. When we have more time than in the plane scenario, it's easier to fall into our defenses of denial, anger, obsession, and depression. And yet the creative response to every situation is the life-affirming one. The creative expression of that co-pilot was his acceptance of the reality of the moment and his willingness to join his friends in a jump to freedom. We are all on this plane ride together. Accepting responsibility for our share of problems, both personal and global, might enable us to successfully "light the lamp" of the world.

.◡ ◡.

Job had to turn on the light of insight in order to get to the final stage of his grief, acceptance, and the blessing of inner peace. First, he had to accept the reality of his life change, as painful as it was. What occurs is a simple fact. Second, he had to accept responsibility for recreating a new life, a stronger, more vivid expression of his interests, values, and dreams. Acceptance means recognizing that life events provide meaningful growth. It also means forgiving ourselves for not being able to control these events.[58] Finally, it means giving thanks for our responsiveness to life change, because that's how we find our true creativity.

Job was so resistant to accepting the nature of the changes in his life that he finally elicited God's longest speech in the entire Bible! God's answer to Job is a declaration of the power, beauty, elegance, and above all else, the chaos and wildness contained in the balance of creation. Job's paradigm paralysis shifted and opened to powerful possibilities in response to the Creation story. Job was healed by being reminded of the goodness and naturalness of the wild world. God spoke of bringing into being the earth, the sea, the heavens, the animals, the neutrality of life and death, and the boundaries and balance in the world. Then the Source of all creation emphasized the significance of being "utterly fearless" (Job 41:33) in the face of these facts.

When he overcame his fear, Job accepted himself in the present, in this world, in relation to the natural order of things. His old paradigm, or world view, involved controlling nature, being afraid of natural events, and holding to moral and legal paradigms—including blaming himself, others, and even God—in the face of formidable life change.

God's powerful poetry allowed Job to see himself anew, to be baptized and made whole by immersion in the awesomeness of all life. The "tonic of wildness," as Thoreau suggested, makes us aware that nothing in nature need be controlled, changed, or rearranged. We need only to become aware of the sacredness of every aspect of life. We must accept the truth that wildness, wilderness, chaos, and peace are all a part of the world order.[59]

Following the Creation speech from the whirlwind, we're told that God was angry with Job's friends for not speaking of God "as they ought." Job was reminded, as we all must be, that insight or revelation is not enough to transform us. We must put our "right thoughts" into action. Job had to set aside his defensive behaviors, angry obsessions, and depressive rationalizations, those "old friends" that limited his life. He then had to demonstrate successful maturation by interceding for others, teaching the grace he had just learned. It was only after giving back in this way that Job's fortunes were restored.

Acceptance, a seemingly passive term, describes a powerful process of dismantling defenses and letting go of our egos. Then we can be reborn into an integrated wholeness where we recognize our uniqueness as well as our connection with all of Life. Of this process, physicist Fred Alan Wolf says, "...having broken through the illusions that imprison our souls, we perceive a shining aura of divinity wherever we go and in whatever we do."[60]

When Job "saw the light," he recognized the God-in-him, the wisdom and integrity that enabled him to create a higher morality (including his daughters in his inheritance) and to create and accept greater abundance in his life (his possessions increased twofold and he lived another one hundred and forty years). When we open our hearts to life change, we accept and acknowledge our integrity, our creativity, our success. And then, like Job, we finally achieve inner peace.

.⁀ ‿·

Earth is a planet of manifestation. Shining your light means giving expression to your creativity.
— Sandra Ingerman, *A Fall to Grace*

Daily Creative Discipline
(Acceptance: Embracing Success)

1. Ask yourself: **What is my crisis? Choose** at least one thing you are learning from being confronted with this change. **Accept** that whatever is happening right now is for your highest good and your long-term **growth**.

2. Ask: **What is my creative response** to this life change? **How well do I grieve? Where do I tend to get stuck** in my grief? Then think about ways you can nurture your **self-expression.** Make a list of seven ways to creatively respond to a particular life change.

3. Develop many ways of **getting to acceptance** or "Getting to Yes" about the facts of crises and life change. Do two things every day that help you **float above the turmoil** like steam floating up off boiling water. Confucius meditated, Jesus prayed, resilient adults demonstrate faith and take positive action.

4. **Exercise your choice** to live in complete awareness, open to Divine guidance. **Affirm your faith** that you are on earth to accomplish something very important. You have a life purpose—to raise healthy children, to be a blessing to your community, to love someone through their crises, to gain wisdom. **Don't miss the miracles** that happen to guide you along your way.

5. **Align your life with love.** Practice the three ways to pray: communication with God, study, and right action. Do one good deed every day and notice your feelings of self-love, pride, and joy. Remember that the stage of acceptance means that you have survived the ups and downs of change—now it's time to **celebrate!** You now live successfully as you love successfully.

6.   Michael Naranjo suggests this creative exercise: With clay, make a representation of **something that feels good.** Work with it until it feels right, then tell yourself, 'I made it. I like it. **It's perfect. It gives me happiness.**' And that's it."

Chapter Eight

Transcendence: Creating Peace, Purpose, and Love

The only power that can effect transformations of the order we have described is love.

— Huston Smith

Creating Peace

I've always loved the sea. Being a child in San Diego in the 1940s was like being Eve before the fall. There was the war, but it was far away, and even newsreels, ration books, and black shades on our windows didn't make it real for me. To me and my sister, the war brought the magic of margarine: we squeezed a clear plastic container until the cherry-red coloring seed popped and was spread effortfully throughout the mass, resulting in something that looked like butter and almost tasted like it. The war meant feeding the chickens so that we could have eggs and tending the miniature vegetable garden alongside the chicken pen. The war also meant greater independence, as my mother and the other women in the neighborhood went to work in the aircraft factories. While we children were responsible for cooking and cleaning, we also had lots of free time, especially in the summers. Bicycling or taking the bus together to the beach brought us a sense of community. Playing, reading, talking, or just staring at the ocean between swims was our group meditation.

The sea was my solitude. I knew there were interesting creatures beneath the water, and good-tasting ones, too. My best friend's older brother would bring home abalones from La Jolla, and we would remove the meat, pound it hard with a mallet, dip it in bread crumbs, and fry abalone for dinner.

It wasn't until many years later, when I began snorkeling in Hawaii, that I discovered how beautiful many sea creatures are, so beautiful that sometimes I'd get so excited I would gasp and breathe in water instead of air through my snorkel.

Undersea viewing became a passion of mine, so much so that I created the necessity for excursions to Grand Cayman, the Bahamas, Tahiti and Bora Bora, Bali, and the Great Barrier Reef. The most fascinating and exquisitely beautiful sea animals I have seen are called nudibranchs, and although they are found throughout the Pacific and Indian Oceans, they are most abundant on the Great Barrier Reef, off the eastern coast of Australia. I first read about them in a *National Geographic* magazine in the early 1980s. I finally saw them with my own eyes, just some of the more than four hundred species present, while snorkeling at the Great Barrier Reef in 1995.

The nudibranchs ("naked lungs") are classified as mollusks. I couldn't imagine why until I learned that they are actually shell-less snails, or sea slugs. While most mollusks' evolution involved changing the shape and color of their shells, the nudibranchs "branched out" in a bold way. They left their shells altogether for the freedom of experimenting with exotic shapes and vivid colors. It is astounding to come upon these creatures, with names like "Spanish Dancer," waving red and pink mantles like a bullfighter's cape, or the "Blue Dragon," stationary when I saw it, but with its many deep-to pale-blue projections undulating around its variegated blue-and-gold body. Another nudibranch is bright white bordered with gold; still another is translucent yellow with black spots.

Their freedom is as astounding as their beauty. These creatures eat and internalize tiny single-celled plants, algae, which then photosynthesize nutrients for them. Imagine being able to manufacture your own food supply while floating on a sunny reef! Not only have they created solar panels to grow their own food, they have also internalized a method of protection. They are able to feed on organisms that bear stinging cells, coating them with mucous so they are not harmed by the poison. These stinging cells end up inside the frilly fronds of the nudibranchs, becoming weapons to protect them from predators.

We too can leave our shells behind. The psychological defenses that protect us while we are growing up restrict our growth and our beauty once we are adults. The denial of disavowed grief, the anger that is projected from hurt, the obsession that controls from fear, and the depression that paralyzes us into the past, must all be shed in order to allow for the freedom of growth. We can learn to grow past and through, and float above life crises, internalizing the learning and transforming the energy of disappointment and fear into creative activities that confirm life. Just as the war brought independence and purpose to me as a child, the crisis I experienced of being sued as an adult prepared me to help many others move out of deep, sometimes suicidal, grief over adversarial entanglements. My experiences with death enabled me to better aid others who face profound loss.

Just like the nudibranch, everyone has all the resources needed to self-create, to give voice to thoughts and emotions, and grow freedom, complete freedom from fear. As artist Paul Klee said, "Shed your shell; try for a moment to think of yourself as God."

Artist Agnes Martin

I am hand in hand with contentment on my own doorstep.

— Agnes Martin

Modern abstract painter Agnes Martin has grown contentment and wisdom during her eighty-six years of life. Her small, simple apartment in Taos, New Mexico, is a short walk from her studio, where she still paints every day. Her work has been compared to Mondrian's, Kandinsky's, and Klee's. It is shown at the Guggenheim and the Metropolitan Museum of Modern Art in New York. Her paintings are also on permanent exhibit at the Harwood Museum in Taos. Although highly esteemed, Agnes Martin is completely unconcerned with what others think about her art. She earned a master's degree from Columbia University, but when I asked who influenced her work, she answered, "I don't believe in influence." Agnes Martin believes in the individual's own Inspiration, with a capital *I*.

"When I first began painting," she told me, "I painted grass and flowers and Indians, but I didn't like my work. I painted for twenty years without liking my work. Then I had an inspiration that was completely abstract, an inspiration of innocence, beyond nature. From then on, I liked my work. It is completely abstract."

Although she refers to her paintings as being "beyond nature," her prose and poetry shimmer with natural images:

> *The underside of the leaf*
> *cool in shadow*
> *Sublimely unemphatic*
> *Smiling of innocence*
> *The frailest stems*
> *Quivering in light*
> *Bend and break*
> *In silence.*
>
> *This poem like the paintings*
> *is not really about nature*
> *It is not what is seen*
> *It is what is known*
> *forever in the mind.[1]*

and,

> *The reflection of a sunset speaks loudly of days.*

Although she writes, "We are in the midst of reality responding with joy," seeing her work and meeting Agnes Martin is much more evocative of her references to another kind of reality, the "transcendent response," as she calls it, the bliss of being "free from and unrelated to the concrete environment."

How did this woman come to achieve "transcendent living?" Could it be her willingness to persevere with her self-expression until she felt pleased? "I thought," she said, "that people would not consider my abstract work to be art. I was surprised that all of my shows sold out. In the 1960s, I had a show at the Smithsonian with some others and we were called 'minimalists,' and the art was called 'impersonal.' My art is not impersonal; it's emotional."

I can see how one might confuse her minimal expression of form on canvas and her minimal expression of emotion in conversation with being dispassionate and indifferent. But, in truth, she is self-contained, aware of her own beliefs and, as one critic summed it up, "a meditative painter."

Agnes Martin's "meditations" are on large canvases, six feet by six feet. "Recently I've had to go to five by five, because I can't handle the larger ones any longer." The pale, translucent colors of white, yellow, or blue sometimes have repetitive forms, lines, or grids of pencil on oil, or ink or watercolor on paper. Agnes said that she originated the use of the grid. She feels there is power in repetition and that straight lines take her beyond the more curved designs of nature.

Agnes told me that she meditated for a number of years when she was younger, and that she read a great deal about Hinduism and Buddhism. These Asian traditions of thought seem to be reflected in the style of her work and in her simple but erudite philosophical statements.

Work is what is possible for you according to your awareness of life.

You have to hold your mind still in order to hear inspiration clearly.

No suffering is unnecessary; all of it is only enlightening.

You may as well go ahead with as little resistance as possible and eat everything on your plate.

Startling moments of awareness are never forgotten.

Inspiration and life are equivalent. Self-expression is inevitable.

Life is an adventure and adventures are difficult.

Happiness is self-sought. It is life.

Surrender to life.

Whether due to the spaciousness of the Canadian prairie where she was raised, the "non-authoritarianism" of her upbringing, or the breadth and depth of her self-education, Agnes Martin exemplifies someone who has dedicated her life to creativity: She has learned to grow her self-expression by creating according to her own definition—"follow inspiration." She notes that the word "inspire" means simply "to breathe," and she chooses to live simply, following one breath after the other, listening to Mind.

Agnes talked about her two life crises—having her heart broken in love and a period of time when she was literally starving. "Looking back, I would say I was as happy then as I am now. I was never unhappy. I have never been depressed. Then I had nothing, and now I have great wealth, but I feel no different."

I asked her what she did when she was starving. Didn't she become desperate? "I did nothing. I believe that people are kind. I came to live in this country because I think Americans are generous and easygoing. I knew I would be helped." What is her advice to those of us who occasionally feel hopeless in grief?

"You must go on in spite of disappointment and defeat. You must always have hope that you will reach inspiration, that you will get exactly what you want."

I asked Agnes what to do when we get stuck, in painting or in life. How do we "go on"? What is the transcendent response?

"Keep your mind open, free to be inspired. It's hard because our minds are so cluttered, but you can empty the mind in order to become aware of inspiration. I always say to Mind, 'What next?' and wait for the next inspiration."

Agnes Martin tells us that living and being creative is as simple as taking the next breath with awareness:

> *The world evolves due to changes that take place in*
> *   individuals...all living things.*
> *The world evolves due to a growing awareness in the lives*
> *   of all things and is expressed in their actions.*
> *The actions of all things are guided by a growing awareness*
> *   of life;*
> *We call it inspiration.*

How can we learn, as Agnes Martin has, to create inner peace? How can we be open to inspiration? We might begin by honoring the power of the mind. With a capital *M*, Mind suggests our connection with Divine Intelligence, unseen Guides, a Higher or Transcendent Self, or at the very least, a recognition that we have far greater capacities for overcoming and self-creation than we typically acknowledge. I believe we also have far greater capacities for peacefulness.

> *The all of all, reality, mind*
> *the process of destiny*
> *like the ocean full to the brim*
> *like a dignified journey with no trouble*
> *and no goal on and on*
> *Solitude*
>
> — Agnes Martin

Relaxation—Trance—Meditation—Prayer

What Agnes Martin calls "solitude" is what Dr. Herbert Benson at Harvard might call the "relaxation response," and Dr. Jon Kabat-Zinn at the University of Massachusetts Stress Clinic might call "meditation."[2] We might also refer to it as a natural, meditative "trance state." Every time we become completely absorbed in focused concentration, we are in a state of self-hypnosis, or trance. Since we in the western world are not raised with a tradition of meditating, recognizing how we regularly move in and out of trance during the day, just as we move in and out of dream states at night, can aid us in our practice of creating and maintaining inner peace.

To learn to recognize our trance states, we can make mental notes when we discover ourselves daydreaming. We can notice how we float off to some other time and place when driving back and forth to work, or during long car trips. By paying special attention to how our bodies feel when we're in this natural biorhythm of trance, we become open to the five responses described earlier: (1) relaxation, (2) time distortion, (3) suspension of critical thinking, (4) heightened imagery, and (5) associational flow. When we dedicate time to solitude through prayer, meditation, contemplation, or self-hypnosis, we are consciously facilitating the creation of inner and outer peace.

When a crisis comes into our lives, we react physiologically with stress, emotionally with feelings of grief, and mentally with fearful thoughts. In order to transform this negative energy into a creative transcendent response, we must learn how to self-calm, how to float in the deep pool of inner calmness that exists inside each and every one of us. Once we are there, each sequence follows easily: physiological and emotional relaxation, time falling away, the absence of judgment, helpful images, the flow of thoughts, or the absence of thoughts as we float in space. Nearly every *Aha!* or insight comes to my mind just before, during, or after my morning meditation.

The antidote to stress and strife is the relaxation response. The remedy for the tension of being defensive and resisting life is nonresistance. To practice nonresistance, we can adopt a prayerful attitude and a meditative mind-set. Integrating these approaches into our everyday lives can bring greater peace to both body and mind.

Professor Margaret Poloma identified four methods of prayer in her study of the practices and benefits of praying—colloquial, petitionary, ritualistic, and meditative.[3] In the colloquial form, we simply talk to God in our own words, expressing concerns, occurrences, or gratitude. When we petition God, we are asking for help with a specific problem, or healing for ourselves or others. The ritualistic form of prayer is reciting from memory a piece like the Lord's Prayer, the rosary, or a portion of the book of Psalms. Meditative prayer is the simple practice of stilling the mind.

"We need to expand our thoughts of what prayer might be and not just confine it to the idea of talking out loud to a male cosmic parent figure who prefers to be addressed in English," says physician and researcher Larry Dossey. "Silence is the language God speaks and everything else is a bad translation," states Father Dick Rice, who directs a spiritual center in St. Paul, Minnesota. There are many references to silence or stillness in the Bible. Possibly the most well-known in our culture is Psalm 46, verse 10, "Be still and know that I am God." When we choose to be still, we can know that we are in the presence of and connected to God, however we understand God—the "still small voice within," the "ground of all being," the Creator of all, the Source of all energy, Divine Intelligence, Great Spirit, Holy Spirit, Father, Mother, Oneness, Love, Life.

.ɔ ↩.

We are a noisy people. And because some of us respond more intensely to auditory stimulation than to visual imagery, stilling the mind and emotions with words, either chanted aloud or silently spoken, can serve as the "mental device" necessary to achieve the focused meditative or prayerful state. Any words or sounds can be used to gently keep bringing the mind back from chatter, obsession, and confusion, to silent peacefulness.

We also tend to be a lazy people. The path most traveled is the one that is familiar. In the early morning, returning to sleep would be more natural than meditating. Practice creating a new path in order to transcend crisis.

The following are suggestions for how to use daily *meditation* to move from crises to creativity.

1. Choose a quiet environment where you won't be inter-rupted. Try earplugs if there's a need to block out family or household sounds, or play "white noise," nature sounds, or New Age music in the background, sounds that won't engage your left-brain intellect by triggering associations.

2. Sit in a comfortable high-backed chair that provides good support. Close your eyes, or stare at something in the distance slightly above eye level, going into "soft focus," letting the image become blurred until you quite naturally allow the eyes to close.

3. Notice where your mind goes: through thoughts, images, blankness, sounds. Observe and enjoy this time of not needing to judge or act on any of your thoughts. The mind is open, receptive, and free to travel, also free to return to the present moment. Try using a word or sound repeatedly to gently bring your mind back to the center stage of focused awareness.

4. You may wish to go deeper into relaxation or use part of your meditation time for traditional prayer. Bring into your mind's eye the issue, the part of your body, the situation, the person or group. Place the image in a bubble of white light and ask God, in your own words, to send life energy, or

healing energy, and even a staff of angels to help the condition. "Send light and love."[4]

5.   If you need guidance, ask God, your Higher Mind, a guardian angel, or a spirit guide to please give you the feedback that you require to complete a project or to conduct yourself properly, in accordance with your values. Listen carefully to the creative input. I keep a pen and pad next to my chair in order to note whatever messages come to me.

6.   End your meditation with several affirmations. These statements can be powerful declarations of intention to transform automatic negative thoughts into positive beliefs. Affirmations also create a vision for accomplishment. They demonstrate faith that whatever resources are needed and whatever learning is required will be provided. Through this discipline, doubt and fear are transformed into the proof of love, which is inner peace.

Remember that every moment of your life can be lived from a prayerful, meditative mind. The Judeo-Christian-Buddhist-Islamic tradition tells us that structured meditation or prayer is only one way to pray. A second way is through service, recognizing that everything we do at work or in the home makes us servants of the God-Love energy force. Here, the word "pray" means "to bring about." When we serve others we help bring about God's kingdom of peace on earth. Every dirty diaper changed, every meal prepared, every project completed, every portion of time devoted to listening to another or to the inner voice that insists on solitude demonstrates a daily prayerful action that is a communication of peace.

Another traditional way to pray is through study and learning. Seeing the mind as a gift of Creation helps us recognize our responsibility to use it to capacity and to honor our achievements at every level. Respect every bit of new learning—mastering a new recipe, learning how to set the clock on the VCR, reading a book through to the end. Applaud all of your learning, knowing that you were designed to grow, learn, love and, in this way, transcend turmoil.

In Buddhism, the prayer that is comparable to the traditional Christian Lord's Prayer alludes to the achievement of inner peace in a most delightful way. It ends with, "...may all beings have a happy heart." When we have inner peace, we have a happy heart.

Creating Purpose

If art speaks clearly about something relevant to people's lives, it can change the way they perceive reality.
— Judy Chicago

While abstract artist Agnes Martin lives in solitude in order to create her "meditative paintings," Judy Chicago creates "participatory art" on a grand scale, flying from one city to the next, coordinating groups of artists, reviewing projects, presenting new ideas, creating her own art, giving lectures, fund-raising, and generally working fourteen-hour-plus days.

Trained in fine art, Judy used to spend long uninterrupted days in the quiet of her own studio, taking at least one hour for meditation or quiet time every morning. But all that changed in the summer of 1971 on a trip to Oregon, where she happened to see a small, hand-painted plate in an antique shop.

Soon she immersed herself in studying the art of china painting and learning about the women who were keeping this ancient art alive. She conceived an enormous project including hundreds of other artists, which would both consume and ignite her energy for the next decade. The resulting work, "The Dinner Party," is a multimedia installation of china painting, ceramics, textiles, needlework, aluminum and wood. The work forms a triangle forty-eight feet on each side, honoring thirty-nine women with place settings, and nine hundred and ninety-nine women on tiles. Judy

Chicago's staff of researchers and hundreds of volunteers helped her to highlight the achievements and historical contributions of women through the ages.

"I feel strongly about being a part of life, rather than separate from it," Judy Chicago wrote in her diary in May of 1973. Succeeding entries verify the grief she experienced through the years as she worked to complete the project: "I've hit some huge pocket of fear, insecurity, terror, something. It started after I told Lloyd that I was trying to create a masterpiece" (December 7, 1974); "...having terrible trouble—alone with floods of feelings which I don't want to feel but must. It is painting again and getting close to my center that is causing the trouble. It is bringing me into contact with layers and layers of longing, loss, fear, disappointment, anger...I don't want to go inside again, but I must—" (February 15, 1977).

The crisis that first propelled Judy to look into her deep "layers of loss" was the death of her father when she was thirteen. Her father was a lively, intelligent man who created a hub of political discussion and activity in their home. A union organizer, he was passionate about social issues. He was also innovative in his parenting, constantly concocting games and play experiences that taught Judy to enjoy life, to think of human values, and to expand her skills in math and logic. Possibly the most important message he gave her was that she could accomplish anything she chose to in life.

Because Judy's mother worked out of the home during the late 1930s and the 1940s, in an era when women were expected to stay home, Judy grew up with the role model of a woman working in the world of men. Even though her father could never relate to her artistic impulse, her parents enjoyed her expressions of intelligence and supported her desire to have art lessons at the Art Institute of Chicago.

During the communist scare and the resulting McCarthy congressional hearings, Judy's father was driven out of the union and threatened and harassed by the FBI. Although he began to work again as an insurance salesman, his health steadily declined until he died suddenly during a hospitalization for bleeding ulcers. Judy has no memory of events in the year following his death. Clearly, his loss informed her grief and growth cycles and her urge toward creativity, her self-expression, for the rest of her life.

At the age of twenty-three, married just one year, Judy suffered another experience of traumatic grief. Her husband, Jerry, was killed when his car plunged over a cliff and crashed. "I knew I was alone forever, that I could lose the people I loved anytime, any moment, and that the only thing I had in this life was myself...I realized that I must build my life on the basis of my own identity, my own work, my own needs, and the only way I could do that was through my art."[5] Judy's recent autobiography documents not only her struggle to find her own voice, but also her dedication to helping all women validate their creativity.

Long before her epic works, "The Dinner Party" and "The Birth Project,"[6] Judy was involved in teaching and encouraging women to create and show their art. In 1970, she originated a women's art class at Fresno State, which evolved into the study of numerous areas of expression, including performance art. She, along with her colleague Miriam Shapiro, put together the first West Coast file on women artists' work for the library at the California Institute of the Arts. In 1971, she developed the Feminist Art Program at the California Institute of the Arts. Two years later, she brought to fruition an exhibition space for women and a community art gallery, Womanspace.

Judy Chicago's passionate purpose was and continues to be having women's work taken seriously. She encourages women to "project emotion directly" and get "plugged into themselves and into their energy sources, an essential step in human and creative development." When we take ourselves seriously and make efforts to learn about our emotional responses to life changes and to oppression, we transform energy from the dark demons of defense to the light awareness of love for ourselves and for others.

Judy Chicago's sense of purpose encompasses recognizing the most basic elements of creativity—women's experiences around being female, giving birth and nurturing life. Judy noticed that not only were women's contributions to civilization overlooked in history books, but that even in the world of art, women's work was rated second to men's. Even more striking, there was a complete absence of birth images throughout the entire Western history of art.[7] During the 1980s, Judy worked to bring forth "The Birth Project," using creation myths and "the physical process of giving birth as a metaphor for the birth of the universe and of life itself."

As with "The Dinner Party," Judy joined efforts with many women across the country in order to create images of the birth experience using her drawings and paintings enhanced with batik, needlepoint, quilting, beading, embroidery, crochet, applique and smocking—the many traditional techniques of needlework used by women to clothe their families, decorate male leaders, and define cultural rituals. The twenty-eight exhibition units included in "The Birth Project" resulted in powerful images, as well as written histories and illustrations of maternity clothes, confinement, and the treatment of women during childbirth.

The passion that Judy Chicago has for learning and teaching through imagery is living proof of her persistent transformation of disappointment and would-be obstacles into creativity and transcendent living. Judy uses her emotions to fuel her work. In order to complete a recent project, it was imperative that she be in touch with her emotions in order to process grief. With her husband, photographer Donald Woodman, Judy took on an intense and emotionally draining collaborative piece of work, "The Holocaust Project: From Darkness Into Light,"[8] which required more than eight years to complete. The experience involved months of travel, research, and immersion into every aspect of the death-camp experience. At times, her discoveries left her "completely undone." At Treblinka, "during our entire stay...I just cried and cried." At Auschwitz, she wrote, "I feel my grasp on sanity faltering." She wondered how she could "find meaning in this world now that I see it clearly in all its horror?"

Periodically overcome by her grief, Judy experienced the depression which reflects compassion; the dark place that incubates our next stage of growth. In grief, she had no idea how or if she could make "art" from the Holocaust images. Only her outrage and pain pushed her on. A visit to Ebensee, Austria, showed her where prisoners were forced to build miles of tunnels in which to assemble weapons for the Nazis and where the inmates were worked to death, often within only three days. This information startled Judy and prompted a new reaction: She got drunk and had a nightmare about being imprisoned. The next day, she found herself irritable with her husband. "I just couldn't take any more horror. I began to see it everywhere…" Judy was experiencing symptoms of traumatic stress, which often affects those who witness or provide service to victims and survivors of physical or sadistic abuse.[9]

So why continue to look? Why didn't she close the door on this project and begin one with more hope, more "life"? By embracing and learning from all aspects of reality, both the dark and the light, we realize our power. It is from a balanced knowing that we find wisdom. We cannot grow in denial, stuck in the quicksand of disavowed grief. Judy Chicago's willingness to be aware of evil allowed her to grieve, incubate, and grow images that can teach others about the dangers of ignorance. The true significance of evil lies in the choice to live in the absence of light.

Judy Chicago chose to shine light on a "universal human experience of victimization." She wanted to bring to light the fact that in the twentieth century alone, more than sixty million people have died from genocidal action. Not only the six million in the Holocaust during World War II, but sixty million people around the world, have been killed. This century has been referred to as "the age of genocide."[10] Judy's purpose was to contribute to a "transformation of consciousness through art." Only by transforming darkness to light can we become aware, compassionate, and loving.

During the last of the eight years required to create "The Holocaust Project," both Judy's mother and her brother, her only sibling, died, and her husband's father died, catalyzing another cycle of deep grief and growth. "Art has made my life worth living," Judy wrote in her recent autobiography.[11]

"Resolutions for the Millennium," Judy Chicago's next creative project, will present a "vision of a different world." The series will show "images of a world transformed into a global community of caring people." A series of traditional proverbs provide images that "reinvigorate our working together as a human race." Judy hopes that her art will teach these values. I believe the poem she wrote at the end of "The Dinner Party" expresses most beautifully the purpose she feels in her life work. This poem was also sung during her wedding ceremony.

The Merger

And then all that has divided us will merge
And then compassion will be wedded to power
And then softness will come to a world that is harsh and unkind
And then both men and women will be gentle
And then both women and men will be strong
And then no person will be subject to another's will
And then all will be rich and free and varied
And then the greed of some will give way to the needs of many
And then all will share equally in the Earth's abundance
And then all will care for the sick and the weak and the old
And then all will nourish the young
And then all will cherish life's creatures
And then all will live in harmony with each other and the Earth
And then everywhere will be called Eden once again.

© 1979 by Judy Chicago

As the world embraces connectedness as a legitimate leadership force, women's natural leadership styles will become mainstream.
— Dorothy Cantor, Toni Bernay, *Women in Power*

Twenty-five women who were elected officials were interviewed by two UCLA psychologists to discover their "secrets of leadership." One question the researchers asked was, "How did you develop enough self-confidence to overcome the obstacles to women achieving political power?" The subjects could not relate to the question. The word "obstacles" puzzled them. They saw no obstacles, only the hard work and dedication necessary to reach their goals. Their minds were set on their purpose, on seeing the possibilities. The important message these women were given growing up was the same message Judy Chicago received, that they could do anything they chose to do! There were five aspects of their learning: (1)They could do anything (2) They had strong family support (3) They developed a sense of being competent (4) They could always see the possibilities (5) They learned how to use "creative aggression."[12]

In the context of the grief and growth and creativity cycles I've been referring to throughout this book, we can see that because these women were consistently helped to overcome crises while they were growing up, they never suffered "paradigm paralysis" or the temptation to live "lies of limitation." Because of their positive mind-set, they were never trapped in disappointment or grief. These women learned to channel their life energy to transform fear into a powerful sense of purpose.

One of my friends has joined the ranks of these "women in power." In 1994, Roberta Cooper Ramo, a native New Mexican, was elected the first women president of the American Bar Association. One of her first international tasks, as representative of this body of over 350,000 lawyers, was to lead a delegation to the United Nations Conference on the Status of Women in Beijing, China.

During her tenure, Roberta focused on the "issue of domestic violence, a problem from which no racial, religious, ethnic or economic group is immune." She also worked to ensure that legal services to the poor continue to be funded. Another goal was to "begin to educate people about the importance of the U.S. Constitution and the Bill of Rights and what the American legal system, with its independent bar and independent judiciary, really means."

Roberta's interest in politics may have been inherited. In her inaugural speech, she told a story about her grandmother, a pioneering homesteader in Wyoming, whose husband was active in Democratic politics. "One day, when Franklin D. Roosevelt was coming to town, her husband came home to change clothes and she asked him where he was going. 'I'm going to meet the president,' he said. My grandmother said she wanted to go to the meeting, too. 'It's only for men,' he told her. 'Not anymore,' my grandmother replied."

Roberta's ability to say "not anymore" was nurtured and supported by her family. Like the women politicians in the UCLA study, Roberta was taught that she could accomplish whatever she set out to do. Her competence was never questioned, only affirmed. Now, she sees the possibilities in any situation. Because self-expression was fostered in her family, Roberta became skilled at transforming aggressive energy into initiative, articulate public speaking, visionary plans, and inspired leadership.

Those who know her well appreciate her fine sense of humor. Any visit with Roberta, public or private, is guaranteed to produce laughter. At one early morning breakfast meeting with the newly-elected mayor of Albuquerque, she introduced him to the group and recognized how difficult it is to be a public person in a small community where everyone knows you and wants to tell you something of personal importance no matter where you happen to be or what you may be engaged in at the moment.

"So, I spotted the mayor the other day in the supermarket," she said, "trying to hide between the lettuce and the broccoli." When the mayor later acknowledged that he was unfamiliar with the way Roberta ran these meetings, she quipped, "Badly." Invariably, her own hilarious laughter follows these flashes of spontaneous good humor, proving that regardless of the seriousness of her purpose, she creates a joyous sense of community.

What about those of us who did not have the good fortune to grow up within an intact, supportive, and loving family? I would guess that more of us must work to grow through crises, recognize the defenses that mark our grief, and find the fortitude to practice self-expression and transcendence. Maybe Roberta's grandmother can remind us to say "not anymore" to our fear, our sadness, our self-doubt. "Not anymore" might signal a turning point, a resolution of grief from the past and fear of the future, so that we may be guided into the possibilities of the present...guided to discover our purpose.

In the book *The Life You Were Born to Live,* author Dan Millman writes: "Our subconscious knows what we are here to do; it reaches out to us, sending messages through our dreams, intuitions, and innermost longings. The call of our destiny manifests as our deepest drives and abilities—the hidden forces behind our personality."[13]

We must learn to "be still" and listen for these messages. In order to find purpose, we must learn to trust the depth of our own awareness.

The splendor of the rising sun can truly be appreciated when you have hope for the future.
    — Daisaku Ikeda, President, Soka Gakkai Buddhism Movement

It's possible to rebuild a broken spirit.
                                              — Sarah Dixon

For many years, Sarah Dixon had no hope for her future. She was born with spina bifida and hydrocephalus, the second most common birth defects (after heart defects) compatible with life. With spina bifida, a neural tube defect, the spinal column does not develop in the usual internal way. In Sarah's case, part of the spinal cord was exposed. Below the point on the spinal cord where the defect occurs, the normal neurological connections are disrupted during fetal growth, leaving these children with atrophied lower limbs and bowel and bladder incontinence.

The night of her birth, Sarah had surgery to place her spinal cord within her back and cover it with a skin graft. Within two weeks, it was found that the cerebrospinal fluid that fills the cavities of the brain and the spinal cord was blocked. This clear liquid bathes the brain, serves as a buffer against shock, and carries substances such as antibodies to nervous-system tissue. Hydrocephalus, or "water on the brain," indicates that the spinal fluid is accumulating instead of circulating and draining to allow for the production of new fluid. Without intervention, seizures, mental retardation, progressive enlargement of the head, and death can occur. Sarah required surgery to install a "shunt," a small tube running from the right side of her head, beneath the skin, to drain fluid down to the abdomen. "I'm very fortunate that I eventually outgrew the hydrocephalus, and they could remove the shunt," Sarah told me. "It's nice to not have a bump on my head where that little pump-like device was."

Sarah is now twenty-five. I remember when she was one, and two, and three years old, and her parents would have huge birthday parties to celebrate each year of her survival in spite of early prognoses that she would not live. Other gloomy predictions were of severe, "vegetable-like" retardation and of total paralysis. While Sarah's body is confined to a wheelchair, her spirit is anything but paralyzed. And while Sarah and her mother told me she went through a time of dark and dangerous depression during adolescence, now her conversation is spiced with words like "fortunate," "incredibly lucky," and "miracle."

Like artist Frida Kahlo, Sarah had to undergo nearly thirty operations. Many involved shunt replacements; some were orthopedic, involving the placement of plates and pins in her hips; the last several involved her bladder, procedures that would give her freedom from catheters and allow for normal bathroom use. When I first interviewed Sarah, she was recovering from surgery and very hopeful about the results.

"The abnormal bodily functions were probably the hardest part of all this for me growing up," she said. "People, especially children, are uncomfortable enough around the handicapped, but add urinary catheters and bowel accidents, and lots of people can't handle it at all. I was teased mercilessly in elementary school. But the hardest time that I remember involved two older women. I was about ten and my father had taken me to the swimming pool that was part of our small housing community. I love the water and was in the pool when these women started telling my father he had to take me out. They saw my catheter and thought urine would get into the pool. I know my father was furious but also embarrassed, and I felt very ashamed."

"Sarah, I remember John Bradshaw differentiating between shame and guilt. He said that guilt is when we make a mistake; shame is when we feel we *are* a mistake. Is that the kind of shame you felt?"

"Sometimes, yes, because I knew from preschool on that I was different from the other children. And yet denial served me well because I kept thinking, 'Someday I'll be like the other kids...by fourth grade, sixth grade, after the next surgery, junior high...' The teasing gave me more drive, strengthened my determination. But by high school, I fell into my grief, as you would say."

"What happened in high school? Were you attending public school?"

"My mother always wanted me to learn to adjust to the world, not to expect the world to adjust to me, so I attended public school. I must have finally become aware that I would never be like the other kids. I would never be able to do what they do. Because of the teasing, I had built a wall around myself and was a loner. I hated my life and felt angry with everyone. You know my wonderful older sister, Heather? At that time, I resented her, sometimes hated her for being healthy, just as I know there were many times that she resented me for being ill. She would have to stay home and look after me when mother was working.

"So I became a rebel. I wore black and acted like I didn't care about anything. I began to drink and use drugs. And my drugs of choice were the hallucinogens. I wanted to live in some other reality, any other reality but my own. I was running away from my life."

"What happened to start bringing you out of this deep grief cycle?"

"The love of my family. I didn't see it or believe it for some time. Basically, they refused to let me go on like that. They put me in therapy, then they agreed with the therapist that I had to be hospitalized. I was only in the Adolescent Unit for two weeks, but it turned me around enough so I could stop the drugs and work in therapy. I saw Dr. Scofield for another year after that and he came to my high school graduation ceremony. I felt so proud and grateful for everyone's help."

"Is there one stage in grief where you tend to get stuck?"

"Yes, it's the depression. I don't have so much anger anymore, but I do occasionally feel depressed. Meditation makes my depression much shorter than in the past. Where it used to last weeks and months, now it's only days."

"How did you learn to meditate?"

"I became a Buddhist two years ago. Some friends invited me to a meeting and I began going regularly and learned to chant. I chant forty minutes each day. The chanting has helped turn my negative thinking into positive. Learning about Buddhism has helped me, just as my mother's traditional religion has helped her, to believe in God and to trust that there is meaning in my life."

"How do you understand the meaning of your life, the meaning in suffering?"

"I believe in 'karma,' not the idea of punishment but of learning. I believe I chose to experience multiple challenges in this lifetime in order to learn about compassion and, of course, about love. Every time I overcome another obstacle or heal from another surgery, I feel much greater self-esteem. Some people speak of God's punishment. I don't believe God punishes; I believe God is love, the Buddha is love, and my Buddha nature is my loving nature." Sarah looked thoughtful for a moment. "Maybe I shouldn't go on and on about this."

"Please go on and on," I encouraged her.

"Well, it's the practice of Buddhism that has reconnected me with the world and with myself, so I get excited about it. I get spiritual breakthroughs, sometimes, but they're hard to hold on to. The practice of meditation, though, brings a continuous flow of energy, and the energy helps me overcome my problems. Because

I've chosen to experience challenges doesn't mean I have to suffer. It just means I have to be responsible for overcoming the problems."

"What is your goal?"

"Spiritually, my goal is to achieve enlightenment—all knowledge, peace, wisdom. Physically, I want to do as much as I can do. I have a friend who's also in a wheelchair and is an amazing athlete. He wants to teach me to play basketball and to ski. I also want to get married someday and have children."

"And I can't keep myself from asking," I said, "since you believe in reincarnation, what would you like to be in your next life?"

"I would like to evolve so that I would not have to come back, but if I do, I'll take anything with a healthy body. Heaven, for me, would be to run, to dance, and to climb mountains. Until then, I visualize my body healing, I do acts of love, I pray for myself and for others every day."

"What about the people who hurt you, how do you handle them?"

"I chant and pray that they'll find their happiness but that they find it as far away from me as possible," Sarah said, with a smile. "One of my biggest breakthroughs was the realization that no one can hurt me unless I allow it. Learning the paradox of selfish/selfless is a part of that. Being selfish, I have good boundaries and clear values, which enable me to be selfless, to create happiness and love for others."

"I've been learning about your beautiful soul," I said to Sarah, "but are you aware that you are physically beautiful?" Sarah has strawberry-blond hair, blue eyes, perfect features, and an elegant mouth.

"People have said that to me beginning in high school, that I was pretty, but I didn't believe it. Since my spirituality has developed, it's easier to see beauty everywhere, even in myself."

Sarah wheeled herself into another room in her apartment and returned with a scrapbook.

"I like your apartment," I told her. "I've always wanted to visit this building."

Sarah brightened. "This is one of my dreams-come-true." I wanted to live independently and have a car. It seems as though everything I pray for happens and happens more and more quickly. I feel very blessed."

Sarah showed me her scrapbook, every part of it made artistically with her own hands. The bold title on the first page declares:

"It's Time to Take the Next Step!"

On January 15, 1996, I attended a large multicultural Martin Luther King Day celebration. I noticed Sarah sitting in the front row and went to find out why she was there. She told me she would be singing with a small choir later in the program. As I took my chair, I wondered how she would be able to get to the performance platform. As the choir was being introduced, Sarah got up out of her chair and, using a cane, walked up the few stairs to the platform and stood during the entire performance! What courage, I thought, and what an example she is of "determined overcoming," of growing inner strength, of transforming loss into love. Later, I went up to Sarah and jokingly asked, "What will you do next, fly?"

"I like that idea," she answered with a soft smile. "Maybe I could visualize growing wings."

"Are there other dreams you haven't told me about?" I asked.

"I'm going back to school. While I've done lots of volunteer work, and also secretarial and computer jobs, I want to be a teacher. I want to teach kindergarten and first grade. My dream is to live and teach in Japan for several years and then in Australia. I've always wanted to live in Australia, work there, see all the different sights, snorkel at the Great Barrier Reef…"

And I could see Sarah flying, doing, enjoying, tasting, creating her lovely dreams.

The following are excerpts from some of Sarah's poetry.

Gum

Sticky, sweet, pink,
swimming through my mouth.
Up and down, round and round,
back and forth, back and forth
mashing against teeth.
Bladed ridges used for tearing,
only squeezing your bouncy, textured body.
Releasing a wet, sweet tasting liquid in my mouth.
Leaving me with a smile.

Starry Night

Twirling circles,
in a sky.
Yellow, dark blue, gold and orange
going round and round
paint meshing together,
forming beauty of a wonderful night.

A portrait's view of a madman who knew how to create beauty.
No one noticing until you were long gone.
Crisp and distinct vision of the night.
Ignored until your gift of art left the world.
Leaving a long legacy of overwhelming talent and profound
influence.

Alice's Trip

...Ladybugs and butterflies climb and kiss me across my entire
    body
A field of daisies surrounds me, and I stay completely focused...

Sarah reminds us to respect every life experience for its inherent growth and creative potential. She told me about waiting after class recently to talk to a professor. She waited and waited until it seemed apparent that he was ignoring her in favor of another student. Finally, "I went to my car, and once inside I broke down, crying uncontrollably for a long time. Then I realized I'd been given the opportunity to release the grief tied up with my physical problems of the last year. I felt so much better the next day." Sarah even commented regarding her last surgery: "I think we have to accept the assault as an act of love." How many of us can do that?

Every time we struggle or suffer in some way, we are working with the raw materials of growth. These experiences are our medium for self-expression, the soil we use to transform ourselves from seedlings to lush, lively, strong and lovely plants.

I return to Job now for the last time, because at some point in life, we are all Job, becoming intimately acquainted with change and the illusion of loss. Every time we get closer to accepting the "assault as an act of love," as Sarah recommends, we recognize our connection with Spirit, accept our growth, and manifest a creative response. Job reached acceptance by a transformation of awareness, a new vision of life, a "transformed seeing,"[14] expressed in his words, "I have spoken of things too wonderful for me to know...I knew of you then only by report, but now I see you with my own eyes..." (Job 42:3-5). We learned from Jacques Lusseyran, the blind French resistance leader, that seeing has little to do with the visual organs, and much to do with opening the spirit to a new world view. When this transformation occurs, our grief miraculously melts away and creative self-expression becomes aligned with love and regeneration.

A miracle is the instant acceptance and manifestation of the world's perfection. Job received a miracle, the insight that cycles of loss and life change are powerful creative agents of growth and creativity, which result in expressions of divine harmony and balance.

With the direct experience of God, Job's old moral constraints, his view of God as an authoritarian arbitrator of life, were replaced by an identification with the Wisdom of the Creative Force. Job, now fearless co-creator of his life, transcends the past, restores his fortunes, doubles his possessions, and lives to a blessed old age. As he declares his recognition of Wisdom, Job achieves inner peace, a sense of purpose, and a greater capacity to create love.

Creating Love

Enjoy the light that you create. Those words came to me during my morning meditation. I had been worrying, about how to end this book and whether it contained profound enough, helpful enough information. I thought I needed to find more famous artists to quote, or philosophers to offer their wisdom. When "Enjoy the light that you create" came to me, I was amused and delighted by the straightforward message. And then followed the words, "Search no further to find brilliance outside of yourself. The light, the love, that you create every single day, from within and in interaction with others, will nourish you and bring you joy." Whatever we need to hear is within each one of us. We only need remember to push up our periscopes, or look to our constant, bubbling creative well-springs, and listen for the Transcendent or Higher Self connected to intuition and to the vast Universal Intelligence.

A loving heart requires trust. Whenever I observe myself in distress, I think of us humans as like highly intelligent missiles with perfect guidance systems. During our failures to trust, we think the system is broken and we act like impatient children in the back seat of the car on a long trip: "When will we be there? I'm hungry. Why did I have to come? I'll bet we're lost." We stay in our fear and doubt until someone, a parent, a mentor, a close friend or family member, or the clear voice of the Higher Self provides reassurance. The love-connection of reassurance reorients and reconnects us to our own inner strength. It enables us to settle down again within a soft sense of safety.

We must learn to trust that our guidance systems are in place and that we have all the equipment we need to withstand every type of stressful test. When the tests begin, the process in which we find ourselves is that of balancing our experience of grief and growth, and creating our signature self-expression.

Daily Creative Discipline
(Transcendence: Creating Peace, Purpose, and Love)

1. Ask yourself if there are remaining **grief reactions** that you still harbor. If so, find ways to "feel the feelings" and **express them.** Talk to someone about them, write about them, draw them, be mindful of them during physical activity. Before falling asleep, ask for a dream that will tell you how to transform these feelings. Visualize them in the clouds and see how they begin to change. Ask for a direct experience of God, Spirit, or the Creative Source.

2. Choose to **practice stilling the mind** in some way every day to create inner peace. Find an opportunity to reassure someone else who you notice is struggling with problems, large or small. Know this as an act of love.

3. For one entire day, **make each behavior purposeful** through awareness and celebration. Declare your intention to honor every meal, every meeting, every piece of work with gratitude. Notice how you feel at the end of the day.

4. **Look for possibilities** for change and growth in every situation. Use your creative imagination to take down your defensive walls, your resistance, and your fear of change. Be sure to include your sense of humor in this endeavor— laughter is a great lubricant for overcoming inflexibility.

5. Endeavor to **transform every negative thought into positive life energy.** Make "alignment with love" your point of view for daily behavior. Notice how everyday problems become smaller and smaller. The sensation of free-flowing energy allows you to transcend old habits of limitation and become everything you have ever wanted to be.

6.   For your next birthday, **give yourself a gift** of your own art. Use the work in your file to make a collage in the shape of a circle. This mandala will represent your own inner cosmos, the unification of all aspects of your Self. **Display your creation proudly.**

Peaceful Reminders:
Meditations, Sayings,
Intentions

Mother-Father-God, Angels, and all Servants
   of the Universal Good,
Help lift me out of my grief.
Help me to see with expansive vision
that I have survived every obstacle in the past.
Strengthen my faith so that I may know now
on every level of my being
that I will survive the present terror.
Help me to see clearly
the learning from this experience,
how I have been guided to my knees,
So that when I stand and walk again
It will be in the Light and Love of clear purpose.

I will not live in fear.
Every day I let that energy flow into awareness.

My anger expresses my hurt.
From now on, I let my anger become the life energy that gives
me the drive to become whole.

I recognize my obsessive thoughts as attempts
to control my anxiety. When I notice them, I stop and
affirm my trust that I am safe in the world. I affirm powerful
possibilities for my life.

In depression, I am dying to the past.
I honor the difficulty of this transition and allow the symptoms
to be the rainfall that will incubate new growth.
Through this adversity, I will discover my life purpose.

In acceptance, I allow the wisdom
of all life cycles to mature within me.
I grow love for myself and everyone around me.

I consistently transform life energy
from the dark demons of defense to the light awareness of love.

From Crisis...

Any full life is going to involve pain.
— Madeleine L'Engle

The vastness of your soul can only be measured by the depths of your sorrow.
— Kahlil Gibran

Time ripens all things: no man is born wise.
— Cervantes

A man should learn to sail in all winds.
— Italian proverb

Nothing endures but change.
— Heraclitus (540-480 B.C.E.)

There is no sun without shadow, and it is essential to know the night.
— Albert Camus

Should his heart break and the grief pour out, it would flow over the whole earth it seems, and yet, no one sees it.
— Chekhov

All of our halos slip. Transforming our grief to creativity radiantly replaces them.
— Gail Carr Feldman

To solve a problem you have to go to where the problem isn't.
— Einstein

Don't worry, things are bound to get worse.
— Sam Roll

All sunshine makes a desert.

— Arabian proverb

And as he was capable of giant joy, so did he harbor huge sorrow.

— John Steinbeck

Satan is all defense.

— W. Ulwelling

Every situation, seen rightly, contains the seeds of freedom.

— Joan Borysenko

No matter how hard the winds of evil blow, the flame of truth can never be extinguished.

— Dalai Lama

The gem cannot be polished without friction, nor man perfected without trials.

— Chinese proverb

Strange as it may sound, the intentional knowing of your feelings in times of emotional suffering contains in itself the seeds of healing.

— Jon Kabat-Zinn

When the mind applies judgment to change, what gets created is loss.

— Deepak Chopra

When one person laughs, the whole world laughs with you. When you cry, you cry alone.

— Leopold Kozlaski

Press on. Nothing in the world can take the place of persistence. Talent will not: nothing is more common than unrewarded talent. Education alone will not: the world is full of educated failures. Persistence alone is omnipotent.
— President Calvin Coolidge

Tribulation is treasure...we get nearer and nearer our home, Heaven, by it.
— John Donne, 1623

To Creativity...

What would life be like if you confidently unleashed the creativity within you?
— Dan Millman

Reach inside where the sky really is.
— Rev. H. Patrick Pollard

The creation of a thousand forests is in one acorn.
— Emerson

My words are my wardrobe.
— Laurie Beth Jones

By the creative act, we are able to reach beyond our own death.
— Rollo May

An astonishing capacity for creative power is built into our genes, ready to unfold.
— Joseph Chilton Pearce

Both I and thou have passed through many births...
— Krishna *(Bhagavad-Gita)*

Eccentricity gives energy.
— Carly Simon

Remember, you are constantly in the act of creating yourself.
— Neale Donald Walsch
— God, in *Conversations with God*

The most beautiful thing we can experience is the mysterious.
— Einstein

Find one hundred ways...

— Quincy Jones

In art you strive to be creative, but in politics if you are too creative you scare the hell out of people.

— Ben Nighthorse Campbell,
Native American U.S. Senator (1995)

Go ahead and scare the hell out of people.

— Gail Carr Feldman

Creativity, like human life itself, begins in darkness.

— Julia Cameron

Artists love their medium. Love your medium.

— Gail Carr Feldman

In the creative process, change is the norm.

— Robert Fritz

We live in a world in which life wants to happen.

— Margaret Wheatley

The inner world deepens and grows more refined as empathy expands.

— Huston Smith

Dare to be great, but first dare to make a fool of yourself.

— E. Lynn Werner

Come home to your creative heart. It's time.

— Gail Carr Feldman

To Transcendence...

To acknowledge God and to live are one and the same thing.

— Tolstoy

The soul's greatest perfection is its capacity for pleasure.

— Anonymous

Transcendent living: The ability to exceed the fear of grief and transform the energy of resistance and defense into an unrestrained vitality of growth, the experience of which is our creativity.

— Gail Carr Feldman

The world is not a place but the vastness of the soul.

— Amy Tan

All souls are one. Each is a spark from the original soul, and this soul is wholly inherent in all souls...

— Martin Buber

Love all, Serve all.

— Sai Baba

The universe conspires to give you what you want.

— Anonymous

Remember many things that start off easily end in misery. Meditation starts with difficulty and ends in pleasure, bliss, harmony.

— Bernard Gunther

We have to allow what is good, beautiful and meaningful in the other's tradition to transform us.

— Thich Nhat Hanh

*Love is the greatest of human virtues, and, in fact,
the dominant virtue of the universe.*
— Erik H. Erikson

*When the heart grieves what it has lost, the spirit
rejoices for what it has found.*
— Sufi saying

Anything is possible if you believe it is.
— Jesus of Nazareth

*And we are put on earth a little space, that we may learn
to bear the beams of love...*
— William Blake

*It takes courage to love, but pain through love is the
purifying fire that those who love generously know.*
— Eleanor Roosevelt

I greet this day with an open heart

I allow myself to be a channel for love

I trust my life to unfold in just the right way

I offer no resistance

I accept the miracles

I see the truth

Notes

Chapter One—Grief Cycles and the Creative Process

1. Elisabeth Kübler-Ross, *On Death and Dying* (New York: Macmillan Publishing, 1969).
2. Leonard Shengold, *Soul Murder* (New York & London: Yale University Press, 1989).
3. Stephen Levine, *Who Dies?* (New York: Anchor Press [Doubleday], 1982).
4. *A Course in Miracles* (Tiburon, CA: Foundation For Inner Peace, 1975).

Chapter Two—Murphy, Job, and Other Tales of Creative Competence

1. Clarissa Pinkola Estes, "Creative Fire" (Boulder, CO: Sounds True Recordings, 1991);
   Helen Luke, *Kaleidoscope* (New York: Parabola Books, 1992).

Chapter Three—Denial: To the Light of Awareness

1. Barbara's recovery from satanic abuse is documented in the author's first book, *Lessons in Evil, Lessons From the Light* (New York: Crown Books, 1993).
2. Pulitzer Prize-winning author and Princeton professor Joyce Carol Oates describes dissociation in her novel about satanic abuse, *Man Crazy* (New York: Dutton, 1997), 212–213, 218.
3. Resistance to the awareness that citizens in our country, the United States, could sexually abuse their children is illustrated by the 1980 Textbook of Comprehensive Psychiatry stating that the incidence of incest is "one in one million families" on the North American continent, diminishing the extent of the problem and suggesting that incest is a greater problem in South America.
4. See de Mause's primer, *Foundations of Psychohistory* (New York: Creative Roots, 1992).
5. Thomas Moore, "On Creativity," audio cassettes, (Boulder, CO: Sounds True Recordings, 1993).
6. From D. McIvor, "How Do Non-Adjudicated Sex Offenders Think?" in *Treating Abuse Today* 3, no. 6 (1993): 29.

7.   To learn about pedophiles who murder, read the historical novel by Caleb Carr, *The Alienist* (New York: Random House, 1994), or forensic psychiatrist and police officer Ron Turco's recent nonfiction book, *Closely Watched Shadows* (Wilsonville, OR: BookPartners, 1997).

8.   I'm indebted to Dr. Larry Morris, of Hillside Community Church, Albuquerque, for his teachings on the transformation of Siddhartha into the Buddha.

9.   Robert Fritz, *The Path of Least Resistance* (New York: Fawcett Columbine, 1984), 17.

10. Andrea Gabor, *Einstein's Wife* (New York: Viking, 1995), 25.

11. Howard Gardener, *Creating Minds* (New York: Basic Books, 1993).

12. Gardener, 129.

Chapter Four—Anger: The Drive to Wholeness

1.   Bill DeFoore, *Anger* (Deerfield Beach, FL: Health Communications Inc., 1991).

2.   Bruno Bettelheim, *The Uses of Enchantment* (New York: Knopf, 1976); Clarissa Pinkola Estes, *Women Who Run with the Wolves* (New York: Ballantine Books, 1992).

3.   Helen Fisher, *Anatomy of Love* (New York: Fawcett Columbine, 1992).

4.   Huston Smith, *World's Religions* (San Francisco: Harper Collins, 1994).

5.   Barry Panter, Mary Lou Panter, Bernard Virshup, and Evelyn Virshup, eds., *Creativity and Madness* (Burbank, CA: AIMED Press, 1995).

Chapter Five—Obsession: The Energy of Passion and Personal Power

1.   *The New Interpreter's Bible,* vol. 4 (Nashville: Abingdon Press, 1996), 625.

2.   Physician Gerald Jampolsky opened the first Center for Attitudinal Healing in order to offer a mental and emotional support system for children and adults who were facing life-threatening illness. He has written a number of books. My favorites are *Love is Letting Go of Fear* and *Teach Only Love.*

3.   A book by psychiatrist Lee Sannella explains the kundalini expe-
      rience as a type of energy or power that is dormant at the base of
      the spine until it is galvanized or "awakened." It then moves up
      the spine to the crown of the head, giving rise to a mystical,
      blissful state of consciousness. For more information about this
      psychophysiological-spiritual transformation see Dr. Sannella's
      book, *The Kundalini Experience* (Lower Lake, CA: Integral
      Publishing, 1992). Barbara Whitfield, in *Spiritual Awakenings*
      (1995), also describes Kundalini energy and how it works; and
      don't miss Caroline Myss's masterpiece, *Anatomy of the Spirit*
      (New York: Harmony Books, 1996).

4.   For those interested in reading about reincarnation or past-life
      therapy, see the following: Brian Weiss, *Many Lives, Many
      Masters* (New York: Simon & Schuster, 1988); Hans Ten Dam,
      Exploring Reincarnation (London: Penguin, 1990); Joseph Head
      and Sylvia Cranston, *Reincarnation: The Phoenix Fire Mystery*
      (San Diego: Point Loma Publications, 1991); James Redfield and
      Carol Adrienne, *The Tenth Insight: Holding the Vision, An
      Experiential Guide* (New York: Warner Books, 1996).

5.   John Bradshaw, *Bradshaw On: The Family* (Deerfield Beach,
      FL: Health Communications Inc., 1988), 89.

6.   John Briere's research published in the Annals of the New York
      Academy of Sciences is reported in Judith Herman's book,
      Trauma and Recovery (New York: Basic Books, 1992).

7.   Herman, 44.

8.   For further reading on cases of reincarnation from the Holocaust,
      see Rabbi Yonassan Gershom's book, *Beyond the Ashes* (Virginia
      Beach, VA: A.R.E. Press, 1992). For further reading on regression
      therapy for obesity and substance abuse, see psychiatrist Brian
      Weiss's book, *Through Time into Healing* (New York: Simon &
      Schuster, 1992).

9.   From Kay Goebel's "Michelangelo's Creativity: The Conquest of
      Adversity," in Panter, et al.

10.   Louis Renou, ed., *Hinduism* (New York: George Braziller, 1962),
      136.

11.   W. G. Archer in Alex Comfort, trans., Koka Shastra (New York:
      Simon & Schuster, 1997).

Chapter Six—Depression: The Dark Road to Discovery

1. Allende's book, *Paula* (New York: Harper Collins, 1995), is a touching tribute to her daughter, a documentation of her grief, and a deeply moving account of her spiritual healing.
2. I thank my colleague, psychologist Kim Smith Ph.D., for sharing his research and knowledge with me about suicide.
3. I later found this poem in one of Elisabeth Kübler-Ross's books, *Death Is of Vital Importance* (Barrytown, NY: Station Hill Press, 1995), 75.
4. R. Maris, *Pathways to Suicide* (Baltimore: Johns Hopkins Press, 1981).
5. "International Classification of the Causes of Death," in the classic text *The Cry for Help* (New York: McGraw-Hill, 1965) by N. Farberow and E. Shneidman.
6. K. Pelletier, *Sound Mind, Sound Body* (New York: Simon & Schuster, 1994).
7. L. Dossey, "Spirituality in Health Care" (Albuquerque, NM: Spirituality in Health Care Conference, February 1997).
8. Stanford psychiatrist David Spiegel cites forty-two studies in this area suggesting that psychosocial connections increase life expectancy in those with cancer. In Pelletier, 133.
9. Pelletier, 138–139. In the U.S., Dr. Kim Smith related, men over sixty-five have the highest rate of suicide. Financial loss seems to be the precipitating factor, while for women it is relationship loss.
10. For more about the concept of "soul clusters" or "soul groups," read James Redfield and Carol Adrienne's *The Tenth Insight: Holding the Vision, An Experiential Guide*.
11. Bernie Siegel's first best-selling book was *Love, Medicine, and Miracles* (New York: Harper & Row, 1986).
12. For many touching examples of dying children teaching us about completing "unfinished business," read Elisabeth Kübler-Ross's *Death Is of Vital Importance*.
13. Researchers have found that those who simply write about traumatic events show a boost in their immune-system activity compared to controls. Scott Sleek, "Rallying the Troops Inside Our Bodies," in *American Psychological Association Monitor* 26, no. 12 (December 1995): 24.

14.   See Harvard psychiatrist Bessel Van der Kolk's book, *Traumatic Stress: The Effects of Overwhelming Experience on Mind, Body, and Society* (New York: Guilford Press, 1996).

15.   Much of the material on Frida Kahlo is taken from Hayden Herrera's excellent biography, *Frida* (New York: Harper & Row, 1983).

16.   Herrera, 75.

17.   Peter Kramer, *Listening to Prozac* (New York: Viking, 1993), 126.

18.   Kübler-Ross, *Death Is of Vital Importance.*

19.   The research of psychologists Antonuccio, Danton, and DeNelsky is described in "Psychotherapy Alone Is As Effective As Drugs in Treating Depression," in the *American Psychological Association Monitor* 27, no. 1 (January 1996): 6.

20.   See the May 5, 1997 *Newsweek,* 74.

21.   E. Vare and G. Ptacek, *Mothers of Invention* (New York: William Morrow, 1987), 89.

22.   For more about the stages and projections of love, read Deepak Chopra's *The Path to Love* (New York: Harmony Books, 1997); another favorite of mine is Sam Keen's *To Love and Be Loved* (New York: Bantam Books, 1997).

Chapter Seven—Acceptance: Embracing Success

1.   Herbert Benson, *The Relaxation Response* (New York: William Morrow, Simon & Schuster, 1975). Also see his latest book, *Timeless Healing* (New York: Simon & Schuster, 1997).

2.   Willis Harman and Howard Rheingold, *Higher Creativity* (New York: C. P. Putnam's, 1984).

3.   This information about Jacques Lusseyran is taken from page 43 of his autobiography, *And There Was Light* (New York: Parabola Books, 1987; first published by Little, Brown & Co., 1963).

4.   Ibid., 23.

5.   Ibid., 29.

6.   Ibid., 281.

7.   Frederic Flach, *Resilience* (New York: Fawcett Columbine, 1988), 113–114.

8.   E. J. Anthony and B. Cohler, eds., *The Invulnerable Child* (New York: Guilford Press, 1987).

9.   Gina O'Connell Higgins, *Resilient Adults* (San Francisco: Jossey-Bass, 1994).

10. Feldman, *Lessons in Evil, Lessons From the Light.*, 289.

11. Ibid.

12. For an excellent account of research on the "near-death experience," or NDE, read Dr. Melvin Morse's book, *Transformed by the Light* (New York: Villard, 1992).

13. Smith, *World's Religions.*

14. Liu Wu-Chi, *Confucius, His Life and Time* (New York: Philosophical Library Inc., 1955), 49.

15. Smith, 110.

16. H. G. Creel, *Confucius, The Man and the Myth* (Westport, CT: Greenwood Press, 1972; original copyright © 1949).

17. Smith, 111.

18. Liu, 11.

19. Ibid., 74.

20. Creel, 92.

21. Winberg Chai, *Confucianism* (Woodbury, NY: Barron's Educational Services Inc., 1973), 39.

22. Stephen Mitchell, *The Gospel According to Jesus* (New York: Harper Collins, 1991), 160.

23. A. N. Wilson, *Jesus, A Life* (New York & London: W. W. Norton, 1992), 128.

24. Josephus, in Wilson, 129.

25. John Crossan, *The Historical Jesus* (San Francisco: Harper Collins, 1991), 99.

26. Ellis Rivkin, *A Hidden Revolution* (Nashville: Abingdon Press, 1978), 40.

27. Exod. 18:21.

28. Rivkin, 57.

29. Wilson, 97.

30. William B. Silverman, *The Sages Speak* (Northvale, NJ & London: Jason Aronson, 1989), 207.

31. Smith, 186.

32. Wilson, 128.

33. Mark 2:17 and Mitchell, 148.

34. British biographer A. N. Wilson offers a persuasive argument that it was actually Paul (or Saul) who was responsible for betraying

Jesus and handing him over to the authorities. This would explain his obsession with the crucifixion and his compensatory need to blame the other Jews, thus separating himself from Judaism altogether. *Jesus, A Life,* 203–206.

35. Because the tendency towards a literal interpretation of "an eye for an eye" persists, we should be reminded that in Exodus 21 Moses, with God's guidance, is setting down laws about compensation for loss, not laws that merely instruct retaliation.

36. Matt. 5:48 in *The Revised English Bible* (Oxford University Press and Cambridge University Press, 1989).

37. Mitchell, 164.

38. Elaine Pagels, *The Gnostic Gospels* (New York: Vintage Books, 1979, 1989), xvii.

39. Ibid., xv.

40. Ibid., 126–127.

41. Gospel of Thomas, in *Pagels,* 128.

42. Mitchell, 173. Italicized "accept" is my wish to highlight the word.

43. Gospel of Thomas, in *Pagels,* 127.

44. Matt. 5:1–10.

45. Rivkin, 302–303.

46. Silverman, 61–62.

47. Abba Hillel Silver, *Where Judaism Differed* (Northvale, NJ & London: Jason Aronson, 1987), 257.

48. Mitchell, 161.

49. Pagels, 127.

50. Ibid., 131.

51. Ibid., 120.

52. Brother David Steindl-Rast, in Thich Nhat Hanh's *Living Buddha, Living Christ,* (New York: G. P. Putnam's, 1995), xiii–xiv.

53. C. G. Jung, "Job," in *The Collected Works of C. J. Jung,* vol. 11, eds. Read, Fordham, Adler and McGuire (Princeton, NJ: Princeton University Press, 1958).

54. Ibid., 387.

55. Wisd. of Sol. 7:25–26.

56. Mitchell, 270.

57.   Roger Fisher, "Elements of Negotiation" (Fullerton, CA: TDM Audio, 1986); Also see his book, *Getting to Yes* (New York: Houghton Mifflin, 1981).

58.   For help with forgiving yourself or others, see Robin Casarjian's book, *Forgiveness: Bold Choice for a Peaceful Heart* (New York: Bantam, 1992).

59.   David Strong's article, "The Promise of Technology Versus God's Promise in Job" (*Theology Today* 48, no. 2 [July 1991]: 170-181) presents Job's story as a meditation on the power of the divine and the need for sacred "wild" places in our world (170).

60.   Fred Alan Wolf, *The Spiritual Universe: How Quantum Physics Proves the Existence of the Soul* (New York: Simon & Schuster, 1996).

Chapter Eight—Transcendence: Creating Peace, Purpose, and Love
1.   All material on Agnes Martin is from personal interview and the following monographs: "Agnes Martin, January 22–March 1, 1973" (Philadelphia: Institute of Contemporary Art, University of Pennsylvania, 1973); Dore Ashton, "Agnes Martin: Paintings and Drawings, 1957–1975" (Arts Council of Great Britain, 1977); and "Agnes Martin, Writings" ed. Dieter Schwarz, accompaniment to exhibition "Agnes Martin: Paintings and Works on Paper, 1960–1989" (Winterthur, Switzerland: Kunstmuseum, January–March 1992).

2.   Jon Kabat-Zinn, *Full Catastrophe Living* (New York: Dell Publishing, 1990).

3.   Poloma's research is described in Tom Kuncl's "Faith and Healing" (Boca Raton, FL: Globe Communications Corp., 1995), 30.

4.   The power of prayer to heal has now been well-documented by research. To learn more, read Larry Dossey's book, *Healing Words* (New York: Harper Collins, 1993).

5.   Judy Chicago, *Through the Flower: My Struggle as a Woman Artist* (New York: Doubleday, 1975), 25–26.

6.   Both projects are described in books by Judy Chicago: *The Dinner Party* (New York: Anchor Books, 1979); and *The Birth Project* (Garden City, NY: Doubleday, 1984).

7. Chicago may not have been aware of Frida Kahlo's work, described in chapter 6 of this book. In 1932, Kahlo rendered a bold, shocking painting of her own birth—shocking because the image of a woman, legs apart, birthing a bloody infant is completely unfamiliar, if not taboo, in our culture.

8. Judy Chicago, *Holocaust Project* (New York: Penguin Books, 1993).

9. I spoke of "secondary post-traumatic stress" in my book *Lessons in Evil, Lessons From the Light.* This concept describes the compassionate suffering of therapists who work with survivors of sadistic abuse.

10. Chicago, *Holocaust Project,* 9. Also see Robert J. Lifton's books: *Nazi Doctors: Medical Killing* and the *Psychology of Genocide* (New York: Basic Books, 1986); Lifton and Eric Markusen, *The Genocidal Mentality: Nazi Holocaust and Nuclear Threat* (New York: Basic Books, 1990).

11. Judy Chicago, *Beyond the Flower* (New York: Penguin Books, 1996).

12. "Creative aggression" is defined as "taking initiative; leading others; speaking out and expressing autonomous opinions; setting goals and making efforts and plans that carry them out; insisting on your rights; and defending yourself when challenged". Ibid., 268.

13. Dan Millman, *The Life You Were Born to Live* (Tiburon, CA: H. J. Kramer, Inc., 1993).

14. J. Andresen, "Biblical Job: Changing the Helper's Mind," *Contemporary Psychoanalysis* 27, no. 3 (1991): 462.

Bibliography

Achenbaum, W. Andrew, and Lucinda Orwoll. "Becoming Wise: A Psycho-Gerontological Interpretation of the Book of Job." *International Journal of Aging and Human Development* 32, no. 1 (1991): 21–39.

Allende, Isabel. *Paula.* New York: Harper Collins, 1995.

Andresen, J. "Biblical Job: Changing the Helper's Mind." *Contemporary Psychoanalysis* 27, no. 3 (1991): 454–481.

Anglund, Joan. *The Way of Love.* New York: Random House, 1992.

Anthony, E. J., and B. Cohler, eds. *The Invulnerable Child.* New York: Guilford Press, 1987.

Archer, W. G. "Preface." *In Koka Shastra.* Translated by Alex Comfort. New York: Simon & Schuster, 1997.

Benson, Herbert. *The Relaxation Response.* New York: William Morrow, 1975.

———. *Timeless Healing.* New York: Simon & Schuster, 1997.

Bettelheim, Bruno. *The Uses of Enchantment.* New York: Knopf, 1976

Borysenko, Joan. *Fire in the Soul.* New York: Warner Books, 1993.

Bradshaw, John. *Bradshaw On: The Family.* Deerfield Beach, FL: Health Communications Inc., 1988.

———. *Creating Love.* New York: Bantam Books, 1994.

Brinkley, Dannion. *Saved by the Light.* New York: Villard Books, 1994.

Cameron, J. *The Artist's Way.* New York: G. P. Putnam's, 1992.

Cantor, Dorothy, and Toni Bernay, with Jean Stoess. *Women in Power.* New York: Houghton Mifflin, 1992.

Carr, Caleb. *The Alienist.* New York: Random House, 1994.

Casarjian, Robin. *Forgiveness: Bold Choice for a Peaceful Heart.* New York: Bantam, 1992.

Chai, Winberg, *Confucianism.* Woodbury, NY: Barron's Educational Services Inc., 1973.

Chicago, Judy. *Through the Flower: My Struggle as a Woman Artist.* New York: Doubleday, 1975.

———. *The Dinner Party.* New York: Anchor Books, 1979.

———. *The Birth Project.* Garden City, NY: Doubleday, 1985.

———. *Holocaust Project.* New York: Penguin Books, 1993.

———. *Beyond the Flower.* New York: Penguin Books, 1996.

Chopra, Deepak. *Creating Health.* Boston: Houghton Mifflin, 1991.

———. *The Path to Love.* New York: Harmony Books, 1997.

A Course in Miracles. Tiburon, CA: Foundation For Inner Peace, 1975.

Comfort, Alex, trans. *Koka Shastra.* New York: Simon & Schuster, 1997.

Creel, H. G. Confucius, *The Man and the Myth.* Westport, CT: Greenwood Press, 1972; original © 1949.

Crossan, John. *The Historical Jesus.* San Francisco: Harper Collins, 1991.

Dalal-Clayton, Diksha. *The Adventures of Young Krishna.* New York: Oxford University Press, 1992.

DeFoore, Bill. *Anger.* Deerfield Beach, FL: Health Communications Inc., 1991.

Degler, Teri. *The Fiery Muse: Creativity and the Spiritual Quest.* Canada: Random House, 1996.

de Mause, Lloyd. *Foundations of Psychohistory.* New York: Creative Roots, 1992.

Dossey, Larry. *Healing Words.* New York: Harper Collins, 1993.

Dreiser, T. *Thoreau.* New York: Premier Books/Fawcett, 1958.

Duncan, Lois. Who Killed My Daughter? New York: Delecorte Press, 1992.

Duncan, Lois, and William Roll. *Psychic Connections.* New York: Delecorte Press, 1995.

Epstein, Mark. *Thoughts without a Thinker.* New York: Basic Books, 1995.

Estes, Clarissa Pinkola. "Creative Fire." Boulder, CO: Sounds True Recordings, 1991.

———. *Women Who Run with the Wolves.* New York: Ballantine Books, 1992.

Erikson, E. *Childhood and Society.* New York: Norton, 1950.

Farberow, N., and E. Schneidman. *The Cry for Help.* New York: McGraw-Hill, 1965.

Feldman, Gail. *Lessons in Evil, Lessons From the Light.* New York: Crown Books, 1993.

Fisher, Helen. *Anatomy of Love.* New York: Fawcett Columbine, 1992.

Fisher, Roger. "Elements of Negotiation." Fullerton, CA: TDM Audio, 1986.

Fisher, Roger., William Ury, and Bruce Patton. *Getting to Yes.* New York: Houghton Mifflin, 1981.

Flach, Frederic. *Resilience.* New York: Fawcett Columbine, 1988.

Fritz, Robert. *The Path of Least Resistance.* New York: Fawcett Columbine, 1984.

Gabor, Andrea. *Einstein's Wife.* New York: Viking, 1995.

Gardener, Howard. *Creating Minds.* New York: Basic Books, 1993.

Gershom, Yonassan. *Beyond the Ashes.* Virginia Beach, VA: A.R.E. Press, 1992.

Greene, Bob, and Oprah Winfrey. *Make the Connection.* New York: Random House, 1996.

Gutierrez, G. *On Job: God-Talk and the Suffering of the Innocent.* Maryknoll, NY: Orbis Books, 1987.

Harman, Willis, and Howard Rheingold. *Higher Creativity.* New York: G. P. Putnam's, 1984.

Haynal, Andre. *Depression and Creativity.* New York: International Universities Press, 1985.

Head, Joseph, and Sylvia Cranston. *Reincarnation: The Phoenix Fire Mystery.* San Diego: Point Loma Publications, 1991.

Helmstetter, S. *Choices.* New York: Pocket Books, 1989.

Herman, Judith. *Trauma and Recovery.* New York: Basic Books, 1992.

Herrera, Hayden. *Frida.* New York: Harper & Row, 1983.

Higgins, Gina O'Connell. *Resilient Adults.* San Francisco: Jossey-Bass, 1994.

Hirshfeld, Robert M. A., and James M. Russell. "Assessment and Treatment of Suicidal Patients." *The New England Journal of Medicine* 337, no. 13 (1997): 910-915.

Ingerman, Sandra. *A Fall to Grace.* Santa Fe, NM: Moon Tree Rising, 1997.

Institute of Contemporary Art. "Agnes Martin, January 22–March 1, 1973." *Monograph.* Philadelphia: University of Pennsylvania, 1973.

Jampolsky, Gerald. *Teach Only Love.* New York: Bantam, 1983.

———. *Love Is Letting Go of Fear.* Berkeley, CA: Celestial Arts Publishing, 1995.

"Job." In *The New Interpreter's Bible,* vol. 4. Nashville: Abingdon Press, 1996.

Jung, C. G. "Job." In *The Collected Works of C.G. Jung,* vol 11. Edited by Read, Fordham, Adler, and McGuire. Princeton, NJ: Princeton University Press, 1958.

Kabat-Zinn, Jon. *Full Catastrophe Living.* New York: Dell Publishing, 1990.

Kahn, J. H. *Job's Illness: Loss, Grief and Integration.* New York: Pergaman, 1975.

Kamins, Michael, prod. "Colores: Michael Naranjo—A New Vision." Albuquerque, NM: KUNM-TV, 1996.

Keen, Sam. *To Love and Be Loved.* New York: Bantam Books, 1997.

Kisch, J. "Job's Friends: Psychotherapeutic Precursors in the Ancient Near East." *Psychotherapy* 27, no. 1 (1990): .

Klausner, J. *Jesus of Nazareth.* New York: Macmillan, 1925; : First Menorah Publishing Co., 1979.

Koehn, Alfred. *Confucius, His Life and Work.* Peking: Lotus Court Publications, 1945.

Kramer, Peter. *Listening to Prozac.* New York: Viking, 1993.

Kübler-Ross, Elisabeth. *On Death and Dying.* New York: Macmillan Publishing, 1969.

———. *Death, the Final Stage of Growth.* Englewood Cliffs, NJ: Prentice-Hall, 1975.

———. *On Life after Death.* Berkeley, CA: Celestial Arts, 1991

———. *Death Is of Vital Importance.* Barrytown, NY: Station Hill Press, 1995.

Kuncl, Tom. *Faith and Healing.* Boca Raton, FL: Globe Communications Corp., 1995.

Levine, Stephen. *Who Dies?* New York: Anchor Press (Doubleday), 1982.

———. *Embracing the Beloved.* New York: Doubleday, 1995.

Lifton, Robert J. *Nazi Doctors: Medical Killing and the Psychology of Genocide.* New York: Basic Books, 1986.

Liu Wu-Chi. *Confucius, His Life and Time.* New York: Philosophical Library Inc., 1955.

Luke, Helen. *Kaleidoscope.* New York: Parabola Books, 1992.

Lusseyran, Jacques. *And There Was Light.* New York: Parabola Books, 1987; first published by Little, Brown & Co., 1963.

Maris, R. *Pathways to Suicide.* Baltimore: Johns Hopkins Press, 1981.

McIvor, D. "How Do Non-Adjudicated Sex Offenders Think?" *Treating Abuse Today* 3, no. 6 (1993): 29.

Millman, Dan. *The Life You Were Born to Live.* Tiburon, CA: H. J. Kramer, Inc., 1993.

Mitchell, Stephen. *The Gospel According to Jesus.* New York: Harper Collins, 1991.

———. *The Book of Job.* New York: Harper Perennial, 1987.

Moore, Thomas. "On Creativity." Boulder, CO: Sounds True Recordings, 1993.
————. *Care of the Soul.* New York: Harper Collins, 1992.
Morse, Melvin. *Transformed by the Light.* New York: Villard, 1992.
Myss, Caroline. *Anatomy of the Spirit.* New York: Harmony Books, 1996.
Nelson, Mary C. *Michael Naranjo.* Minneapolis, MN: Dillon Press, 1975.
————. *Artists of the Spirit.* Sonoma, CA: Arcus Publishing Co., 1995.
Oates, Joyce Carol. *Man Crazy.* New York: Dutton, 1997.
Pagels, Elaine. *The Gnostic Gospels.* New York: Vintage Books, 1989.
Panter, Barry, Maru Lou Panter, Bernard Virshup and Evelyn Virshup, eds. *Creativity and Madness.* Burbank, CA: Aimed Press, 1995.
Pelletier, K. *Sound Mind, Sound Body.* New York: Simon & Schuster, 1994.
Peterson, E. H. *Job.* Colorado Springs, CO: NavPress, 1996.
Poloma, Margaret. "Religious Domains and General Well-Being," *Social Indicators Research* (May 1, 1990): 255; *Journal for Scientific Study of Religion* (December 1, 1989): 415.
Powell, Robert A. "The Sophia Teachings." Boulder, CO: Sounds True Recordings, 1997.
Redfield, James. *The Celestine Prophecy.* New York: Warner Books, 1993.
————. *The Tenth Insight.* New York: Warner Books, 1996.
Redfield, James, and Carol Adrienne. *The Tenth Insight: Holding the Vision, An Experiential Guide.* New York: Warner Books, 1996.
Renou, Louis, ed. *Hinduism.* New York: George Braziller, 1962.
The Revised English Bible, with the Apocrypha. Oxford University Press, Cambridge University Press, 1989.
Rivkin, Ellis. *A Hidden Revolution.* Nashville: Abingdon Press, 1978.
Rodegast, P., and J. Stanton. *Emmanuel's Book.* New York: Bantam, 1987.
Rohr, Richard. *Job and the Mystery of Suffering.* Crossroad Publishing, 1996.
Rumsey, Celia. "Chronic." Annandale-on-Hudson, NY: The Center for Curatorial Studies, Bard College, October 28–December 22, 1995.
Sandblom, Philip. *Creativity and Disease.* Philadelphia: G. B Lippincott Co., 1989.
Sannella, Lee. *The Kundalini Experience.* Lower Lake, CA: Integral Publishing, 1992.

Scovel Shinn, Florence. *The Wisdom of Florence Scovel Shinn.* New York: Simon & Schuster, 1989.

Schwarz, Dieter, ed. "Agnes Martin,Writings." Monograph accompanying exhibition "Agnes Martin: Paintings and Works on Paper, 1960–1989." Winterthur, Switzerland: Kunstmuseum, 1992.

Selye, Hans. *The Stress of Life.* New York: McGraw-Hill, 1956.

Siegel, Bernie. *Love, Medicine and Miracles.* New York: Harper & Row, 1986.

Shengold, Leonard. *Soul Murder.* New York & London: Yale University Press, 1989.

Shlain, Leonard. *Art and Physics.* New York: William Morrow, 1991.

Silver, Abba Hillel. *Where Judaism Differed.* Northvale, NJ & London: Jason Aronson, 1987.

Silverman, William B. *The Sages Speak.* Northvale, NJ & London: Jason Aronson, 1989.

Smith, Huston. *World's Religions.* San Francisco: Harper Collins, 1994.

Smith, Jean Kennedy, and George Plimpton. *Chronicles of Courage: Very Special Artists.* New York: Random House, 1994.

Storr, Anthony. *Solitude—A Return to the Self.* New York: Macmillan (The Free Press), 1988.

Strong, David. "The Promise of Technology Versus God's Promise in Job." *Theology Today* 48, no. 2 (July 1991): 170–181.

Tavris, Carol. *Anger: The Misunderstood Emotion.* New York: Touchstone, 1989.

Ten Dam, Hans. *Exploring Reincarnation.* London: Penguin, 1990.

Thich Nhat Hanh. *Living Buddha, Living Christ.* New York: G. P. Putnam's, 1995.

Turco, Ron. *Closely Watched Shadows.* Wilsonville, OR: BookPartners, 1997.

Van der Kolk, Bessel. *Traumatic Stress: The Effects of Overwhelming Experience on Mind, Body, and Society.* New York: Guilford Press, 1996.

Vare, E., and G. Ptacek. *Mothers of Invention.* New York: William Morrow, 1987.

Walsch, Neale Donald. *Conversations with God,* Book 1. New York: G. P. Putnam's Sons, 1996.

Weisberg, R. W. *Creativity: Genius and Other Myths.* New York: W. H. Freeman & Co., 1986.

Weiss, Brian. *Many Lives, Many Masters.* New York: Simon & Schuster, 1988.

———. *Through Time into Healing.* New York: Simon & Schuster, 1992.

———. *Only Love Is Real.* New York: Warner, 1996.

Whitfield, B. *Spiritual Awakenings.* Deerfield Beach, FL: Health Communications Inc., 1995.

Wilson, A. N. *Jesus, A Life.* New York & London: W. W. Norton, 1992.

Williamson, M. *Return to Love.* New York: Harper Collins, 1993.

———. *Illuminata.* New York: Random House, 1994.

———. *The Healing of America.* New York: Simon & Schuster, 1997.

Wohlgelernter, D. "Goal Directedness: Understanding the Development of the Book of Job," *Individual Psychology* 44, no. 3 (September 1988): 296–306.

Wolf, Fred Alan. *The Spiritual Universe: How Quantum Physics Proves the Existence of the Soul.* New York: Simon & Schuster, 1996.

Woolger, R. *Other Lives, Other Selves.* New York: Bantam, 1988.

Yancey, P. "Riddles of Pain." *Christianity Today* 29 (December 1985): 80.

Index

About the Author

Gail Carr Feldman Ph.D. is a clinical psychologist, an award-winning author, and a popular public speaker. Her early professional experience as a social worker involved service to Los Angeles gang groups, prison parolees, and welfare families. In New Mexico she worked at the Family and Child Guidance Center, which has a cross-cultural clientele of children, adolescents, and families. She has been in private practice for twenty-seven years serving a wide range of clients with a special focus on hypnotherapy. She served for twenty-two years as clinical assistant professor, Psychiatry Department, University of New Mexico School of Medicine. She has appeared on radio and television programs across the country, including *Larry King Live*. Her powerful message is how to transform the energy focused on life crises into creative self-expression and transcendent living.

To contact Dr. Gail Feldman to arrange for lectures or workshops, write to her office:

300 San Mateo Blvd. N.E., Suite 805
Albuquerque, New Mexico 87108

Call: 505-266-8488
Fax: 505-268-5161
E-mail: GFWrites@aol.com

To order additional copies of

From Crisis to Creativity

Book: $15.95   Shipping/Handling: $3.50

Contact: ***BookPartners, Inc.***
P.O. Box 922, Wilsonville, OR 97070
Fax: 503-682-8684
Phone: 503-682-9821
Phone: 1-800-895-7323